ABC GUIDE TO AUSTRALIAN TEST CRICKETERS

G000037608

from Heather & John
1995

ABC GUIDE TO AUSTRALIAN TEST CRICKETERS

RICK SMITH

WITH A FOREWORD BY
ALAN McGILVRAY

Queen Anne Press

A QUEEN ANNE PRESS BOOK

First published in 1994 by
Queen Anne Press, a division of
Lennard Associates Ltd
Mackerye End, Harpenden
Herts AL5 5DR

British Library Cataloguing in Publication Data
is available

ISBN 1 85291 541 2

THE AUTHOR

Rick Smith was born in Launceston, Tasmania, in 1955. He graduated from the University of Tasmania and began a teaching career in 1978. He is a former A grade cricketer with a deep interest in the history of the game. A collector of cricket memorabilia, Rick also has an interest in photography and can frequently be seen at games attempting to capture the action on film. He is the author of a number of limited edition books on various aspects of cricket history.

FOREWORD

It has always been my view that cricket is a game that generates character—and characters—like no other. It is a game first of all for people, and it irritates me that so much of its history and its accomplishment seems to be measured by figures and statistics. They're part of it, of course, but they're not the only part, and it is important that the literature of the game recognises that. Too often it does not.

In flicking through the pages of Rick Smith's marvellous work *The ABC of Australian Test Cricketers*, I was very pleased to find that the character and the characters of this great game have come to life. It is a stunningly complex task to have undertaken, involving research of awesome proportions, but the author has not allowed himself to be dominated by performances and figures. He has delved into the people, and in so doing has brought them to life, and that makes his book something special.

My involvement in cricket spans a great number of years now, from the time I first had instruction from the great M A Noble back in my days at Sydney Grammar School in the 1920s. Of the more than 350 Test players whose deeds are recorded in this book, I suppose I knew personally about 70 per cent. Many of them I have counted as very good friends, and nearly all of them have been people to admire.

Cricket is a game that sorts people out very quickly. There is a requirement to be a team man; to be steadfast and strong; to be patient and tolerant and self-sacrificing. It is an unforgiving game in many ways, a game that can bring sudden disappointment, and a game that teaches some very hard lessons. It has been my experience that virtually all of those who make it to the top in cricket have a strength of character that stands above the norm, and it is these men that this book honours.

From my own viewpoint, the record here is fascinating, because I can remember so many of the central figures. I can see their faces and hear their voices, and the marvellous moments in which they were involved come flooding back. But this book provides a service, too, for those who have never seen these people, or know little of them, for cricket can only flourish when it has a history to build upon. The men and the deeds recorded here should be an inspiration for all who follow, for every generation has its champions, and those who have gone before provide the stick by which those who follow are measured. I am constantly looking at the players of today and conjuring up visions of those who have preceded them. Rick Smith talks of Michael Slater, for instance, as 'nimble-footed' and 'aggressive', and in picturing Slater's dynamic start to Test cricket in England in 1993, I have to agree that footwork is the key to everything he does.

When you talk of footwork the mind automatically rushes back, without any prodding at all, to the dancing feet of the inimitable Don Bradman. On the subject of footwork I have to say that Slater is as good as just about anybody I have seen since Bradman. The way he gets into position to play the on-drive for instance, that hardest of all shots to play, is reminiscent of the great Bradman, though I hasten to say I am talking here merely of footwork. I would not be so unfair as to burden young Slater with any Bradman tags when it comes to the overall art of batsmanship.

In reading the account of Keith Miller I had to chuckle. The point is made that Miller's unpredictability was one of the features of his cricket, and that his desire always to see cricket as a game to be enjoyed perhaps counted against his being appointed captain of Australia, as he undoubtedly should have been. As I read the pen picture I could see Miller leading a club team on to the ground, and placing his field with a regal sweep of the hand and the command 'scatter'. I could see him haring into a ground in Britain, late for duty because he had been to the races. And I could see him charming everybody with his wit and his love of cricket.

The book talks of Bill Woodfull's stoic dignity, of Ian Chappell's claim to being the finest of Australia's captains, and his equally forceful capacity for being an 'administrator's nightmare'. It tells of the tragic life and death of Billy Midwinter, who played in the very first Test and finished up representing both Australia and England. And it tells of the famous Lindsay Hassett sense of humour which tended to 'distract' attention at times from his capacity as a leader.

One of the inevitable side issues in a book such as *The ABC of Australian Test Cricketers* is the changing image of cricket and cricketers. We read of Woodfull's reserve, and the fun-loving ways of Miller and Hassett, and compare them to the modern player, where the pressures seem to be infinitely greater. Smith makes the point, for instance, that Allan Border would have been quite happy to divest himself of the Australian captaincy when the pressures of a disappointing Australian run were at their greatest in the middle 1980s. I cannot help but sympathise with those who live under the pressure of the modern game. The invasive media attention, and the commercial pressures that exist, are very hefty indeed. In this scenario Border has proved himself a marvellous survivor, having worn the hard times, risen above his depressions, and gone on to be a fine and very successful captain of his country.

Pressure, of course, is a relative thing. Back in the days of Warwick Armstrong and Bill O'Reilly and the like, there was not the media attention of today, but there were pressures of other kinds. Of hard weeks' travelling, and world wars, and Great Depressions. Those players wore their pressures too, as modern players do, and the character always seems to shine through, no matter which generation we consider.

This book paints that. From Ted a'Beckett to Tim Zoehrer, and the 350-odd names alphabetically listed in between, the character and the characters cannot be suppressed. I know that I will pick it up and read through it again and again and glow within at the memories.

To those who have not seen these men as I have seen them, I can only commend the reference it provides, and the images it paints of a wonderful game.

Alan McGilvray AM, MBE

ACKNOWLEDGMENTS

Producing a work of this nature is not a solo effort, and a number of people must be thanked for their assistance:
Ric Finlay for doing his considerable best to ensure statistical accuracy, and for allowing me to use photographs from his collection. Maurice Blunden, Gordon Vidler, Brian Bassano, and Ron Williams for allowing me to use pictures from their collections; and to the latter pair for helping to proofread the manuscript; Mrs E McNamara for permission to use pictures from her brother's, the late Arthur James, collection; Mrs Carol Badcock, for permission to use pictures from her late husband's collection; Moss Seigert and Doug Crampton, who have expended much time and effort photographing cricketers over many years, for permission to use their work; The Tasmanian Cricket Association and the Northern Tasmanian Cricket Association for permission to reproduce pictures held in their collections; The Mitchell Library in Sydney for permission to use photographs of EJ Gregory and RJ Pope; The General Reference Library, State Library of NSW for permission to use pictures of RC Allen, FJ Burton, BB Cooper, JT Cottam, JR Hodges, AP Marr, and NFD Thomson; The State Archives Office of Tasmania for permission to use photographs from their collections; *The Examiner* newspaper for allowing access to their extensive photo files; Australian Consolidated Press for permission to reproduce the photograph of Bill Watson; *The Advertiser* - Adelaide for permission to reproduce the photograph of Barry Shepherd; Don Wigan for permission to use his photograph of David Boon; Ken Williams for calculating the number of first-class fifties scored by all Australian Test players; Ray Webster, for help in locating photographs, for offering valuable suggestions concerning the manuscript, and for allowing me to use his diligent research which has uncovered previously unknown information and corrected long-standing errors on players such as Jack Hodges and Nat Thomson; Ross Dundas, the Honorary Librarian of the NSWCA, for his help in locating photographs, and the Association for allowing me to publish them; Jena Pulman and the staff of the Melbourne Cricket Club for permission to use pictures of TJD Kelly and J McIlwraith from their collection. The VCA for permission to use the photograph of G Tribe.

Finally, my thanks to all the Australian Test cricketers who answered my questions and provided pictures of themselves for use in this book, particularly the late Harry Alexander, Geff Noblet, Ernie Toshack, Arthur Morris, Ron Hamence and Peter Allan.

Without the assistance of all the above, the task of producing this work would have been far more difficult, if not impossible.

The photographs used in this book come from the sources mentioned above, and from the author's own collection. Although every effort has been made to contact the copyright owners of the photographs, I hope any omission will be excused.

Finally, many thanks to Alan McGilvray who (with Norman Tasker) agreed to write the Foreword to this book.

Rick Smith
Prospect
Tasmania, 1993

INTRODUCTION

Australian Test cricket, indeed all Test cricket, began on 15 March, 1877 when an English professional touring team captained by James Lillywhite played a combined New South Wales and Victorian team led by Dave Gregory. Other English teams had visited Australia previously, but this was the first time a combined group of colonials had met an English team on even terms, eleven-a-side.

It was not regarded as a game between England and Australia at the time, and the English team was far from representative of that country's cricketing strength. But the game was accepted later as the first Test, and the colonial players became Australia's first Test cricketers.

The side, in batting order, was C Bannerman, NFD Thompson, TP Horan, DW Gregory (capt.), BB Cooper, WE Midwinter, EJ Gregory, JM Blackham, TW Garrett, T Kendall, JH Hodges.

Thanks to a brilliant innings of 165 (retired hurt) by Bannerman, 5/78 by Midwinter in the visitors' first innings and 7/55 by Kendall in the second, the Australians won by 45 runs and began a tradition of cricketing excellence which continues to the present day.

Over 350 individuals have represented Australia since the commencement of Test cricket in 1877. A privileged few have become legends of the game; others have disappeared almost without trace, their period at the top being so brief or so unsuccessful that they were unable to enjoy the long and glorious career hoped for at the outset. A few were the victims of circumstances, with war, illness or injury destroying what could have been great careers. The likes of Ross Gregory, killed in the Second World War, or Archie Jackson, dead of tuberculosis at the age of twenty-three, fall into this category.

While it is undeniable that some players are better or more successful than others, it is equally undeniable that all those who played for Australia possessed some ability at the game. Events like World Series Cricket, or the 1885 fiasco which led to the selection of an entirely new Australian team, or the dispute in 1912 which saw six leading players refuse to tour England, certainly gave Test chances to players who may have otherwise missed out, but bad cricketers don't wear the 'baggy green cap'. A number failed to make the most of their opportunities, but all those selected had some claim to be chosen.

In the space available, this book cannot, and does not, give a full and detailed account of every Australian Test cricketer, but it will serve to provide a summary of each player's career and statistical details. Any of the publications listed in the bibliography, or the multitude of books written about the game in this country, will help to extend knowledge of a particular player, performance or series.

Every Australian who ever picked up a bat or ball has dreamed of representing his country. The players described in this book made that dream come true; and if they didn't all produce glorious deeds in front of packed crowds on the world's finest grounds, they each had their moment of opportunity, which is more than can be said for the vast majority of cricket fans and weekend players. For this they deserve to be remembered, every single one of them.

KEY

The following standard abbreviations have been used throughout the text.

RHB_____ Right Hand Batsman
RaB_____ Right Arm Bowler
Rab(r)_____ Right Arm Round Arm Bowler
RF_____ Right Arm Fast Bowler
RF(r)_____ Right Arm Fast Round Arm Bowler
RFM_____ Right Arm Fast Medium Bowler
RFM(r)_____ Right Arm Fast Medium Round Arm Bowler
RM_____ Right Arm Medium Bowler
RM(r)_____ Right Arm Medium Round Arm
LB_____ Right Arm Leg Break Bowler
LBG_____ Right Arm Leg Break/Googly Bowler
OB_____ Right Arm Off Break Bowler
LHB_____ Left Hand Batsman
LaB_____ Left Arm Bowler
Lab(r)_____ Left Arm Round Arm Bowler
LF_____ Left Arm Fast Bowler
LF(r)_____ Left Arm Fast Round Arm Bowler
LFM_____ Left Arm Fast Medium Bowler
LFM(r)_____ Left Arm Fast Medium Round Arm Bowler
LM_____ Left Arm Medium Bowler
LM(r)_____ Left Arm Medium Round Arm
SLA_____ Left Arm Slow Orthodox Bowler
SLC_____ Left Arm Slow 'Chinaman' Bowler
WK_____ Wicket-keeper

a'BECKETT, Edward Lambert

Vic, RHB/RFM
Born: 11 August 1907
East St. Kilda, Victoria
Died: 2 June 1989
Terang, Victoria

The tall Victorian all-rounder had an all too brief first-class career, retiring at a time when his best was probably still to come. a'Beckett made his first-class debut at twenty and was a Test player, against England in 1928–29, after only six games. Although he toured England in 1930, he took only 19 wickets and made just over 300 runs, playing one Test. In his four games at Test level he failed to reproduce any of the form he displayed in first-class cricket. Ted a'Beckett retired in 1932, after a first-class career of barely four seasons, to pursue a legal career, his rich cricket potential largely unfulfilled. A fractured skull suffered while playing amateur football in 1932 may have influenced his decision to retire.

BATTING	M	Inn	NO	HS	Runs	Ave	100s	50s	C/S
Tests	4	7	0	41	143	20.42	–	–	4
First-class	47	64	8	152	1636	29.21	2	7	35

BOWLING	Balls	Runs	Wkts	Ave	BB	5wI	10wM
Tests	1062	317	3	105.66	1/41	–	–
First-class	–	3062	105	29.16	6/119	3	–

ALDERMAN, Terrence Michael

WA, RHB/RFM
Born: 12 June 1956
Subiaco, Western Australia

Terry Alderman has had something of an up and down career. In 1981 against England, he took a record 42 wickets in his first Test series. At Perth two years later his shoulder was badly injured in a scuffle with a spectator who ran onto the field, and in 1985 he elected to join a rebel tour of South Africa, earning himself a three-year ban. Alderman returned to Test cricket in 1989 and was the leading bowler in the regaining of the Ashes, again taking over 40 wickets. Stints in county cricket with Kent and Gloucestershire made him a master of English conditions. He has not produced the same results in Australia, although his best Test figures were recorded against England at Brisbane in 1990–91. A disappointing 1991 tour of the West Indies may have signalled the end of his Test career, but he continued on at first-class level, and in 1992–93 he was playing coach of Western Australia.

BATTING	M	Inn	NO	HS	Runs	Ave	100s	50s	C/S
Tests	41	53	22	26*	203	6.54	–	–	27
First-class	245	265	108	52*	1307	8.32	–	1	190

BOWLING	Balls	Runs	Wkts	Ave	BB	5wI	10wM
Tests	10181	4616	170	27.15	6/47	14	1
First-class	–	22701	956	23.75	8/46	53	8

ALEXANDER, George

Vic, RHB/RM(r)
Born: 22 April 1851
Fitzroy, Victoria
Died: 6 November 1930
Melbourne, Victoria

George Alexander played an important part in the formative years of Test cricket. Making his debut for Victoria in 1875–76, he was a hard-hitting batsman and round-arm bowler, who played two Tests: one in England at The Oval in 1880 and the other at Adelaide in 1884. His highest score of 33 was made in the first of those games, in a partnership with his captain Murdoch which forced England to bat again. More importantly, he managed the 1880 and 1884 Australian teams in England, while in 1882–83 he managed the Hon. Ivo Bligh's English team in Australia. This was the side which came 'to reclaim the Ashes', did so, and created a legend.

BATTING	M	Inn	NO	HS	Runs	Ave	100s	50s	C/S
Tests	2	4	0	33	52	13.00	–	–	2
First-class	24	35	5	75	466	15.33	–	2	16

BOWLING	Balls	Runs	Wkts	Ave	BB	5wl	10wM
Tests	168	93	2	46.50	2/69	–	–
First-class	–	607	33	18.39	5/57	–	–

ALEXANDER, Harry Houston

Vic, RHB/RF
Born: 9 June 1905
Ascot Vale, Victoria
Died: 15 April 1993
East Melbourne, Victoria

A big, strong fast bowler, 'Bull' Alexander was widely touted as the man to give Bodyline back to Jardine's side when he was chosen for the fifth Test of that unpleasant 1932–33 series. Although he took only one wicket, Alexander did manage to hit Jardine a few times, much to the delight of the crowd. He never operated with a Bodyline field because Australian captain, Bill Woodfull, refused to adopt such tactics. This was Alexander's sole Test, although he did tour India with Frank Tarrant's side in 1935-36 at the end of his career. Making his first-class debut in 1928–29, he produced some excellent displays for Victoria, none better than his 7/95 against New South Wales in 1932.

BATTING	M	Inn	NO	HS	Runs	Ave	100s	50s	C/S
Tests	1	2	1	17*	17	17.00	–	–	–
First-class	41	51	14	23*	228	6.16	–	–	17

BOWLING	Balls	Runs	Wkts	Ave	BB	5wl	10wM
Tests	276	154	1	154.00	1/129	–	–
First-class	–	3222	95	33.91	7/95	2	–

ALLAN, Francis Erskine

Vic, LHB/LFM(r)
Born: 2 December 1849
Allansford, Victoria
Died: 9 February 1917
Melbourne, Victoria

Allan was one of the early prominent Australian players. In 1873–74, a few seasons before Test cricket began, he made a name for himself with some excellent bowling against WG Grace's English team. Although he missed the historic first Test in 1877 because he couldn't spare the time, his left-arm bowling was well regarded, and he toured England under Dave Gregory in 1878. There were no Tests played and Allan didn't perform as well as Fred Spofforth and Harry Boyle. His only Test was against Lord Harris's team at Melbourne in 1879. He was the mainstay of the Victorian attack for many years, making his debut in 1867–68, and was so effective that he was at one time labelled 'the bowler of the century'. While he did exceptionally well at first-class level, he may have been a little past his best when Test cricket became established.

BATTING	M	Inn	NO	HS	Runs	Ave	100s	50s	C/S
Tests	1	1	0	5	5	5.00	–	–	–
First-class	31	50	16	35*	371	10.91	–	–	14

BOWLING	Balls	Runs	Wkts	Ave	BB	5wI	10wM
Tests	180	80	4	20.00	2/30	–	–
First-class	–	1638	124	13.20	8/20	11	2

ALLAN, Peter John

Qld, RHB/RFM
Born: 31 December 1935
Brisbane, Queensland

A strong, fast-medium bowler, Peter Allan is one of only three bowlers to take all ten wickets in a Sheffield Shield innings. He took 10/61 against Victoria in Melbourne, the only instance at the MCG, in 1965–66. This was Allan's big year, as it also saw him play his only Test, in Brisbane against England. He was also chosen for the fourth Test, but had to withdraw due to injury. Allan had previously toured the West Indies in 1964–65 without playing a Test. He made his debut for Queensland in 1959 and spent three seasons in Victoria before returning to Queensland in 1963–64. By the time he retired in 1969 he had amassed an impressive haul of wickets for his home state.

BATTING	M	Inn	NO	HS	Runs	Ave	100s	50s	C/S
Tests	1	–	–	–	–	–	–	–	–
First-class	57	84	19	41	689	10.60	–	–	23

BOWLING	Balls	Runs	Wkts	Ave	BB	5wl	10wM
Tests	192	83	2	41.50	2/58	–	–
First-class	–	5377	206	26.10	10/61	12	3

ALLEN, Reginald Charles

NSW, RHB
Born: 2 July 1858
Glebe, New South Wales
Died: 2 May 1952
Sydney, New South Wales

Allen was a solid right-hand bat who played in the final Test of the 1886–87 series against England. With innings of 14 and 30, in a game which Australia lost by 71 runs, he performed creditably. In fact, he looked like giving his side a chance until he had the unusual distinction of being caught by team-mate Charles Turner, who was fielding substitute for England. After a reasonably encouraging start, it could be considered something of a mystery that he wasn't given another Test. The answer may lie in his first-class career, which began in 1878–79, and suggests nothing extraordinary. Allen was a member of a prominent Sydney legal practice and in later life became involved in horse racing.

BATTING	M	Inn	NO	HS	Runs	Ave	100s	50s	C/S
Tests	1	2	0	30	44	22.00	–	–	2
First-class	17	34	3	41	382	12.32	–	–	9

BOWLING	Runs	Wkts	Ave	BB	5wl	10wM
First-class	117	2	58.50	1/4	–	–

ANDREWS, Thomas James Edwin

NSW, RHB/LBG
Born: 26 August 1890
Newtown, New South Wales
Died: 28 January 1970
Sydney, New South Wales

Tommy Andrews was an important member of the successful Australian sides following the First World War. A free-scoring right handed batsman, an excellent cover fieldsman who brought off many run outs, and a competent leg-break bowler, Andrews had an impressive record in a first-class career which lasted from 1912–13 to 1930–31. He made a significant early impression and was chosen to tour South Africa in 1914, but the trip was cancelled because of the War, and he had to wait until 1921 to make his Test debut. His Test figures were useful rather than spectacular, and his best efforts were two nineties against England in 1921, 92 at Leeds and 94 at The Oval. He toured England again in 1926, but was not as successful. Andrews was a stonemason by trade and made the headstones for team-mates Victor Trumper and Archie Jackson.

BATTING	M	Inn	NO	HS	Runs	Ave	100s	50s	C/S
Tests	16	23	1	94	592	26.90	–	4	12
First-class	151	222	17	247*	8095	39.48	14	43	85

BOWLING	Balls	Runs	Wkts	Ave	BB	5wI	10wM
Tests	156	116	1	116.00	1/23	–	–
First-class	–	3050	95	32.10	6/109	3	–

ANGEL, Jo

WA, LHB/RF
Born: 22 April 1968
Subiaco, Western Australia

A very tall, right-arm fast bowler, Angel was something of a surprise selection for the deciding fifth Test of the 1992–93 series against the

West Indies. Although he took 1/72, he bowled a little better than his figures suggest, and could have had a wicket in his first over when a catch was dropped at deep fine leg. To add insult to injury the ball went over the fence for six. Angel made his first-class debut in 1991–92 when injuries struck key bowlers. He did well enough, taking 31 wickets at 25.38, to ensure a regular place at the start of the next season. An early five-wicket haul against the West Indies must have placed him in contention for a Test place. While still very raw, he does have pace, and his height enables him to gain lift from the pitch. With continued work there could well be a place for him in future Australian Test teams.

BATTING	M	Inn	NO	HS	Runs	Ave	100s	50s	C/S
Tests	1	2	1	4*	4	4.00	–	–	–
First-class	18	26	10	25*	177	11.06	–	–	5

BOWLING	Balls	Runs	Wkts	Ave	BB		5wl	10wM
Tests	114	72	1	72.00	1/72		–	–
First-class	–	1899	63	30.14	6/71		2	–

ARCHER, Kenneth Alan

Qld, RHB/OB
Born: 17 January 1928
Yeerongpilly, Queensland

Ken Archer had the misfortune to play in an era when Australia had a wealth of opening batsmen, and although he managed five Tests, he could not make the big score which would have given him an extended run in the Test team. Competition from the likes of Arthur Morris, Jim Burke, and later Colin McDonald gave the selectors plenty of options. Archer toured South Africa in 1949–50, but was twelfth man in all five Tests. Later when the chance did come he couldn't quite seize it. In three Tests against England in 1950–51 and two in the next season against the West Indies his highest score was 48 and his average 26. Archer opened Queensland's batting from 1946 to 1956 and captained the State on a number of occasions. He was also a superb out-fieldsman, a legacy of his other sport, baseball, at which he was an extremely good player.

BATTING	M	Inn	NO	HS	Runs	Ave	100s	50s	C/S
Tests	5	9	0	48	234	26.00	–	–	–
First-class	82	139	13	134	3774	29.95	3	25	56/1

BOWLING	Runs	Wkts	Ave	BB	5wI	10wM
First-class	698	13	53.69	2/16	–	–

ARCHER, Ronald Graham

Qld, RHB/RFM
Born: 25 October 1933
Brisbane, Queensland

The younger brother of Ken, Ron Archer was a top line all-rounder, the man groomed to replace Keith Miller in the Australian side. His hard-hitting batting, lively bowling and excellent slips fielding made him a natural candidate for the job, and he had already played 19 Tests when knee injuries forced his retirement at the age of twenty-five. In that short time he produced a number of excellent performances, including a century against the West Indies and 5/53 against England at The Oval on his second trip there. Archer toured England in 1953 and 1956, the West Indies in 1955 and Pakistan in 1956, and was chosen to tour South Africa in 1957–58 but withdrew due to injury. He played on principally as a batsman until 1958–59, but his Test career, which lasted from 1951–52 to 1956 shows an extremely talented all-rounder. The abiding memory is of a player whose great potential went largely unfulfilled.

BATTING	M	Inn	NO	HS	Runs	Ave	100s	50s	C/S
Tests	19	30	1	128	713	24.58	1	2	20
First-class	98	137	19	148	3768	31.93	4	21	105

BOWLING	Balls	Runs	Wkts	Ave	BB	5wI	10wM
Tests	3576	1318	48	27.45	5/53	1	–
First-class	–	5958	255	23.36	7/56	9	1

ARMSTRONG, Warwick Windridge

Vic, RHB/LB
Born: 22 May 1879
Kyneton, Victoria
Died: 13 July 1947
Darling Point, New South Wales

One of Australia's cricket legends, Warwick Armstrong played 50 Tests from 1902 to 1921, the last ten as undefeated captain. Beginning with a slim, athletic build, the passing years saw his weight increase from 10 to 22 stone, perhaps because he enjoyed a drink or two, and he became known as 'the Big Ship'. Throughout his career Armstrong had the reputation of being very much a man of strong opinions, which he was more than capable of expressing. Such was his strength of character that he usually emerged victorious from such arguments. His clashes with authority were legendary (he was one of the 'Big Six' who refused to tour England in 1912), and they tend to obscure his ability as a player.

He was a top-class all-rounder: a fine batsman, particularly powerful on the drive, and a leg-break and top-spin bowler capable of maintaining a length for hours on end. In fact he exceeded 100 wickets on each of the 1905, 1909 and 1921 English tours, the last occasion when he was forty-two years old. For such a big man he was surprisingly light on his feet and a very safe catcher.

After the First World War he was the logical choice as captain, although the authorities must have loathed giving him the job. It was rumoured that he was elected by just one vote. However, he was a total success, leading Australia to eight successive victories over England, still a record. In the 1920–21 series he led from the front, scoring three of his six Test centuries. Armstrong's 1921 team is described as one of the finest of all time, and his ruthless use of fast bowlers Jack Gregory and Ted McDonald showed the way for future dual speed attacks. If officials and opponents hated him, his players gave him their whole-hearted support, and if success is the yardstick for captaincy, then Warwick Armstrong is justifiably regarded as one of Australia's greatest captains.

BATTING	M	Inn	NO	HS	Runs	Ave	100s	50s	C/S
Tests	50	84	10	159*	2863	38.68	6	8	44
First-class	269	406	61	303*	16158	46.83	45	57	274

BOWLING	Balls	Runs	Wkts	Ave	BB	5wI	10wM
Tests	8022	2923	87	33.59	6/35	3	–
First-class	–	16406	832	19.71	8/47	50	5

B

BADCOCK, Clayvel Lindsay

Tas, RHB
Born: 10 April 1914
Exton, Tasmania
Died: 13 December 1982
Exton, Tasmania

The short, stocky Badcock was a child batting prodigy, making his debut against Victoria at the age of fifteen in 1929–30. In 1933–34 he set the Tasmanian record score of 274 among a series of big innings, setting an aggregate record which lasted for 50 years. Next season he moved to South Australia, and in 40 games there scored 3282 runs at 56.58 with 12 centuries. His highest score was a massive 325 against Victoria in 1936. Badcock made his Test debut against England in 1936–37, scoring 118 in the fifth Test after some early failures. In fact it was to be his only double figure score in Tests. Touring England in 1938 he made plenty of runs, 1659 in all, but failed in the Tests, scoring just 32 runs, and collecting a pair at Lord's. Badcock never considered that he played well on the tour, and cited faulty footwork as the cause. He continued to make mountains of runs in Shield cricket until the War and sciatica ended chances of a comeback and he returned to the family farm.

BATTING	M	Inn	NO	HS	Runs	Ave	100s	50s	C/S
Tests	7	12	1	118	160	14.54	1	–	3
First-class	97	159	16	325	7371	51.54	26	21	41

BOWLING	Runs	Wkts	Ave	BB	5wl	10wM	
First-class	44	0	–	–	–	–	

BANNERMAN, Alexander Chalmers

NSW, RHB/RM(r)
Born: 21 March 1854
Paddington, New South Wales
Died: 19 September 1924
Paddington, New South Wales

Little 'Alick' Bannerman was a great stonewaller and an integral part of early Australian teams. While the strokemakers went for their shots Bannerman held up an end, and by doing so was responsible for many victories. He was not popular with the crowds, but he was of immense value to his team. He toured England in 1878, 1880, 1882, 1884, 1888 and 1893, driving bowlers to distraction on all visits. His seemingly endless patience was typified by an innings of 91 against England in 1891–92 which took seven and a half hours. Bannerman preferred to open the batting, and if he lacked the flair of older brother Charles, he was no less a valuable player. Cricket was a serious business to 'Alick' Bannerman and Australia can thank him for much of its early success.

BATTING	M	Inn	NO	HS	Runs	Ave	100s	50s	C/S
Tests	28	50	2	94	1108	23.08	–	8	21
First-class	219	381	28	134	7816	22.14	5	30	154

BOWLING	Balls	Runs	Wkts	Ave	BB	5wI	10wM
Tests	292	163	4	40.75	3/111	–	–
First-class	–	656	22	29.81	3/12	–	–

BANNERMAN, Charles

NSW, RHB
Born: 23 July 1851
Woolwich, Kent, England
Died: 20 August 1930
Surry Hills, New South Wales

Charles Bannerman has a secure place in the history of Australian cricket. Against England at Melbourne in 1877 he faced the first delivery in Test cricket and went on to compile the first Test century on his

11

way to a score of 165 (retired hurt). He made the runs off an attack of Lillywhite, Shaw and Southerton, while no one else made more than 18 in a total of 245. His innings ended with a broken finger, but he had done enough to ensure victory. He did not do quite so well in the second game, making 10 and 30. Bannerman topped the averages and aggregates in England in 1878, scoring the first Australian hundred on English soil. There were no Tests on that tour and he played only once more for Australia, against England in 1878–79, although he continued in first-class cricket until 1887–88.

BATTING	M	Inn	NO	HS	Runs	Ave	100s	50s	C/S
Tests	3	6	2	165*	239	59.75	1	–	–
First-class	44	84	6	165*	1687	21.62	1	9	20

BOWLING	Runs	Wkts	Ave	BB	5wl	10wM
First-class	44	0	–	–	–	–

BARDSLEY, Warren

NSW, LHB
Born: 7 December 1882
Nevertire near Warren, New South Wales
Died: 20 January 1954
Collaroy, New South Wales

A very talented opening batsman, Warren Bardsley was the first to make a century in each innings of a Test, 136 and 130 against England at The Oval in 1909, and the oldest to bat through a Test innings, making 193 not out against England in 1926, when he was 43. Bardlsey toured England in 1909, 1912, 1921 and 1926 where he averaged over 50 on each each tour but the first, where he was just under that figure. Bardsley was a rather solemn character, but if he lacked flair he possessed incredible dedication and a nearly flawless technique honed by hours of practice. Such an approach made him a great success on English wickets where his record was better than at home. He retained his skills to the end of his career, scoring 1558 runs at 50.25 on that last tour. For a man of his age it was a fitting testimony to the countless hours spent improving his technique.

BATTING	M	Inn	NO	HS	Runs	Ave	100s	50s	C/S
Tests	41	66	5	193*	2469	40.47	6	14	12
First-class	250	376	35	264	17025	49.92	53	73	112

BOWLING	Runs	Wkts	Ave	BB	5wl	10wM
First-class	41	0	–	–	–	–

BARNES, Sidney George

NSW, RHB/LBG
Born: 5 June 1916
Charters Towers, Queensland
Died: 16 December 1973
Collaroy, New South Wales

A controversial and talented opening batsman, Barnes was chosen to tour England in 1938, but a broken wrist spoiled his trip. He did recover in time to make his debut in the fifth Test, where he scored 41 and 33. After the War he emerged as a key member of the Test team, forming a solid opening partnership with the left-handed Arthur Morris. Against England in 1946–47 he made 234 in a partnership of 405 for the fifth wicket with Don Bradman. Following the triumphant 1948 tour, in which he made a century at Lord's after a duck in the first innings, controversy dogged him. Officials didn't like his clowning and he never played for Australia again. When his selection was rejected by the Board, he took them to court. He became an acidic writer on the game, a job he continued until his death from an overdose of sleeping pills. Of all Australians who have played as many Tests, only Bradman has a better average. Barnes was also a brilliant and brave close to the wicket fieldsman.

BATTING	M	Inn	NO	HS	Runs	Ave	100s	50s	C/S
Tests	13	19	2	234	1072	63.05	3	5	14
First-class	110	164	10	234	8333	54.11	26	37	80/4

BOWLING	Balls	Runs	Wkts	Ave	BB	5wI	10wM
Tests	594	218	4	54.50	2/25	–	–
First-class	–	1836	57	32.21	3/0	–	–

BARNETT, Benjamin Arthur

Vic, LHB/WK
Born: 23 March 1908
Auburn, Victoria
Died: 29 June
Newcastle, New South Wales

Barnett was the surprise choice as reserve wicket-keeper for the 1934 English tour. He had made his first-class debut in 1929–30, but it was his taking of fellow Victorian Fleetwood-Smith's left-arm spinners which probably won him selection as Bert Oldfield's deputy, a task he also performed in South Africa in 1935–36. He returned to England as first choice 'keeper in 1938, where he played his only Tests, and settled there after the War, during which he had been a prisoner of war in Malaya. In retirement he became a skilled administrator representing Australia at many ICC (International Cricket Council) conferences. Barnett is credited with Test cricket's most expensive miss. At The Oval in 1938 he missed stumping Len Hutton when he had made only 40 of an eventual 364. In addition to his 'keeping skills he was a more than useful batsman.

BATTING	M	Inn	NO	HS	Runs	Ave	100s	50s	C/S
Tests	4	8	1	57	195	27.85	–	1	3/2
First-class	173	242	42	131	5531	27.51	4	31	216/142

BOWLING	Runs	Wkts	Ave	BB	5wl	10wM
First-class	20	1	20.00	1/3	–	–

BARRETT, John Edward

Vic, LHB/RM
Born: 15 October 1866
South Melbourne, Victoria
Died: 6 February 1916
Peak Hill, Western Australia

A tall all-rounder, Barrett made his representative debut at 18 in 1885. In addition to his batting he was a useful bowler, once taking 11 wickets in a game against South Australia, 5/31 and 6/49, at Melbourne in 1884–85. Medical studies, which greatly curtailed his career, prevented him from achieving national selection until he toured England in 1890. He performed well, finishing second to Murdoch in the averages with 1227 runs at 24.06, and at Lord's becoming the first Australian to bat through a Test innings when he made 67 out of 176. Barrett's performance on this tour suggested a long Test career, but his chosen profession consumed too much time and he never played for Australia again.

BATTING	M	Inn	NO	HS	Runs	Ave	100s	50s	C/S
Tests	2	4	1	67*	80	26.66	–	1	1
First-class	50	91	12	97	2039	25.81	–	13	16

BOWLING	Runs	Wkts	Ave	BB	5wl	10wM
First-class	336	21	16.00	6/49	3	1

BEARD, Graeme Robert

NSW, RHB/RM
Born: 19 August 1950
Auburn, New South Wales

A capable all-rounder, Beard was a useful middle order batsman and a naggingly accurate bowler of medium pace and off cutters. He made his first-class debut in 1975–76, but World Series Cricket brought him to prominence when Australia was trying to rebuild its national team. He played his 3 Tests against Pakistan when he toured there in 1979–80. Beard also toured England in 1981, but was given few opportunities on wickets which should have suited his style of bowling. After just one more season he announced his retirement from first-class cricket.

BATTING	M	Inn	NO	HS	Runs	Ave	100s	50s	C/S
Tests	3	5	0	49	114	22.80	–	–	–
First-class	54	71	16	75	1441	23.62	–	11	22

BOWLING	Balls	Runs	Wkts	Ave	BB	5wl	10wM
Tests	259	109	1	109.00	1/26	–	–
First-class	–	3524	125	28.19	5/33	7	1

BENAUD, John

NSW, RHB/RM
Born: 11 May 1944
Auburn, New South Wales

The younger brother of Richie, John Benaud was a hard-hitting batsman who could well have played more than 3 Tests. A strong-willed character, he lost the NSW captaincy because he disobeyed an order not to wear ripple-soled shoes. Benaud's best performance was an innings of 142 against Pakistan in Melbourne in 1972–73, shortly after being told he had been dropped for the next Test. In addition to embarrassing the selectors, it clinched a tour of the West Indies, where, unfortunately, he had little success. Benaud's promising career was cut short by his work as a journalist. In recent years he has moved into administration with his appointment as a national selector. Benaud was a considerable player in his own right and by no means just 'Richie's little brother'.

BATTING	M	Inn	NO	HS	Runs	Ave	100s	50s	C/S
Tests	3	5	0	142	223	44.60	1	–	–
First-class	47	85	6	142	2888	36.55	4	16	30

BOWLING	Balls	Runs	Wkts	Ave	BB	5wI	10wM
Tests	24	12	2	6.00	2/12	–	–
First-class	–	176	5	35.20	2/12	–	–

BENAUD, Richard

NSW, RHB/LBG
Born: 6 October 1930
Penrith, New South Wales

Richie Benaud was one of Australia's greatest captains as well as being a magnificent all-rounder. He was the most successful leg spinner since the Second World War, a hard-hitting batsman and a brilliant fieldsman close to the wicket. Making his first-class debut in 1948–49 he quickly rose to Test level, playing his first Test in 1951–52. The selectors saw his obvious potential and persisted with him through some mediocre performances until his great talent came to fruition in South Africa on the 1957–58 tour.

With illness to Ian Craig, Benaud was the surprise choice as skipper for the 1958–59 series against England. Most had favoured Neil Harvey for the job, but Benaud emerged with a 4-0 victory over what was thought to be one of England's strongest ever teams. He suffered only four defeats in 27 Tests as captain, and never lost a series. His leadership was noted for extracting the maximum from his players, particularly Alan Davidson, who became a devastating left-arm opening bowler. Benaud's desire to attack where possible was as vital an ingredient to the classic 1960–61 series as anything the West Indies contributed. Training as a journalist made him a master at dealing with the press, and he gave Australian cricket a high public profile.

Benaud is the only Australian to score 2000 runs and take 200 wickets in Tests, and he held the Test wicket record for his country until it was overtaken by Dennis Lillee in 1980–81. The finest performance among those 248 wickets was an effort of 6/70 against England at Old Trafford in 1961, when by going around the wicket and pitching into the bowlers' footmarks he won a game which appeared all but lost. In the process he also regained the Ashes for his side. It was Benaud's desire for a win which led to Australia chasing runs on the last day at Brisbane in 1960, creating the drama of the first tied Test.

Benaud's part in World Series Cricket made him few friends among the 'Establishment', but that would have caused him little worry as he was always a players' man. As anchor man for televised cricket in England and Australia he remains one of the game's best known and most respected figures.

BATTING	M	Inn	NO	HS	Runs	Ave	100s	50s	C/S
Tests	63	97	7	122	2201	24.45	3	9	65
First-class	259	365	44	187	11719	36.50	23	61	254

BOWLING	Balls	Runs	Wkts	Ave	BB	5wl	10wM
Tests	19108	6704	248	27.03	7/72	16	1
First-class	–	23370	945	24.73	7/18	56	9

BENNETT, Murray John

NSW, RHB/SLA
Born: 6 November 1956
Brisbane, Queensland

A steady left-arm orthodox spinner and handy batsman, Bennett used the turning Sydney wicket to his advantage in a rapid rise from his first-class debut in 1982–83 to Test selection against the West Indies at Melbourne in 1984–85. He was more successful in the next game at Sydney, taking 2/45 and 3/79 to help leg spinner Bob Holland create an unexpected victory. That season his 33 wickets at 20.52 ensured a trip to England in 1985, where he played one Test without success. After leading NSW on a few occasions he gradually drifted out of first-class cricket. With Bob Holland, Peter Taylor and Greg Matthews there were too many spinners for too few places, even in Sydney.

BATTING	M	Inn	NO	HS	Runs	Ave	100s	50s	C/S
Tests	3	5	2	23	71	23.66	–	–	5
First-class	67	85	25	59*	1437	23.95	–	4	49

BOWLING	Balls	Runs	Wkts	Ave	BB	5wl	10wM
Tests	664	325	6	54.16	3/79	–	–
First-class	–	4856	157	30.92	6/32	5	–

BLACKHAM, John McCarthy

Vic, RHB/WK
Born: 11 May 1854
North Fitzroy, Victoria
Died: 28 December 1932
Melbourne, Victoria

Blackham, known as 'the Prince of Wicket-keepers', was responsible for turning the job from one of backstop into a vital position. In fact many early critics believed he raised it to an art form. He was Australia's 'keeper for nearly 20 years, taking part in the first 9 tours of England between 1878 and 1893. He was Australia's skipper on the last tour, and until injury forced his retirement after the first Test of the 1894–95 series. However, he was a conservative and unsuccessful leader. In addition to his keeping, Blackham was a stubborn batsman, and his top score of 74 was made in his last Test. But it was his skill in taking bowlers like Spofforth, Turner and Ferris which created his reputation. Ironically, Spofforth refused to play in the first Test in 1877 because Blackham, not Murdoch was the keeper. The demon bowler soon changed his mind when he saw the Victorian in action behind the stumps.

BATTING	M	Inn	NO	HS	Runs	Ave	100s	50s	C/S
Tests	35	62	11	74	800	15.68	–	4	36/24
First-class	275	442	61	109	6395	16.78	1	26	273/180

BOWLING	Runs	Wkts	Ave	BB	5wl	10wM			
First-class	138	2	69.00	1/8	–	–			

BLACKIE, Donald Dearness

Vic, LHB/OB
Born: 5 April 1882
Bendigo, Victoria
Died: 18 April 1955
South Melbourne, Victoria

Don Blackie had one of cricket's more unusual careers, making his Test debut at a record-breaking 46 years, 253 days, an age when most had well and truly retired. Persuaded to make a comeback to grade cricket with St Kilda, his partnership with another veteran, left-armer Bert Ironmonger, was so successful that the two were paired up for Victoria. In 1928–29 he was chosen for 3 Tests against England. His figures testify to the fact that he did not bowl badly. Against a strong English line up, which easily won the series, his off spin could not be taken lightly. His best performance of 6/94 was achieved in the third Test at Melbourne. Sadly, time to continue his career was not on his side. While it might be a mystery to many that he was chosen at such an age, perhaps the greater mystery is why he was ignored by the selectors until he was, in cricketing terms, a very old man.

BATTING	M	Inn	NO	HS	Runs	Ave	100s	50s	C/S
Tests	3	6	3	11*	24	8.00	–	–	2
First-class	47	61	16	55	548	12.17	–	1	34

BOWLING	Balls	Runs	Wkts	Ave	BB	5wl	10wM
Tests	1260	444	14	31.71	6/94	1	–
First-class	–	5087	213	23.88	7/25	12	2

BONNOR, George John

NSW, RHB/RM
Born: 25 February 1855
Bathurst, New South Wales
Died: 27 June 1912
East Orange, New South Wales

A 6ft 6in giant, George Bonnor was one of cricket's great hitters. There was little skill or science to his batting, which simply involved hitting the ball as hard and as far as possible. He was not consistent, but if he came off he could win a game, and such were his capabilities that he was chosen to tour England in 1880, 1882, 1884, 1886 and 1888. One occasion when he did succeed was at Melbourne in 1884–85, when he made his only Test century, leading Australia to victory in the process. During this season he played for both Victoria and New South Wales in first-class cricket, prompting calls for some kind of residential qualifications to be brought into force. His power was enormous—when Fred Grace caught him at The Oval in 1880 off a huge skier, the batsmen were on their third run. Bonnor was also a fine fieldsman who could throw a cricket ball over 100 yards (almost 100 metres), but it was his hitting for which he will be forever remembered.

BATTING	M	Inn	NO	HS	Runs	Ave	100s	50s	C/S
Tests	17	30	0	128	512	17.06	1	2	16
First-class	148	244	17	128	4820	21.23	5	18	127/1

BOWLING	Balls	Runs	Wkts	Ave	BB	5wl	10wM
Tests	164	84	2	42.00	1/5	–	–
First-class	–	470	12	39.16	3/34	–	–

BOON, David Clarence

Tas, RHB/RM
Born: 29 December 1960
Launceston, Tasmania

The stocky Tasmanian had been touted as a future Test player since primary school; a prophecy he fulfilled against the West Indies in 1984–85, scoring 51 in his second innings. He toured England in 1985, but found difficulties with the English spinners. His early struggles to establish his position were overcome when he was paired with Geoff Marsh, and they became Australia's most successful openers since Simpson and Lawry.

Boon has shown his fighting qualities on many occasions. Dropped for poor form against England in 1986–87, he came back to win the International Cricketer of the Year award next season. In 1988–89 he was the leading scorer against the West Indies, and followed this with a successful tour of England. He made his highest Test score of 200 against New Zealand in Perth, but had the remainder of his season ruined by a knee injury in 1989–90. He recovered to score over 500 runs in successive summers against England and India, batting at number three where he dominated, scoring centuries in three successive Tests, and establishing himself as one of the best batsmen in world cricket.

Returned to the role of opener against the fearsome West Indies pace attack in 1991–92, he was far and away the best Australian batsman, scoring 490 runs at an average of over 60. He was the one player who looked able to counter the bowling of Curtly Ambrose. In this summer Boon took his Test aggregate past 5000 runs. For the 1993 England tour he returned to number three.

At the beginning of his career Boon's fielding could be ordinary, but he has worked hard to make himself one of the world's finest close to the wicket fieldsmen. Some of his catches at short leg have to be seen to be believed.

With the bat or in the field he is a brave and determined character. When a ball from a West Indies' pace bowler cut his chin in Jamaica, he calmly stood and had the wound stitched on the field before continuing on to an undefeated century.

Boon is a vital component of today's Australian teams, able to tailor his batting to suit any situation, and is at his best when runs are most needed or the bowling most difficult. His imposing record in limited-overs cricket is a further testimony to his versatility. He is, without doubt, the finest batsman produced by Tasmania.

BATTING	M	Inn	NO	HS	Runs	Ave	100s	50s	C/S
Tests	80	145	16	200	5869	45.50	17	25	78
First-class	220	372	36	227	15940	47.44	51	69	186

BOWLING	Balls	Runs	Wkts	Ave	BB	5wI	10wM
Tests	18	5	0	–	–	–	–
First-class	–	363	6	60.50	1/12	–	–

BOOTH, Brian Charles

NSW, RHB/RM, OB
Born: 19 October 1933
Perthville near Bathurst, New South Wales

A cultured and stylish middle order batsman, Brian Booth was one of the country's most successful players in the early to mid-sixties. He made his Test debut on tour in England in 1961 and was a constant member of the side until he was dropped after captaining Australia to a defeat against England in 1965–66. He had been vice-captain to Bob Simpson since 1963–64. He had also led Australia in the first Test of that 1965–66 series. In addition to his elegant batting he was a superb fieldsman. Booth's best series was against South Africa in 1963–64, when he made two of his Test centuries, including his highest score, 169, in the first game, at Brisbane. Booth was a sportsman in every sense of the word, both on and off the field, and was a double international, being a member of Australia's 1956 Olympic Hockey Team.

BATTING	M	Inn	NO	HS	Runs	Ave	100s	50s	C/S
Tests	29	48	6	169	1773	42.21	5	10	17
First-class	183	283	35	214*	11265	45.42	26	60	119

BOWLING	Balls	Runs	Wkts	Ave	BB	5wI	10wM
Tests	436	146	3	48.66	2/33	–	–
First-class	–	956	16	59.75	2/29	–	–

BORDER, Allan Robert

NSW, Qld, LHB/SLA
Born: 27 July 1955
Cremorne, New South Wales

Allan Border will certainly be remembered as one of Australia's finest players. A tough, determined, little left hander, he was the basis of Australia's batting through the eighties; in fact there were times when many believed he *was* the batting, such was the level of performance he maintained.

Border came into the Test side during World Series Cricket and established himself so successfully that he held his place after the 'peace' settlement was reached. As the old guard gradually retired Border found himself in sides with increasingly less experience, and when Kim Hughes tearfully resigned the captaincy in 1984–85 he was the obvious alternative. It was not a task he relished, and it would be fair to say it took him some time to come to terms with it. The indifferent form of many teams he captained would not have helped and, while there must have been times when he felt like quitting, he kept going, developing first into a good limited-overs skipper and, finally, into an excellent Test captain.

Along the way he has established records which may never be beaten. No one has played as many Tests, scored as many runs or taken as many catches. Border is the only man to score 150 in each innings of a Test, a feat he achieved against Pakistan at Lahore in 1979–80. Of all Australians who have played more than 20 Tests, only Bradman and Greg Chappell have a higher average. He has also appeared in more Limited-overs Internationals than any other player. Other scoring records would take too long to list, but it must be remembered that for much of his career he alone stood between Australia and defeat. Perhaps the best example of this came at Queens Park Oval, Trinidad in 1983–84, when his innings of 98 not out and 100 not out saved what was apparently a lost cause. To have done so well for so long under such pressure is a sure sign of his greatness.

In addition to his batting prowess, Border is an outstanding fieldsman and a much under-used slow bowler, as his 11-wicket demolition of the West Indies at Sydney in 1988–89 shows, and he is always a threat in limited-overs cricket.

Recently the struggle has at last been rewarded, with Border developing a team capable of winning. A surprise victory in the 1987 World Cup and the 1989 Ashes slaughter of England have been his leadership highlights. In recent times Border has not batted with the freedom of his younger days, but he remains a player to be reckoned with, particularly when the going gets tough. Despite not registering a Test century for four years, he maintained his fifty-plus average. The long awaited hundred came against Sri Lanka in 1992 and he followed it with another against the West Indies at Melbourne later the same season.

Border's 1993 tour of England was as much a triumph as 1989 with the Australians dominating the series. The captain proved he still possessed the skills at the highest level with an innings of 200 not out in the fourth Test at Headingly.

BATTING	M	Inn	NO	HS	Runs	Ave	100s	50s	C/S
Tests	147	252	43	205	10695	51.17	26	61	148
First-class	350	570	89	205	24770	51.50	66	129	335

BOWLING	Balls	Runs	Wkts	Ave	BB	5wI	10wM
Tests	3901	1499	39	38.44	7/46	2	1
First-class	–	3836	99	38.75	7/46	3	1

BOYLE, Henry Frederick

Vic, RHB/RM(r)
Born: 10 December 1847
Sydney, New South Wales
Died: 21 November 1907
Bendigo, Victoria

The bearded 'Harry' Boyle was a key member of the first Australian sides and his bowling partnership with Fred Spofforth helped establish the reputation of Australian cricket. In 1878 the two bowled a strong MCC side out for 33 and 19 to ensure Australia would never be underestimated again. Boyle also toured England in 1880 and 1882, when he took part in the famous Ashes match at The Oval. He tied up an end for Spofforth and even took the final wicket to create the legend. His figures of 2/24 and 3/19 showed his value in a tense, close-scoring game. The tall, round-arm bowler toured England on two more occasions, in 1884 and 1888, as player-manager, but nothing would equal the memory of that immortal moment in 1882 when he put the ball through Edmund Peate's defence.

BATTING	M	Inn	NO	HS	Runs	Ave	100s	50s	C/S
Tests	12	16	4	36*	153	12.75	–	–	10
First-class	140	215	48	108	1711	10.24	1	1	125

BOWLING	Balls	Runs		Wkts	Ave	BB	5wl	10wM
Tests	1744	641		32	20.03	6/42	1	–
First-class	–	5692		370	15.38	7/32	26	6

BRADMAN, Donald George

NSW, SA, RHB/LB
Born: 27 August 1908
Cootamundra, New South Wales

If batting is the art of scoring runs then Don Bradman is the finest of all batsmen because he scored runs in a quantity and manner that has never been challenged by any other player. In a first-class career of over 20 years he averaged a century every third innings and his first-class average of 95.14 and Test average of 99.94 are unapproachable. He is the only player to score one hundred first-class centuries without playing English county cricket, and no one has come anywhere near the low number of innings he took to achieve them. Measured on any scoring scale he is at least a third better than any other batsman, and his scoring feats would, and have, filled books. In fact he has had more written and spoken about him than any other cricketer.

Bradman spent most of his youth in the NSW country town of Bowral, quickly showing an extraordinary aptitude for the game. His rise through the ranks of representative cricket was meteoric. He made his first-class debut in 1927–28, scoring 118. The next season he was in the Test side against England. Although he did little in his first game, and was actually dropped for the second Test, he returned to complete the series with scores of 79, 112, 40, 58, 123 and 37 not out. When doubts were expressed about his technique on English wickets the 21-year-old scored 974 runs at 139.14 in the 1930 series, with innings of 8, 131, 254, 1, 334, 14 and 232. At Headingly he made 309 of those 334 in a single day. He tortured bowlers everywhere, even averaging 56 against Bodyline, which was invented specifically to curb his scoring.

In 1936–37 Bradman became captain of Australia, and after losing the first two Tests to England, his side came back to win the remaining three. His innings of 270, 212 and 169 in those three games played a major part in the result.

After the war he returned to lead Australia to victories at home against India and England, before ending his Test career when he led his side undefeated through England in 1948. Nimble footwork, lightning reactions, an ability to sight the ball sooner than others, and an insatiable appetite for runs had all combined to produce the nearest thing to a batting machine.

As captain of Australia, Bradman was cool and calculating, with a tactical skill that almost matched his ability with the bat. Australia never lost a series while he was in charge. After retirement and a knighthood he continued to direct Australia's cricket fortunes as selector and administrator.

An intensely private man, Bradman's rare public appearances attract enormous media attention. Such is his influence that more than 40 years after his retirement as a player he was rightfully referred to as 'the greatest living Australian'. He is unique. There will never be another Bradman.

BATTING	M	Inn	NO	HS	Runs	Ave	100s	50s	C/S
Tests	52	80	10	334	6996	99.94	29	13	32
First-class	234	338	43	452*	28067	95.14	117	69	131/1

BOWLING	Balls	Runs	Wkts	Ave	BB	5wl	10wM
Tests	160	72	2	36.00	1/8	–	–
First-class	–	1367	36	37.97	3/35	–	–

BRIGHT, Raymond James

Vic, RHB/SLA
Born: 13 July 1954
Footscray, Victoria

Ray Bright proved a great stayer. Just when it seemed the slow left-armer had played his last Test he would fight his way back into the side. In fact one of his last Test performances was among his best, five wickets in the second innings of the Madras tied Test in 1986–87. Relying more on flight and changes of pace than spin, Bright made his first-class debut in 1972–73 and his Test debut in England in 1977. Although he never fully established himself, he was a useful foil to

Lillee and Alderman in 1981 and had success in Pakistan, where he took 7/87 at Karachi in 1980. A competent batsman with a number of impressive first-class innings to his credit, and captain of Victoria, Bright's determination took him further than many players of greater skill. At the end of his career he had the honour of leading the Australian team in a limited-overs competition in Sharjah.

BATTING	M	Inn	NO	HS	Runs	Ave	100s	50s	C/S
Tests	25	39	8	33	445	14.35	–	–	13
First-class	184	247	51	108	4130	21.07	2	12	107

BOWLING	Balls	Runs	Wkts	Ave	BB	5wl	10wM
Tests	5541	2180	53	41.13	7/87	4	1
First-class	–	15114	471	32.08	7/87	24	2

BROMLEY, Ernest Harvey

WA, Vic, LHB/SLA
Born: 2 September 1912
Fremantle, Western Australia
Died: 1 February 1967
Clayton, Victoria

Ern Bromley was born in Western Australia and made his debut for his home state in 1929–30. After some promising innings, but lacking regular competition there, he moved to Victoria where he was an instant success, earning a place in the fourth Test of the Bodyline series. It was thought that left handers might counter the English line of attack. Although he failed in that game, his good Shield form won him a trip to England in 1934. Sadly the moving ball found holes in his technique, particularly around off stump, and he averaged only 16.42. In less exacting conditions he could reveal a useful range of strokes. Bromley was also an excellent fieldsman with a strong throwing arm.

BATTING	M	Inn	NO	HS	Runs	Ave	100s	50s	C/S
Tests	2	4	0	26	38	9.50	–	–	2
First-class	52	78	6	161	2055	28.54	3	12	43

BOWLING	Balls	Runs	Wkts	Ave	BB	5wl	10wM
Tests	60	19	0	–	–	–	–
First-class	–	1651	39	42.33	4/50	–	–

BROWN, William Alfred

NSW, Qld, RHB
Born: 31 July 1912
Toowoomba, Queensland

Bill Brown was a talented opening batsman who toured England in 1934, 1938 and 1948, passing 1000 runs on each occasion, and South Africa in 1935–36. Taken on that first English tour as a promising young player, he made 73 on debut at Trent Bridge and a century at Lord's. 1938 was his most successful tour, coming second to Bradman with 1887 runs at 57.18, and carrying his bat for 206 at Lord's, his finest innings. Brown returned to Queensland from NSW in 1939 to captain his home State. After the War he captained the Australian team to New Zealand in 1945–46, but was soon replaced in the Test side by the partnership of Arthur Morris and Sid Barnes. Although he toured England in 1948, making 1448 runs at 57.92, he could not command a regular Test place. Brown retired in 1950 leaving behind an impressive Test and first-class record.

BATTING	M	Inn	NO	HS	Runs	Ave	100s	50s	C/S
Tests	22	35	1	206*	1592	46.82	4	9	14
First-class	189	284	15	265*	13838	51.44	39	66	110/1

BOWLING	Runs	Wkts	Ave	BB	5wl	10wM			
First-class	110	6	18.33	4/16	–	–			

BRUCE, William

Vic, LHB/LM
Born: 22 May 1864
South Yarra, Victoria
Died: 3 August 1925
St Kilda, Victoria

William Bruce, who toured England in 1886 and 1893, was an elegant left-hand batsman, bowler and good fieldsman. He was an outstanding

schoolboy cricketer and was quickly introduced into the Victorian team in 1882–83, continuing to represent them until 1903–04. His two tours of England produced fewer runs than his ability appeared to warrant, although in 14 Tests for Australia his performances were consistent without being spectacular. Despite never scoring a Test century, he passed fifty on five occasions and his average is a very creditable one for the period in which he played. Bruce was a solicitor by profession, and committed suicide by drowning at the age of 61.

BATTING	M	Inn	NO	HS	Runs	Ave	100s	50s	C/S
Tests	14	26	2	80	702	29.25	–	5	12
First-class	145	250	11	191	5731	23.97	4	28	103

BOWLING	Balls	Runs	Wkts	Ave	BB	5wI	10wM
Tests	958	440	12	36.66	3/88	–	–
First-class	–	4244	143	29.67	7/72	5	–

BURGE, Peter John Parnell

Qld, RHB
Born: 17 May 1932
East Brisbane, Queensland

A solidly built righthander, Peter Burge hit the ball with tremendous power, representing Australia in 42 Tests between 1954–55 and 1965–66. He took part in every tour during that period, and at first-class level was the key player in the Queensland batting line up. Burge took some time to establish himself in Test cricket, before he came of age in England in 1961 when he scored 1376 runs at 55.04, including 181 in the fifth Test. Three years later he turned the vital Headingley Test with a spectacular 160, a display which ensured the retention of the Ashes. This innings showed the best of his batting: thunderous hooks, pulls, sweeps and drives, all hit with the power that made him one of the world's most dangerous players.

BATTING	M	Inn	NO	HS	Runs	Ave	100s	50s	C/S
Tests	42	68	8	181	2290	38.16	4	12	23
First-class	233	354	46	283	14640	47.33	38	68	166/4

BOWLING	Runs	Wkts	Ave	BB	5wI	10wM	
First-class	129	1	129.00	1/0	–	–	

BURKE, James Wallace

NSW, RHB/OB
Born: 12 June 1930
Mosman, New South Wales
Died: 2 February 1979
Manly, New South Wales

Jimmy Burke was a dour, determined opening batsman for Australian teams in the fifties. He made his first-class debut at 18 in 1948–49, and in 1950–51 scored 101 not out against England in his first Test. Burke was one of the few successes on the 1956 tour of England, making 1339 runs at 47.82. He formed a strong partnership with Colin McDonald, giving the side a sound start and frustrating bowlers with his stay-put style. Spectators also found his style hard to take, but his value to his side in wearing down the opposition bowlers was immense. As an off-spin bowler Burke took some valuable wickets, but his action was very suspect indeed. One critic described it 'like a policeman laying a truncheon over a short offender's head'. After his playing days, Burke became a much respected ABC Radio commentator. Sadly, health and financial troubles contributed to his suicide when he shot himself at the age of 48.

BATTING	M	Inn	NO	HS	Runs	Ave	100s	50s	C/S
Tests	24	44	7	189	1280	34.59	3	5	18
First-class	130	204	36	220	7563	45.01	21	35	59

BOWLING	Balls	Runs	Wkts	Ave	BB	5wl	10wM
Tests	814	230	8	28.75	4/37	–	–
First-class	–	2941	101	29.11	6/40	3	–

BURN, Edwin James Kenneth

Tas, RHB/RM
Born: 17 September 1862
Richmond, Tasmania
Died: 20 July 1956
Hobart, Tasmania

Kenny Burn's selection as reserve 'keeper in the 1890 team to tour England is one of cricket's legends. He had never kept wicket in his

29

life! During the tour all the players, except Burn, had a turn behind the stumps to spell Blackham. He was a batsman pure and simple, not a wicket-keeper. However, he was a talented batsman who represented Tasmania from 1883–84 to 1909–10, captaining them for 20 years. A solid, no frills player, Burn could, and did, score runs off all comers in his long career, and was one of Tasmania's finest batsmen. In 1907–08, aged 45, he took a century off the touring English side. At club level he was phenomenal, his best scores being 365 and 361. He played both Tests on the 1890 tour without success, but his skill should have warranted another chance, particularly in Australian conditions, where he was a much better player. When he died at the age of 93, he was the oldest living Test cricketer, having outlasted all his team mates, a fact which would have appealed to his dry Scottish humour.

BATTING	M	Inn	NO	HS	Runs	Ave	100s	50s	C/S
Tests	2	4	0	19	41	10.25	–	–	–
First-class	48	90	8	119	1750	21.34	2	5	31

BOWLING	Runs	Wkts	Ave	BB	5wI	10wM
First-class	320	14	22.85	3/15	–	–

BURTON, Frederick John

NSW, Vic, RHB/WK
Born: 2 November 1865
Collingwood, Victoria
Died: 25 August 1929
Wanganui, New Zealand

Fred Burton was a wicket-keeper and right-hand batsman whose career unfortunately coincided with that of John McCarthy Blackham. This undoubtedly prevented Burton from playing more than two Tests. He actually played the second of those as a batsman, the only game against England in 1887–88. He had played his other Test, also against England, the previous season. Although he looked a good prospect, he never really proved his ability in performances and his career figures are disappointing. Eventually he settled in New Zealand, where he spent the latter part of his life. After his playing days were over he spent some time as a first-class umpire.

BATTING	M	Inn	NO	HS	Runs	Ave	100s	50s	C/S
Tests	2	4	2	2*	4	2.00	–	–	1/1
First-class	22	38	10	47	376	13.42	–	–	25/7

CALLAWAY, Sydney Thomas

NSW, RHB/RFM
Born: 6 February 1868
Redfern, Sydney, New South Wales
Died: 25 November 1923
Christchurch, New Zealand.

Syd Callaway was a competent all-rounder who represented New South Wales from 1888 to 1896. Although he played only 3 Tests he had one memorable moment. He played two Tests against England in 1891–92 with little success. However, in the third Test of the 1894–95 series at Adelaide, he made 41, at number eleven, and took 5/37 in England's first innings, thus helping his side to a massive 382 run victory. Strangely enough, this was his only game of the series. Callaway toured New Zealand with New South Wales teams and liked the country so much that he eventually settled there. He represented Canterbury for a number of seasons, where he was particularly effective with the ball, proving to be a matchwinner on numerous occasions.

BATTING	M	Inn	NO	HS	Runs	Ave	100s	50s	C/S
Tests	3	6	1	41	87	17.40	–	–	–
First-class	62	112	8	86	1747	16.79	–	10	48

BOWLING	Balls	Runs	Wkts	Ave	BB	5wI	10wM
Tests	471	142	6	23.66	5/37	1	–
First-class	–	5460	320	17.06	8/33	33	12

CALLEN, Ian Wayne

Vic, LHB/RFM
Born: 2 May 1955
Alexandra, Victoria

A tall, fast-medium bowler, Ian Callen burst onto the first-class scene in 1976–77 with a series of fine performances, taking 31 wickets, including what remained his best figures of 8/42 against Queensland. World Series Cricket gave him an early shot at Test level, against India at Adelaide in the final game of the 1977–78 series. He bowled well to take six wickets in an Australian victory. Despite touring the West Indies in 1978 and Pakistan in 1982 Callen never made it onto the Test arena again. Injuries certainly restricted his chances, particularly in the West indies, and his career must seem to be rather unsatisfactory for one who promised so much in the beginning. Even Victoria seemed to discard him while he still had something to offer.

BATTING	M	Inn	NO	HS	Runs	Ave	100s	50s	C/S
Tests	1	2	2	22*	26	–	–	–	1
First-class	53	68	21	34	578	12.30	–	–	19

BOWLING	Balls	Runs	Wkts	Ave	BB	5wI	10wM
Tests	440	191	6	31.83	3/83	–	–
First-class	–	5412	197	27.47	8/42	7	1

CAMPBELL, Gregory Dale

Tas, RHB/RFM
Born: 10 March 1964
Launceston, Tasmania

Greg Campbell was the surprise choice of the 1989 Australian team to England, gaining the selectors' nod over more experienced campaigners like Mike Whitney. The young fast-medium bowler had played one first-class game in 1986–87, and none in the next season, but he returned in 1988–89 to capture 36 wickets and impressed all with his ability. Injuries to key bowlers put him in Australia's team at Headingley, where he failed to do himself justice. He bowled well in other games on tour and certainly displayed the potential to be an investment for the future. He showed the benefit of the tour with some good performances in 1989–90, including some steady bowling in three Tests against Sri Lanka and Pakistan. His career since then has been restricted with knee and wrist injuries, and he had played few games during the previous two years before he moved to Queensland at the start of the 1992–93 season.

BATTING	M	Inn	NO	HS	Runs	Ave	100s	50s	C/S
Tests	4	4	0	6	10	2.50	–	–	1
First-class	44	50	9	41	347	8.46	–	–	10

BOWLING	Balls	Runs	Wkts	Ave	BB	5wI	10wM
Tests	951	503	13	38.69	3/79	–	–
First-class	–	4016	120	33.47	6/80	5	–

CARKEEK, William

Vic, LHB/WK
Born: 17 October 1878
Walhalla, Victoria
Died: 20 February 1937
Prahran, Victoria

Bill 'Barlow' Carkeek made his Victorian debut in 1903–04 and proved to be a steady, rather than spectacular, wicket-keeper. He went to England as Hanson Carter's deputy in 1909. When Carter withdrew from the 1912 tour, as one of six players in dispute with the authorities, Carkeek was chosen as the number one keeper. He played in all six Tests in the Triangular Series, but the wet English summer prevented him from performing at his best. He was again unlucky in 1914–15, when he was selected to tour South Africa and the outbreak of War caused the trip to be cancelled. His career effectively over, Carkeek returned to his trade as a blacksmith.

BATTING	M	Inn	NO	HS	Runs	Ave	100s	50s	C/S
Tests	6	5	2	6*	16	5.33	–	–	6
First-class	95	146	32	68	1388	12.17	–	2	114/45

CARLSON, Phillip Henry

Qld, RHB/RM
Born: 8 August 1951
Nundah, Queensland

Phil Carlson played two Tests for Australia in 1978–79, during the second season of World Series Cricket. The national selectors were searching for an all-rounder to boost an inexperienced team, but despite his fine first-class record, he was unable to grasp the opportunity. Carlson made his debut in 1968–69, but the strong Australian sides of the early seventies forced him to spend ten years playing for Queensland before Test selection came his way. He finally made the side by performing the rare feat of taking 10 wickets and scoring a century, which he did against New South Wales in 1978–79. Carlson retired after a loss of form in 1981, ending a career which ultimately failed to live up to its early promise.

BATTING	M	Inn	NO	HS	Runs	Ave	100s	50s	C/S
Tests	2	4	0	21	23	5.75	–	–	2
First-class	91	161	14	110*	4167	28.34	5	19	59

BOWLING	Balls	Runs	Wkts	Ave	BB	5wI	10wM
Tests	368	99	2	49.50	2/41	–	–
First-class	–	3096	124	24.96	7/42	5	1

CARTER, Hanson

NSW, RHB/WK
Born: 15 March 1878
Halifax, Yorkshire, England
Died: 8 June 1948
Bellevue Hill, New South Wales

A Yorkshire-born undertaker, 'Sammy' Carter was a fine 'keeper for Australia before and after the First World War. Small, but tough, Carter toured England in 1902, 1909 and 1921. He missed out in 1912 when he was one of the 'Big Six' who refused to go. His first-class career, which began in 1897–98, lasted 27 years, and he was an important part of many Australian sides. Warwick Armstrong particularly valued the little man's advice, and his knowledge of the game's laws. It was Carter who told Armstrong that a declaration by England's captain, Lord Tennyson, in 1921 was illegal, forcing the captain to rescind his decision. Towards the end of his Test career, after the War, his position came under threat from the emerging talents of Bert Oldfield, but Carter was still able to claim his share of Tests, even when he was over 40. Throughout his career he was a useful batsman, capable of holding up an end or going on the attack according to the situation.

BATTING	M	Inn	NO	HS	Runs	Ave	100s	50s	C/S
Tests	28	47	9	72	873	22.97	–	4	44/21
First-class	128	175	31	149	2897	20.11	2	13	182/89

CHAPPELL, Gregory Stephen

SA, Qld, RHB/RM
Born: 7 August 1948
Unley, South Australia

Greg Chappell was one of the most stylish and consistently successful batsmen ever to play for Australia. The second of three brothers, he developed an almost faultless technique, and his classic, upright drives were as close to perfection as it is possible to be. In addition to his awesome batting skills, Chappell was a much under-rated medium pace bowler and an outstanding fieldsman in any position.

Making his first-class debut in 1966–67 at the age of 18 against Victoria, he made 53 and 62 not out. Two seasons with Somerset in English county cricket honed his skills before his inevitable Test selection, against England at Perth in 1970–71. Coming in at 5/107 he made a superb 108 to immediately secure his place in the side. On his first tour of England in 1972, he made 131 at Lord's and 113 at The Oval, there adding 201 with his elder brother Ian. Australia won both games. As the seventies progressed he continued to score heavily, his batting being an important part of what had become the world's best team. When Ian resigned the captaincy in 1975 Greg was the obvious successor and confirmed it with a century in each innings of his first Test as captain, against the West Indies at Brisbane in 1975–76. As a leader he was less aggressive than his brother, but a capable and competent skipper all the same.

Greg Chappell's captaincy had only two low points: leading the unhappy 1977 tourists to England amidst the revelations of World Series Cricket, which he subsequently joined, and the notorious underarm incident in a 1981 World Series Cup game, when he instructed his brother Trevor to bowl the last delivery underarm to prevent New Zealand hitting a six to win the match. That apart, he was always the model of what a cricketer should be.

After World Series Cricket he returned to the Test team and led the side whenever he indicated his willingness to do so. In this latter part of his career he was not always in the peak of fitness, but he was still the side's best batsman. Chappell's last Test, against Pakistan in 1983–84, was the perfect end—his 182 made him Australia's highest run scorer, and he set a new record for the most catches as well. Bill Ponsford and Reggie Duff are the only other Australians to make hundreds in their first and last Tests. Against all opposition, under all conditions, Australia can have had few better players.

BATTING	M	Inn	NO	HS	Runs	Ave	100s	50s	C/S
Tests	87	151	19	247*	7110	53.86	24	31	122
First-class	321	542	72	247*	24535	52.20	74	111	376

BOWLING	Balls	Runs	Wkts	Ave	BB		5wI	10wM
Tests	5227	1913	47	40.70	5/61		1	–
First-class	–	8717	291	29.95	7/40		5	–

CHAPPELL, Ian Michael

SA, RHB/LB
Born: 26 September 1943
Unley, South Australia

The eldest of the Chappell brothers, Ian could justly lay claim to being Australia's finest captain. A tough right-hand batsman, part-time leg spinner and excellent slips fieldsman, he had all the necessary skills to be a Test player, making his first-class debut in 1961–62 and his Test debut three years later, against Pakistan in 1964–65.

It took him some time to really establish himself at the highest level, which he did on the 1968 English tour, topping the averages with 1261 runs at 48.50. His skills blossomed against the West Indies in 1968–69, when he scored hundreds in each of the first two Tests. He also became the side's vice-captain. The only problem came in South Africa in 1970, when, after skipper Lawry had called him 'the best batsman in the world', he made just 32 runs in 8 innings. It proved only a temporary setback to a player who sought to impose his dominance. His liking for the hook typified his aggressive approach, and if it sometimes led to his dismissal, it also brought him plenty of runs.

When the selectors sacked Lawry for the last Test in 1970–71, Chappell was the natural replacement. Although he lost that match, and the Ashes too, it was really the start of a new era for Australian cricket. Within three years he had taken the team from also-rans to the best side in the world. Although he could be an administrator's nightmare, Chappell inspired fanatical loyalty in his players, enabling them to produce performances matched by few Australian teams. He resigned the captaincy in 1975 and retired from Test cricket the next year, but was back in the news by 1977 as one of the organisers of World Series Cricket. Always a fighter for better conditions for his players, it was only natural such an organisation would appeal to him.

After World Series Cricket he returned for one more season in 1979–80, and while he still possessed considerable batting talent, reclaiming his place in the Test team, his on-field behaviour created controversy. Chappell retired to television and journalism where his work has shown his great understanding of the game, and as expected, a fearlessness in expressing his opinions.

Conservative followers like to highlight his clashes with authority, but they must never obscure his pugnacious batting skills and outstanding leadership. In 30 Tests as captain he won 15 and lost only 5. Ian Chappell seemed to thrive on pressure, and if you had to choose someone to play an innings for your life he would be an obvious choice.

BATTING	M	Inn	NO	HS	Runs	Ave	100s	50s	C/S
Tests	75	136	10	196	5345	42.42	14	26	105
First-class	262	448	41	209	19680	48.35	59	96	312/1

BOWLING	Balls	Runs	Wkts	Ave	BB	5wl	10wM
Tests	2873	1316	20	65.80	2/20	–	–
First-class	–	6614	176	37.57	5/29	2	_

CHAPPELL, Trevor Martin

SA, WA, NSW, RHB/RM
Born: 21 October 1952
Glenelg, South Australia

The youngest of the Chappell brothers, Trevor was a useful player, although lacking the superb skills of Ian and Greg. After a brilliant school career, his progress in the first-class arena was more sedate. Like his brothers he took part in World Series Cricket, then settled in New South Wales where he produced his best form. Chappell's sound batting, steady medium pace bowling and brilliant fielding won him a place on the 1981 tour of England where he played his only Tests. He proved a useful limited-overs player, despite the infamous underarm delivery, and he scored a century against India in the 1983 World Cup. It is hard to say how much his brothers' success damaged his own career, but he must have suffered to some extent. Following two such great players could not have been easy.

BATTING	M	Inn	NO	HS	Runs	Ave	100s	50s	C/S
Tests	3	6	1	27	79	15.80	–	–	2
First-class	88	151	14	150	4049	29.55	5	21	47

BOWLING	Runs	Wkts	Ave	BB	5wl	10wM			
First-class	1462	59	24.77	4/12	–	–			

CHARLTON, Percie Chater

NSW, RHB/RFM
Born: 9 April 1867
Surry Hills, New South Wales
Died: 30 September 1954
Pymble, New South Wales

Percie Charlton was a right-handed all-rounder who toured England in the wet summer of 1890, where he played in both Tests. On tour he scored 534 runs at 14.83 and took 42 wickets at 19.04. His work as a doctor and personal ill-health reduced his representative cricket after that tour, but he continued to play club cricket, mostly with I Zingari,

38

with whom he was associated for over half a century. In later life Charlton was also involved in administration with the NSWCA for a number of years. His first-class record shows considerably more success with the ball than the bat, and he was also a very capable fieldsman.

BATTING	M	Inn	NO	HS	Runs	Ave	100s	50s	C/S
Tests	2	4	0	11	29	7.25	–	–	–
First-class	40	65	13	50	648	12.46	–	1	38

BOWLING	Balls	Runs	Wkts	Ave	BB	5wI	10wM
Tests	45	24	3	8.00	3/18	–	–
First-class	–	1937	97	19.96	7/44	6	1

CHIPPERFIELD, Arthur Gordon

NSW, RHB/LB
Born: 17 November 1905
Ashfield, New South Wales
Died: 29 July 1987
Ryde, New South Wales

Arthur Chipperfield had a meteoric rise to the top, being chosen to tour England in 1934 after only three first-class innings. In 1932–33 he had made 152 for Northern Districts against the visiting English side in a non-first-class game. It proved a sound selection as he scored 899 runs at the reasonable average of 40.86. He is the only Australian to make 99 on his Test debut; at Trent Bridge, on that tour. Left not out at lunch he was dismissed immediately after the break and without obtaining that elusive single. His useful leg-spin bowling and outstanding slips fielding were other bonuses. Chipperfield made his sole Test century on tour against South Africa in 1935–36 and he visited England again in 1938, but without the same success as previously. In fact Chipperfield's whole career was typified by its inconsistency. Good performances were interspersed with bouts of disappointing form, but on his day he was an extremely good cricketer.

BATTING	M	Inn	NO	HS	Runs	Ave	100s	50s	C/S
Tests	14	20	3	109	552	32.47	1	2	15
First-class	96	129	17	175	4295	38.34	9	22	91

BOWLING	Balls	Runs	Wkts	Ave	BB	5wI	10wM
Tests	924	437	5	87.40	3/91	–	–
First-class	–	2582	65	39.72	8/66	1	–

CLARK, Wayne Maxwell

WA, RHB/RFM
Born: 19 September 1953
Perth, Western Australia

World Series Cricket gave Wayne Clark the opportunity to play for Australia in 1977–78, after three years of good work in the Sheffield Shield. Clark played well against India, forming a successful opening partnership with Jeff Thomson, then had a reasonable tour of the West Indies with Bob Simpson's youthful team. Strangely, he played for Australia only once more, although he continued to represent his State with distinction for many years. Whether murmurings about the legality of his action were responsible will never be known, and no one could have been disappointed with the form of his replacements, Rodney Hogg and Alan Hurst, against England in 1978–79. However, there remains the thought that his performances suggested he was worth a few more opportunities.

BATTING	M	Inn	NO	HS	Runs	Ave	100s	50s	C/S
Tests	10	19	2	33	98	5.76	–	–	6
First-class	62	82	25	46*	717	12.57	–	–	23

BOWLING	Balls	Runs	Wkts	Ave	BB	5wI	10wM
Tests	2793	1265	44	28.75	4/46	–	–
First-class	–	6169	210	29.37	7/26	6	1

COLLEY, David John

NSW, RHB/RFM
Born: 15 March 1947
Mosman, Sydney, New South Wales

David Colley was a talented all-rounder who had the misfortune to be at his peak at a time when Australian cricket was endowed with many talented players. He made his first-class debut in 1969–70, and, following some good all-round performances, was selected in the 1972 team to tour England, where he played his only three Tests. Although he performed usefully in those games, making 54 at Trent Bridge and bowling well without collecting many wickets, he was never given another chance. Players like Lillee, Massie, Walker and Gilmour emerged on the scene, and that, combined with injury, relegated Colley to Shield cricket and an early retirement, a disappointing end for one with such talent.

BATTING	M	Inn	NO	HS	Runs	Ave	100s	50s	C/S
Tests	3	4	0	54	84	21.00	–	1	1
First-class	87	123	23	101	2374	23.74	1	13	44

BOWLING	Balls	Runs	Wkts	Ave	BB	5wl	10wM
Tests	729	312	6	52.00	3/83	–	–
First-class	–	7459	236	31.60	6/30	8	–

COLLINS, Herbert Leslie

NSW, RHB/SLA
Born: 21 January 1889
Darlinghurst, New South Wales
Died: 28 May 1959
Sydney, New South Wales

A tough, poker-faced batsman of endless patience, Herbie 'Horseshoe' Collins was one of the key members of Australia's post-World War I teams. Collins' first-class debut came in 1909–10, but it was in leading the AIF team through England in 1919 that he really made his mark. In 1920–21 he entered Test cricket at the age of 31 and scored 557 runs in the series. He made 70 and 104 on debut at Sydney, and 162 at Adelaide. Collins toured England in 1921 and showed his stubborn streak by making 40 in 289 minutes at Old Trafford to save a Test. When Warwick Armstrong retired, he took over the captaincy, making 203 against South Africa in his second game in charge. He performed well against England in 1924–25, retiring in 1926 after England won back the Ashes. Collins then returned to his chosen profession of bookmaker.

BATTING	M	Inn	NO	HS	Runs	Ave	100s	50s	C/S
Tests	19	31	1	203	1352	45.06	4	6	13
First-class	168	258	10	282	9924	40.01	32	40	115

BOWLING	Balls	Runs	Wkts	Ave	BB	5wl	10wM
Tests	654	252	4	63.00	2/47	–	–
First-class	–	3871	181	21.38	8/31	8	2

CONINGHAM, Arthur

NSW, Qld, LHB/LFM
Born: 14 July 1863
Emerald Hill, Victoria
Died: 13 June 1939
Gladesville, New South Wales

An extremely talented all-rounder, Arthur Coningham's cricket ability was submerged by his eccentric character and the scandal which appeared to follow him. After touring England in 1893 with little success, although he lit a fire in the outfield at Lord's on a cold day, he moved to Queensland at the end of season 1893–94 and had the distinction of scoring their initial first-class century when he made 151 against New South Wales in 1895 after appearing in Sheffield Shield matches for New South Wales earlier in the season. His sole Test was against England at Melbourne in 1894–95, and he took the wicket of Archie MacLaren with his first ball. Scandal took over in 1899 when he sued his wife for divorce on the grounds of her committing adultery with a Roman Catholic priest. Coningham conducted his own case in two spectacular trials, but lost. He moved to New Zealand and later spent six months in gaol for fraud. He was finally divorced in 1912, but his health declined, and his last years were spent in an asylum.

BATTING	M	Inn	NO	HS	Runs	Ave	100s	50s	C/S
Tests	1	2	0	10	13	6.50	–	–	–
First-class	35	59	2	151	896	15.71	1	2	27

BOWLING	Balls	Runs	Wkts	Ave	BB	5wI	10wM
Tests	186	76	2	38.00	2/17	–	–
First-class	–	2603	112	23.24	6/38	2	–

CONNOLLY, Alan Norman

Vic, RHB/RFM
Born: 29 June 1939
Skipton, Victoria

Alan Connolly was a big, fast-medium bowler who formed an effective opening partnership with Graham McKenzie in the latter half of the 'sixties, taking 102 wickets in his 29 Tests. Although he made his first-class debut in 1959–60, it wasn't until 1963–64 that he played Test cricket, against South Africa in Brisbane. He was not a success, but managed a place on the team to England in 1964. He failed to appear in a Test there, and missed the 1964–65 tour of the West Indies, but fought his way back into the side in 1967–68, becoming an invaluable team member. By cutting down his pace and bowling fast medium cutters he became a successful Test bowler. Connolly took 23 wickets against England in 1968, and 20 against the West Indies in 1968–69. Even against the overwhelming strength of South Africa in 1969–70, he managed 20 wickets at 26.10 in the four Tests. His performances then declined until a back injury finally forced his retirement.

BATTING	M	Inn	NO	HS	Runs	Ave	100s	50s	C/S
Tests	29	45	20	37	260	10.40	–	–	17
First-class	201	215	93	40	1073	8.79	–	–	77

BOWLING	Balls	Runs	Wkts	Ave	BB	5wI	10wM
Tests	7818	2981	102	29.22	6/47	4	–
First-class	–	17974	676	26.58	9/67	25	4

COOPER, Bransby Beauchamp

Vic, RHB/WK
Born: 15 March 1844
Dacca, India
Died: 7 August 1914
Geelong, Victoria

Born in India, BB Cooper was educated at Rugby in England and played his early cricket there. He represented Middlesex in their initial first-class game and played for MCC with WG Grace. In fact, his only first-class century was made in a Gentleman v Players game in 1869, when he added 283 with WG. After spending some time in the USA, he settled in Victoria in 1869–70. Over the next few years he played in many representative matches, culminating in the very first Test at Melbourne in 1877. He scored 15 and 3 in Australia's triumphant win. In addition to his batting he was also a useful wicket-keeper. With his English amateur background and knowledge of the game, Cooper played a leading part in Australian cricket's formative years.

BATTING	M	Inn	NO	HS	Runs	Ave	100s	50s	C/S
Tests	1	2	0	15	18	9.00	–	–	2
First-class	50	83	5	101	1600	20.51	1	7	41/20

COOPER, William Henry

Vic, RHB/LBG
Born: 11 September 1849
Maidstone, Kent, England
Died: 5 April 1939
Malvern, Melbourne, Victoria

WH Cooper was a leg-break bowler who made his first-class debut in 1878–79 for Victoria against England, a mere three years after taking up the game. Although he played only two Tests, his best effort was an impressive 6/120 against England at Melbourne in 1881–82, after taking 3/80 in the first innings. Cooper was chosen to tour England in 1884 and big things were expected of him, but a severe hand injury sustained on the voyage out robbed him of a golden opportunity. In fact, he took only seven wickets on the tour and retired on his return. William Cooper's great-grandson is former Australian Test batsman Paul Sheahan.

BATTING	M	Inn	NO	HS	Runs	Ave	100s	50s	C/S
Tests	2	3	1	7	13	6.50	–	–	1
First-class	26	39	15	46	247	10.29	–	–	16

BOWLING	Balls	Runs	Wkts	Ave	BB	5wI	10wM
Tests	466	226	9	25.11	6/120	1	–
First-class	–	1739	71	24.49	7/37	5	–

CORLING, Grahame Edward

NSW, RHB/RFM
Born: 13 July 1941
Newcastle, New South Wales

A fast-medium bowler with a good action, Grahame Corling was capable of moving the ball either way, and in conditions which gave him the slightest help he could be very dangerous indeed. Sadly, his only chance came on the 1964 tour of England when he played in all five

Tests, and the 12 wickets he took at 37.25 do not reflect how well he bowled. Although he deserved a further chance it was never given. The presence of Graham McKenzie, Neil Hawke and the emerging Alan Connolly terminated what should have been a much longer and more impressive Test career.

BATTING	M	Inn	NO	HS	Runs	Ave	100s	50s	C/S
Tests	5	4	1	3	5	1.66	–	–	–
First-class	65	78	32	42*	484	10.52	–	–	11

BOWLING	Balls	Runs	Wkts	Ave	BB	5wI	10wM
Tests	1159	447	12	37.25	4/60	–	–
First-class	–	5546	173	32.05	5/44	6	–

COSIER, Gary John

Vic, SA, Qld, RHB/RM
Born: 25 April 1953
Richmond, Victoria

Gary Cosier was a schoolboy cricketer of great talent (at 15 he opened the Northcote batting with Bill Lawry), and at Melbourne against the West Indies in 1975–76 he made 130 to become the 11th Australian to score a hundred on his Test debut. The glittering career, which seemed there for the taking, failed to materialise. The solidly built, red-headed right hander could hit the ball enormous distances, but apart from a thunderous 168 against Pakistan in 1976–77, his Test career has little to enthuse over. Too many innings were terminated by reckless-ness and lapses of concentration. Cosier was Australia's vice-captain for a time during World Series Cricket, touring the West Indies in 1977–78 and playing in the 1979 World Cup, but continued poor form saw him dropped from the team. For a batsman of such talent and power, and a more than useful medium pace bowler, his career is a case of what might have been.

BATTING	M	Inn	NO	HS	Runs	Ave	100s	50s	C/S
Tests	18	32	1	168	897	28.93	2	3	14
First-class	91	161	9	168	5005	32.92	7	27	75

BOWLING	Balls	Runs	Wkts	Ave	BB	5wI	10wM
Tests	899	341	5	68.20	2/26	–	–
First-class	–	2301	75	30.68	3/20	–	–

COTTAM, John Thomas

NSW, RHB/LB
Born: 5 September 1867
Strawberry Hills, New South Wales
Died: 30 January 1897
Coolgardie, Western Australia

JT Cottam's solitary Test was against England at Sydney in 1886–87, and he made just four runs. He was a promising junior batsman and was only 19 at the time. As the late eighties was a period of rebuilding for Australian cricket, it is strange that the youngster wasn't given a further chance to establish himself in the Test side. He toured New Zealand with a New South Wales team in 1889–90 where he performed reasonably well. Unfortunately, after that tour he played very little cricket. Cottam died of typhoid fever at the age of only 29 in the Western Australian mining town of Coolgardie where he had been lured by the prospect of a gold find. Davis' Australian Cricket Annual of 1896–97 said of him in an obituary, 'He had a great physique, polished style and high ability.'

BATTING	M	Inn	NO	HS	Runs	Ave	100s	50s	C/S
Tests	1	2	0	3	4	2.00	–	–	1
First-class	7	13	1	62	273	22.75	–	3	4

BOWLING	Runs	Wkts	Ave	BB	5wI	10wM
First-class	98	3	32.66	2/48	–	–

COTTER, Albert

NSW, RHB/RF
Born: 3 December 1884
Sydney, New South Wales
Died: 31 October 1917
Beersheba, Palestine

'Tibby' Cotter was Australia's fastest bowler in the decade before World War I. Although not always accurate, he was very quick and pictures show a slinging action not unlike Jeff Thomson's. He made his Test debut in the 1903–04 series, and his figures of 6/40 and 2/25 in the final game helped win back the Ashes. Cotter toured England in 1905 and 1909, and would have gone again in 1912, but withdrew as one of the 'Big Six' over a management dispute. At The Oval in 1905 he recorded his best figures of 7/148 in 40 overs of sustained hostility. In 1907–08 he took 14 wickets in the first two Tests, the only games he played in the series. There was still plenty of pace in 1909 when he produced returns of 5/38 and 6/95 in Australia's success. His speed was such that in his heyday he had a reputation for smashing stumps and scaring batsmen. Cotter joined the Light Horse in World War I and was killed by a sniper at Beersheba in Palestine.

BATTING	M	Inn	NO	HS	Runs	Ave	100s	50s	C/S
Tests	21	37	2	45	457	13.05	–	–	8
First-class	113	157	10	82	2484	16.89	–	4	63

BOWLING	Balls	Runs	Wkts	Ave	BB	5wl	10wM
Tests	4633	2549	89	28.64	7/148	7	–
First-class	–	10730	442	24.27	7/15	31	4

COULTHARD, George

Vic, RHB/RM
Born: 1 August 1856
Boroondara, Victoria
Died: 22 October 1883
Carlton, Victoria

George Coulthard was a prominent figure in the early years of Australian cricket as a player and an umpire, and he was also a fine Australian Rules footballer. He possesses the strange record of umpiring a Test before actually playing in one. As a cricketer he was a useful all-rounder, but with an ordinary first-class record, who played against England at Melbourne in 1882. As an umpire he was well thought of, although he was the central figure in one of cricket's most sensational incidents, giving star batsman Billy Murdoch run out at Sydney in the 1878–79 game between New South Wales and England, thus precipitating the worst riot in the country's cricket history when Lord Harris's team was threatened by a large and angry crowd. Coulthard's sport had little chance to prosper, as he was struck down by tuberculosis at the age of 27.

BATTING	M	Inn	NO	HS	Runs	Ave	100s	50s	C/S
Tests	1	1	1	6*	6	–	–	–	–
First-class	6	11	3	31	92	11.50	–	–	3

BOWLING	Runs	Wkts	Ave	BB	5wl	10wM
First-class	125	5	25.00	3/29	–	–

COWPER, Robert Maskew

Vic, WA, LHB/OB
Born: 5 October 1940
Kew, Victoria

Bob Cowper was a highly talented all-rounder who retired at the age of 28 with plenty of Test cricket still left in him. From a sporting family, Cowper made his first-class debut in 1959–60 and his Test debut during the 1964 tour of England. From then until his retirement in 1968, he was a key member of the Australian team. There were many fine performances in his short career, including two centuries against the firepower of Wes Hall and Charlie Griffith on the 1964–65 tour of the West Indies. However, the highlight was a monumental innings of 307 against England at Melbourne in 1965–66, after he had been dropped for the previous Test. Cowper was also a very capable off spinner. At Old Trafford in 1968 his figures of 4/48 and 2/82 helped Australia to its only victory of the series. After his early retirement Cowper moved to Monaco and the world of high finance.

BATTING	M	Inn	NO	HS	Runs	Ave	100s	50s	C/S
Tests	27	46	2	307	2061	46.84	5	10	21
First-class	147	228	31	307	10595	53.78	26	58	151

BOWLING	Balls	Runs	Wkts	Ave	BB	5wl	10wM
Tests	3005	1139	36	31.63	4/48	–	–
First-class	–	5709	183	31.19	7/42	1	–

CRAIG, Ian David

NSW, RHB
Born: 12 June 1935
Yass, New South Wales

At 17 years 239 days Ian Craig became Australia's youngest Test player when he was selected against South Africa in 1952–53. Although he made 53 and 47 on debut, he was unable to establish his place in the side. He had secured his selection with an innings of 213 not out against the tourists for New South Wales. Craig toured England in 1953, but was disappointing. After a break to complete pharmacy studies he returned to big cricket in time to tour England again in 1956 when he fared much better, making 872 runs at 36.33. Despite the fact that he was far from an automatic choice he was given the captaincy for the tour of South Africa in 1957–58, making him the youngest Test captain. The side was a success, but Craig's batting was disappointing. Sadly, a bout of hepatitis ended his Test career just when he might have established it. Although he successfully played for, and captained, New South Wales, he never made a Test comeback.

BATTING	M	Inn	NO	HS	Runs	Ave	100s	50s	C/S
Tests	11	18	0	53	358	19.88	–	2	2
First-class	144	208	15	213*	7328	37.96	15	38	70

BOWLING	Runs	Wkts	Ave	BB	5wl	10wM
First-class	127	1	127.00	1/3	–	–

CRAWFORD, William Patrick Anthony

NSW RHB/RF
Born: 3 August 1933
Sydney, New South Wales

Pat Crawford was a tall fast bowler able to swing the ball either way. He made his first-class debut in 1954–55 and created such a good impression that he was chosen to tour England in 1956. Unfortunately, he broke down after just a few overs in his Lord's Test debut. It was one of a series of injuries which restricted his career to just four Tests; the remaining three were played against India on the way home in 1956. When fit and bowling well he could generate considerable speed and his Test return of seven wickets at 15.28 certainly suggests potential. Sadly, the potential never came to fruition.

BATTING	M	Inn	NO	HS	Runs	Ave	100s	50s	C/S
Tests	4	5	2	34	53	17.66	–	–	1
First-class	37	42	20	86	424	19.27	–	1	18

BOWLING	Balls	Runs	Wkts	Ave	BB	5wI	10wM
Tests	437	107	7	15.28	3/28	–	–
First-class	–	2313	110	21.02	6/55	5	1

D

DARLING, Joseph

SA, LHB
Born: 21 November 1870
Glen Osmond, South Australia
Died: 2 January 1946
Hobart, Tasmania

A tough, uncompromising cricketer, Joe Darling was an excellent left-handed batsman and a fine captain. He toured England in 1896, 1899, 1902 and 1905, the last three occasions as captain. Darling made his first-class debut in 1893–94 and played his first Test one year later against AE Stoddart's English team. As a captain he is best remembered for the 1902 series, when his side emerged 2-1 winners in an epic contest which saw a game lost by one wicket and another won by three runs. As a batsman his best series was at home in 1897–98 when he scored all three of his Test centuries, his attacking approach being a key factor in his side's victory. After his cricket career he moved to Tasmania where he became a farmer and subsequently a Member of Parliament from 1921 until his death.

BATTING	M	Inn	NO	HS	Runs	Ave	100s	50s	C/S
Tests	34	60	2	178	1657	28.56	3	8	27
First-class	202	333	25	210	10635	34.52	19	55	148

BOWLING	Runs	Wkts	Ave	BB	5wl	10wM	
First-class	55	1	55.00	1/5	–	–	

DARLING, Leonard Stuart

Vic, LHB/RM
Born: 14 August 1909
South Yarra, Victoria
Died: 24 June 1992
Daw Park, South Australia

Len Darling was a talented left-handed batsman who made his debut in 1926–27, but took some years to establish himself as a Test candidate. A good season in 1931–32 helped him gain selection for the fourth Test of the 1932–33 series. He handled the Bodyline of Larwood and Voce better than most and registered his highest score, 85, in the last Test. His efforts earned a tour of England in 1934 where he exceeded a thousand runs and played in the first four Tests. Touring South Africa in 1935–36 he appeared in all five Tests, and at the end of the 1936–37 season, in which he played one Test, Darling retired to live in Adelaide in order to further his employment. In his 12 Tests he achieved a number of useful innings, but failed to make the big score that would have established his place in the team.

BATTING	M	Inn	NO	HS	Runs	Ave	100s	50s	C/S
Tests	12	18	1	85	474	27.88	–	3	8
First-class	100	143	7	188	5780	42.50	16	26	59

BOWLING	Balls	Runs	Wkts	Ave	BB	5wl	10wM
Tests	162	65	0	–	–	–	–
First-class	–	1504	32	47.00	3/57	–	–

DARLING, Warwick Maxwell

SA, RHB
Born: 1 May 1957
Waikerie, South Australia

'Rick' Darling came into the Australian side in 1977–78, during World Series Cricket, as a right-handed opening batsman and brilliant cover fieldsman. He played 14 Tests, never seeming able to do justice to his considerable talent, but on his day he could destroy any attack. In many of these games he formed a frenetic partnership with Graeme Wood, an association that seemed almost always to end in a run out. His liking for the hook led to him collecting a number of blows, including one from Bob Willis in 1978–79 that was almost fatal, and his nervousness often restricted his performances. Darling toured the West Indies in 1977–78 and India in 1979–80, but he was unable to hold his Test place when World Series ended.

BATTING	M	Inn	NO	HS	Runs	Ave	100s	50s	C/S
Tests	14	27	1	91	697	26.80	–	6	5
First-class	98	177	22	134	5554	35.83	9	32	30

BOWLING	Runs	Wkts	Ave	BB	5wI	10wM	
First-class	23	0	–	–	–	–	

DAVIDSON, Alan Keith

NSW, LHB/LF
Born: 14 June 1929
Lisarow near Gosford, New South Wales

One of Australia's best all-rounders, Alan Davidson was a devastating left-arm opening bowler, a batsman capable of turning a match with a few well struck blows and a fieldsman so good he was known as 'the claw'. Although he made his first-class debut in 1949–50 and toured England in 1953 and 1956, it was not until he visited South Africa in 1957–58 that he developed into a match-winning cricketer. Off a 15-pace run he could move the ball both ways, and no batsman in the world could claim to play him with any confidence. His Test bowling average of 20.53 amply attests to this, comparing more than favourably with anyone who ever played the game.

When Richie Benaud became Australia's captain in 1958–59 it was Davidson who was his chief destroyer. While bowlers with suspect actions took the headlines in that series against England, Davidson emerged with 24 wickets. In the Tied Test of 1960–61 he became the first to score 100 runs and take 10 wickets in a Test, with 5/135 and 6/87, 44 and 80. The last innings was played in partnership with Benaud and took Australia to the verge of victory. In that series he took 33 wickets, despite missing the fourth Test. He was the leading bowler in the 1961 series against England, as well as playing an innings of 77 not out in the crucial Old Trafford Test which added 98 for the last wicket with Graham McKenzie, and gave Benaud enough runs to produce a sensational win. Had he not been required to do so much bowling, Davidson may have produced many more runs, as he was certainly a talented batsman. In his last series in 1962–63, also against England, he took 24 wickets to again be the chief agent in retaining the Ashes.

Davidson seemed constantly subject to limps and strains, but Benaud's understanding captaincy could always produce one more over, and often the breakthrough wicket. Certainly Davidson's success owes much to the way Benaud handled him, always managing to cajole that extra effort.

After his retirement as a player Davidson served as a national selector and as president of the New South Wales Cricket Association.

BATTING	M	Inn	NO	HS	Runs	Ave	100s	50s	C/S
Tests	44	61	7	80	1328	24.59	–	5	42
First-class	193	246	39	129	6804	32.86	9	36	168

BOWLING	Balls	Runs	Wkts	Ave	BB	5wI	10wM
Tests	11587	3819	186	20.53	7/93	14	2
First-class	–	14048	672	20.90	7/31	33	2

DAVIS, Ian Charles

NSW, Qld, RHB
Born: 25 June 1953
North Sydney, New South Wales

Ian Davis had a meteoric rise, making his Test debut in 1973–74 after only a handful of first-class games. Despite some promising innings against New Zealand in that season he lost his place in the Test side. He did not return to Test cricket until 1976–77 when he made 105 against Pakistan, his only Test century. That innings and some good play in the Centenary Test, particularly his 68 in the second innings, saw him selected to tour England in 1977, but he struggled in the different conditions. Like many of that team he joined World Series Cricket, but made little impact. After that venture ended he returned to

Shield cricket, and although he played some fine innings he was never again a serious candidate for Test selection. Ian Davis retired after season 1982–83 at the early age of 29.

BATTING	M	Inn	NO	HS	Runs	Ave	100s	50s	C/S
Tests	15	27	1	105	692	26.61	1	4	9
First-class	76	128	9	156	3985	33.48	5	28	36

BOWLING	Runs	Wkts	Ave	BB	5wI	10wM
First-class	7	0	–	–	–	–

DAVIS, Simon Peter

Vic, RHB/RFM
Born: 8 November 1959
Brighton, Victoria

A miserly fast-medium bowler, Simon Davis had considerable success in limited-overs cricket, representing Australia in numerous internationals. He was extremely difficult to score off and frustrated many batsmen into losing their wickets. In the longer game he produced some useful performances for Victoria, most notably 7/104 on his first-class debut. Towards the end of his career he captained Victoria on a number of occasions. His single Test was the first on the 1985–86 tour of New Zealand, and although he bowled steadily, he lacked the penetration to succeed at the highest level. While he might prove difficult to score off, he was unlikely to crash through a batting line-up. A genial and engaging character, Simon Davis gave his all, regardless of the situation, making up in determination what he may have lacked in natural ability.

BATTING	M	Inn	NO	HS	Runs	Ave	100s	50s	C/S
Tests	1	1	0	0	0	0.00	–	–	–
First-class	48	47	28	15*	98	5.15	–	–	13

BOWLING	Balls	Runs	Wkts	Ave	BB	5wI	10wM
Tests	150	70	0	–	–	–	–
First-class	–	4345	124	35.04	7/104	5	–

DE COURCY, James Harry

NSW, RHB
Born: 18 April 1927
Newcastle, New South Wales

'Jimmy' de Courcy made his first-class debut for New South Wales in 1947–48, but it was not until he was selected for the 1953 tour of England that he graduated to the highest level of the game. He scored over a thousand runs on the tour, gaining selection in the last three Tests. His top score of 41 was made on debut at Old Trafford. Three of his six first-class centuries were scored on that tour, including his top score of 204 against the Combined Services. De Courcy continued to play first-class cricket until 1957–58, but he never threatened to regain his place in the Australian team. The large number of scores over fifty show his ability to get a start, but not to convert good beginnings into high scores. For a player of such talent his record must be considered slightly disappointing.

BATTING	M	Inn	NO	HS	Runs	Ave	100s	50s	C/S
Tests	3	6	1	41	81	16.20	–	–	3
First-class	79	113	11	204	3778	37.03	6	23	51

BOWLING	Runs	Wkts	Ave	BB	5wl	10wM		
First-class	67	0	–	–	–	–		

DELL, Anthony Ross

Qld, RHB/LFM
Born: 6 August 1947
Lymington, Hampshire, England

A big, slow-moving, left-arm opening bowler, Tony Dell was capable of swinging and seaming the ball in an awkward fashion, despite a lumbering approach to the wicket. Dell made his Test debut in the last game of the 1970–71 series against England, taking 2/32 and 3/65, opening the bowling with Dennis Lillee. His only other Test was against New Zealand in 1973–74 and a single wicket was not enough to keep him in the side. Slowness in the field, plus the emergence of players like Bob Massie, Max Walker, Gary Gilmour and Geoff Dymock all conspired to restrict his Test career. Dell produced some excellent figures for Queensland before he retired from first-class cricket in 1974.

BATTING	M	Inn	NO	HS	Runs	Ave	100s	50s	C/S
Tests	2	2	2	3*	6	–	–	–	–
First-class	41	57	27	13*	169	5.63	–	–	18

BOWLING	Balls	Runs	Wkts	Ave	BB	5wl	10wM
Tests	559	160	6	26.66	3/65	–	–
First-class	–	3658	137	26.70	6/17	6	1

DODEMAIDE, Anthony Ian Christopher

Vic, RHB/RFM
Born: 5 October 1963
Williamstown, Victoria

All-rounder Tony Dodemaide's Test debut was nothing short of sensational. Against New Zealand at Melbourne in 1987–88 he scored a valuable 50, then took 6/58 in the visitors' second innings. Another seven wickets in the sole Test against Sri Lanka and some excellent limited-overs performances, including 5/21 on debut, led Australians to believe a top flight all-rounder had been discovered. He added to that impression with some good bowling under difficult conditions in Pakistan in 1988–89, but after just two Tests against the West Indies later that season he was out of the side, and within a year he was dropped from the Victorian team. The loss of his once lethal outswinger had been the major cause of a dramatic loss of form. Dodemaide played English county cricket for Sussex with some success, before fighting his way back into the Victorian side in 1990–91. He was a major factor in Victoria's Sheffield Shield win of that season. His outstanding form next season, when he was named Shield Player of the Year, saw his

Test recall to tour Sri Lanka. He played two Tests on tour to complete his rehabilitation, but was unable to claim a place at home against the West Indies, or a trip to England in 1993.

BATTING	M	Inn	NO	HS	Runs	Ave	100s	50s	C/S
Tests	10	15	6	50	202	22.44	–	1	6
First-class	160	243	61	123	5448	29.93	5	25	81

BOWLING	Balls	Runs	Wkts	Ave	BB	5wl	10wM
Tests	2184	954	34	28.06	6/58	1	–
First-class	–	14916	469	31.47	6/58	13	–

DONNAN, Henry

NSW, RHB/RM(r)
Born: 12 November 1864
Liverpool, New South Wales
Died: 13 August 1956
Bexley, New South Wales

A right-handed batsman and round-arm bowler, but a poor fieldsman, 'Harry' Donnan was a defensive player in the mode of 'Alick' Bannerman, whom he resembled in stature. Donnan's patient batting for New South Wales earned him a trip to England in 1896, although he had begun his Test career against WG Grace's team in 1891–92, playing in two of the three games. His other three Tests were all played on that 1896 tour. For one who did so well at first-class level (he also exceeded a thousand runs in England), his Test record gives no indication of his true ability. There were no other chances at Test level, but Donnan continued making runs for New South Wales until he retired after the 1900–01 season.

BATTING	M	Inn	NO	HS	Runs	Ave	100s	50s	C/S
Tests	5	10	1	15	75	8.33	–	–	1
First-class	96	160	14	167	4262	29.19	6	22	37

BOWLING	Balls	Runs	Wkts	Ave	BB	5wl	10wM
Tests	54	22	0	–	–	–	–
First-class	–	1191	29	41.06	3/14	–	–

DOOLAND, Bruce

SA, RHB/LBG
Born: 1 November 1923
Adelaide, South Australia
Died: 8 September 1980
Adelaide, South Australia

Bruce Dooland had the misfortune to arrive on the Test scene in the period following the Second World War, an era when Australia's cricketing riches were overflowing. For such a fine leg spinner, two Tests against England in 1946–47 and one against India in the next season were scant reward for his talent. When he missed selection to tour England in 1948 Dooland took his skills first to Lancashire League, then to county cricket with Nottinghamshire for whom he made his debut in 1953. He was a sensation, taking 368 wickets in his first two seasons. Also a competent batsman, he twice completed the double of 1000 runs and 100 wickets. Dooland returned to Adelaide at the end of the 1957 season, but his county career certainly showed that a great player had slipped through Australia's fingers.

BATTING	M	Inn	NO	HS	Runs	Ave	100s	50s	C/S
Tests	3	5	1	29	76	19.00	–	–	3
First-class	214	326	33	115*	7141	24.37	4	41	186

BOWLING	Balls	Runs	Wkts	Ave	BB	5wI	10wM
Tests	880	419	9	46.55	4/69	–	–
First-class	–	22332	1016	21.98	8/20	84	23

DUFF, Reginald Alexander

NSW, RHB/RM
Born: 17 August 1878
Sydney, New South Wales
Died: 13 December 1911
North Sydney, New South Wales

Reggie Duff was Victor Trumper's opening partner for New South Wales and Australia in the early years of this century, but he was a fine aggressive player in his own right. He made 104 on debut against England at Melbourne in 1901–02, the only Australian to score a century from number ten, when captain Joe Darling held him back in the order. Duff toured England in 1902 and 1905, making an excellent 146 to save the fifth Test on the 1905 tour. That score gave Duff a century in both his first and last Tests, a feat subsequently equalled for Australia only by Bill Ponsford and Greg Chappell. He scored a thousand runs on each of his tours at just under 30.00. Duff's attacking play was a perfect foil for Trumper's genius, and the two formed Australia's first substantial opening partnership. Duff retired in 1908, but his life went into a sad decline and he died three years later, aged only 33.

BATTING	M	Inn	NO	HS	Runs	Ave	100s	50s	C/S
Tests	22	40	3	146	1317	35.59	2	6	14
First-class	121	197	9	271	6589	35.04	10	33	73

BOWLING	Balls	Runs	Wkts	Ave	BB	5wI	10wM
Tests	180	85	4	21.25	2/43	–	–
First-class	–	478	14	34.14	2/17	–	–

DUNCAN, John Ross Frederick

Qld, Vic, RHB/RFM
Born: 25 March 1944
Brisbane, Queensland

Ross Duncan gave sterling service to Queensland as a fast-medium bowler from his debut in 1964–65 until he moved to Victoria in 1971. It was a 13-wicket haul against that state which gave Duncan his one Test match, against England at Melbourne in 1970–71. Injury reduced his effectiveness and he failed to take a wicket in his 14 overs. He did not bowl in the second innings. His move to Melbourne saw him playing for Victoria for the next two years. He bowled just as effectively as he did for his home state, taking 31 wickets at 27.45, but he was never again a serious Test candidate.

BATTING	M	Inn	NO	HS	Runs	Ave	100s	50s	C/S
Tests	1	1	0	3	3	3.00	–	–	–
First-class	71	106	29	52	649	8.42	–	1	33

BOWLING	Balls	Runs	Wkts	Ave	BB	5wI	10wM
Tests	112	30	0	–	–	–	–
First-class	–	6801	218	31.19	8/55	9	1

DYER, Gregory Charles

NSW, RHB/WK
Born: 16 March 1959
Parramatta, New South Wales

Greg Dyer was a competent wicket-keeper-batsman, who made his first-class debut in 1983–84. His initial Test came against England in Adelaide in 1986–87 when regular keeper Tim Zoehrer was injured. His glovework was smooth, and 'keeping at Sydney had made him adept at taking the spinners. Also a talented batsman, Dyer became Australia's 'keeper when Zoehrer was dropped next season. He looked set to have the job for a number of years, despite the controversy surrounding the disputed catching of Kiwi Andrew Jones, when it appeared that the ball had bounced. His stay at the top was a short one as he in turn was replaced by the little known Ian Healy for the 1988–89 tour of Pakistan. Dyer's dismissal from the New South Wales team was equally dramatic when he was replaced as captain by Geoff Lawson and as 'keeper by Phil Emery half way through the 1988–89 season.

BATTING	M	Inn	NO	HS	Runs	Ave	100s	50s	C/S
Tests	6	6	0	60	131	21.83	–	1	22/2
First-class	51	66	8	106	1671	28.81	1	10	123/18

DYMOCK, Geoffrey

Qld, RHB/LFM
Born: 21 July 1945
Maryborough, Queensland

Geoff Dymock was a talented left-arm opening bowler, who made his first-class debut in 1971–72. Two years later he took 5/58 against New Zealand in his first Test. The presence of Lillee, Thomson, Walker and Gilmour prevented him from establishing a regular Test place, but the advent of World Series Cricket saw him selected for the Australian team again, and after a successful tour of India in 1979–80, where he took 5/99 and 7/67 at Kanpur, Dymock held his place in the full strength Test side. He bowled exceptionally well in that 1979–80 summer, taking 28 wickets at 19.60 against England and the West Indies, with a best effort of 3/52 and 6/34 against the former in Perth. The dramatic improvement in his bowling was due to the development of an inswinger late in his career. At the time of his retirement he was Queensland's leading wicket-taker.

BATTING	M	Inn	NO	HS	Runs	Ave	100s	50s	C/S
Tests	21	32	7	31*	236	9.44	–	–	1
First-class	126	159	54	101*	1518	14.45	1	3	41

BOWLING	Balls	Runs	Wkts	Ave	BB	5wl	10wM
Tests	5545	2116	78	27.12	7/67	5	1
First-class	–	11438	425	26.91	7/67	13	1

DYSON, John

NSW RHB
Born: 11 June 1954
Randwick, New South Wales

A right-handed opening batsman and brilliant fieldsman, John Dyson made his first-class debut in 1975–76. World Series Cricket gave him an opportunity to play at Test level against India in 1977–78. He did little of note in his three Tests, but continued to make runs for his State, forcing himself back into the side for the 1980 Centenary Test tour. For the next few seasons he was a regular member of the team. Although scoring 102 against England in 1981 and 127 not out against the West Indies in 1981–82, he could never produce the level of consistency necessary to make him a top Test player. In 1985 Dyson ended his Test career by choosing to tour South Africa with the rebel Australian team. Following those tours he played a few more games for New South Wales before drifting out of first-class cricket.

BATTING	M	Inn	NO	HS	Runs	Ave	100s	50s	C/S
Tests	30	58	7	127*	1359	26.64	2	5	10
First-class	156	278	31	241	9935	40.22	19	53	99

BOWLING	Runs	Wkts	Ave	BB	5wl	10wM	
First-class	66	2	33.00	1/0	–	–	

E

EADY, Charles John

Tas, RHB/RF
Born: 29 October 1870
Hobart, Tasmania
Died: 20 December 1945
Hobart, Tasmania

Charlie Eady was a fine all-round cricketer and a key player in Tasmanian sides from his debut in 1889–90 until he retired in 1907–08. A big man, he was a very good fast bowler and an effective, if sometimes ungainly, batsman. Against Victoria in 1894–95 Eady became the first Australian to hit centuries in each innings of a first-class game. He was selected to tour England in 1896 and played in the first Test, but ill-health and injury ruined his tour. Continued good form for Tasmania, including another century against Victoria, saw him return for the fifth Test against England in 1901–02. He bowled well, taking 3/30, but missed the subsequent tour of England. Instead, he returned to Tasmania and made 566 in the Association Grand Final, hitting 68 fours and 13 fives, the world's highest club score. After his retirement Eady served as president of the Australian Board of Control in 1910–11, and was a member of Tasmania's Parliament for many years.

BATTING	M	Inn	NO	HS	Runs	Ave	100s	50s	C/S
Tests	2	4	1	10*	20	6.66	–	–	2
First-class	42	71	6	116	1490	22.92	3	6	45

BOWLING	Balls	Runs	Wkts	Ave	BB	5wl	10wM
Tests	223	112	7	16.00	3/30	–	–
First-class	–	3146	136	23.13	8/34	12	5

EASTWOOD, Kenneth Humphrey

Vic, LHB/SLC
Born: 23 November 1935
Chatswood, New South Wales

Ken Eastwood was a surprise selection to replace Bill Lawry in the Australian team for the final Test of the 1970–71 series against England. At the age of 35 he appeared out of his depth, although his form had been good—he had made two double centuries earlier the same season, 201 not out against New South Wales and 221 against South Australia. He had been an excellent opening batsman at first-class level, making his debut in the 1959–60 season, although he had taken some time to establish a place in the side. No doubt he deserved a Test at some stage in his career, but the opportunity came a little too late for him to grasp it. Eastwood continued to play grade cricket with success before giving it away in his mid-forties.

BATTING	M	Inn	NO	HS	Runs	Ave	100s	50s	C/S
Tests	1	2	0	5	5	2.50	–	–	–
First-class	42	68	3	221	2722	41.87	9	8	27

BOWLING	Balls	Runs	Wkts	Ave	BB	5wl	10wM
Tests	40	21	1	21.00	1/21	–	–
First-class	–	383	6	63.83	1/10	–	–

EBELING, Hans Irvine

Vic, RHB/RFM
Born: 1 January 1905
Avoca, Victoria
Died: 12 January 1980
East Bentleigh, Victoria

Hans Ebeling was an accurate fast-medium bowler, capable of moving the ball both ways. Business commitments prevented him from playing on a regular basis for several years after his first-class debut in 1923–

24. When he found the time to play, as he did in 1933–34, he was a great success, gaining a place in the side which toured England in 1934. On the trip he took 62 wickets at 20.83, figures which suggest he deserved more than one Test. He turned down a visit to South Africa in 1935–36, where he would certainly have added to his Test record. As a captain he was responsible for leading Victoria to two Sheffield Shields. After his playing days Ebeling became an administrator of great skill, his masterpiece being the organisation of Melbourne's Centenary Test in 1977. He was also a driving force behind the development of the MCG's cricket museum.

BATTING	M	Inn	NO	HS	Runs	Ave	100s	50s	C/S
Tests	1	2	0	41	43	21.50	–	–	–
First-class	73	83	12	76	1005	14.15	–	3	38

BOWLING	Balls	Runs	Wkts	Ave	BB	5wI	10wM
Tests	186	89	3	29.66	3/74	–	–
First-class	–	5768	217	26.58	7/33	7	2

EDWARDS, John Dunlop

Vic, RHB/LB
Born: 12 June 1862
Prahran, Victoria
Died: 31 July 1911
Hawksburn, Victoria

Principally an aggressive right-handed batsman and good fieldsman, John Edwards could also bowl leg breaks if required. His three Tests were played on the 1888 tour of England, where he was not a great success, scoring just over 500 runs at 12.85. A hand injury also added to a miserable tour. He had a reputation as a more than useful player, but his figures represent a disappointing return, passing the half century only four times in 50 first-class games. He certainly never lived up to his early promise. In an obituary *Wisden* said, 'There was nothing brilliant about his batting' and that 'he had a good defence as well as hitting powers.'

BATTING	M	Inn	NO	HS	Runs	Ave	100s	50s	C/S
Tests	3	6	1	26	48	9.60	–	–	1
First-class	50	84	14	65	961	13.72	–	4	19

BOWLING	Runs	Wkts	Ave	BB	5wI	10wM
First-class	194	7	27.71	2/6	–	–

EDWARDS, Ross

WA, NSW, RHB/WK
Born: 1 December 1942
Cottesloe, Western Australia

Ross Edwards was a key member of Ian Chappell's all-conquering sides of the seventies. A former wicket-keeper, he became a brilliant cover fieldsman and dependable batsman, usually gathering his runs when they were most needed. He made his debut in 1964–65 as a 'keeper, but returned a few seasons later and scored enough runs to make the team to England in 1972. When an opening batsman was required at Trent Bridge he made 170 not out. He toured the West Indies in 1973, then missed a couple of seasons before returning to make 115 at Perth against England in 1974–75, holding an end up while Doug Walters made a hundred in a session. At Lord's in 1975, with Australia 7/81, Edwards made 99 to save the game. That innings typified his cricket, always there in a crisis—and it was worth the admission price just to see him field.

BATTING	M	Inn	NO	HS	Runs	Ave	100s	50s	C/S
Tests	20	32	3	170*	1171	40.37	2	9	7
First-class	126	212	25	170*	7345	39.27	14	42	111/11

BOWLING	Balls	Runs	Wkts	Ave	BB	5wl	10wM
Tests	12	20	0	–	–	–	–
First-class	–	75	1	75.00	1/24	–	–

EDWARDS, Walter John

WA, LHB/LBG
Born: 23 December 1949
Subiaco, Western Australia

Wally Edwards made such a promising start to his first-class career in 1973–74 that within a year he was chosen to open the batting for Australia in the first three Tests against England. While he produced a couple of useful stands with Ian Redpath, he could not go on and make a big score. In fact, that was the essence of his cricket: he would get a start and when it looked as if he had the bowlers at his mercy he would lose his wicket. His first-class career, which ended in 1977–78, is very much a case of what might have been, because on his day he was an attractive and entertaining batsman.

BATTING	M	Inn	NO	HS	Runs	Ave	100s	50s	C/S
Tests	3	6	0	30	68	11.33	–	–	–
First-class	25	46	1	153	1381	30.68	2	9	16

BOWLING	Runs	Wkts	Ave	BB	5wl	10wM
First-class	141	2	70.50	1/11	–	–

EMERY, Sidney Hand

NSW, RHB/LBG
Born: 16 October 1885
Sydney, New South Wales
Died: 7 January 1967
Petersham, New South Wales

Sid Emery was a leg-spin bowler whose chance in Test cricket came when he was selected to tour England in 1912. With six of Australia's top players refusing to tour, the trip was a difficult and unsuccessful one. While Emery turned in some useful spells, he bowled too many bad balls to be a regular Test performer. He delivered his leg spin at medium pace and on the days when he had it under control, sadly not many, he was a matchwinner. His best figures of 7/28 and 5/85 were taken against Victoria in 1909–10, and must have gone some way towards securing a place in the Australian team which toured New Zealand at the end of that season. Emery also had a reputation for wild behaviour, and the nickname 'Mad Mick' was apparently well earned.

BATTING	M	Inn	NO	HS	Runs	Ave	100s	50s	C/S
Tests	4	2	0	5	6	3.00	–	–	2
First-class	58	80	15	80*	1192	18.33	–	6	30

BOWLING	Balls	Runs	Wkts	Ave	BB	5wl	10wM
Tests	462	249	5	49.80	2/46	–	–
First-class	–	4355	183	23.79	7/28	11	3

EVANS, Edwin

NSW, RHB/RFM
Born: 6 March 1849
Emu Plains, New South Wales
Died: 2 July 1921
Walgett, New South Wales

Evans was a medium pace bowler who used great variation of pace and length. He was a team mate of the great Spofforth and there were many who believed him to be the better bowler. Although Evans turned in some remarkable performances, he seemed reluctant to tour, and could not be persuaded to go to England until 1886, when he was 37 and well past his best. As a result he took only 30 wickets. This lack of desire to play away from Sydney caused him to miss many games, and was a major factor in his disappointing Test career. A look at Evans' first-class figures will give some idea of what he was capable of in his prime.

BATTING	M	Inn	NO	HS	Runs	Ave	100s	50s	C/S
Tests	6	10	2	33	82	10.25	–	–	5
First-class	65	105	23	74*	1006	12.26	–	2	63

BOWLING	Balls	Runs	Wkts	Ave	BB	5wI	10wM
Tests	1247	332	7	47.42	3/64	–	–
First-class	–	3356	201	16.69	7/16	18	4

FAIRFAX, Alan George

NSW, RHB/RFM
Born: 16 June 1906
Summer Hill, New South Wales
Died: 17 May 1955
Kensington, London, England

Alan Fairfax was a talented all-rounder who ended his cricket career in Australia in 1932 in order to play in the Lancashire League. England's gain was certainly Australia's loss, as Fairfax had produced a number of useful performances at Test level. He made 65 on debut in the fifth Test of the 1928–29 series, then toured England in 1930, providing useful back up to the bowling of Grimmett and making runs when they were most needed. After a successful series against the West Indies in 1930–31 he declined his Test place to return to England. In addition to his batting and bowling, Fairfax was a brilliant fieldsman, usually in the gully. After his playing days he became a successful coach and writer, until a heart attack claimed him at the age of 48.

BATTING	M	Inn	NO	HS	Runs	Ave	100s	50s	C/S
Tests	10	12	4	65	410	51.25	–	4	15
First-class	55	76	10	104	1910	28.93	1	9	41

BOWLING	Balls	Runs	Wkts	Ave	BB	5wl	10wM
Tests	1520	645	21	30.71	4/31	–	–
First-class	–	3735	134	27.87	6/54	2	–

FAVELL, Leslie Ernest

SA, RHB/RM
Born: 6 October 1929
Arncliffe, New South Wales
Died: 14 June 1987
Magill, South Australia

Les Favell is one of South Australia's cricket legends, despite being born in New South Wales. He moved to Adelaide in order to play first-class cricket, which he succeeded in doing in 1951–52, making a century on debut. He retired in 1969–70 as the State's leading run-scorer, having captained the side 95 times, a record. Favell's aggressive nature made him into a wonderful attacking batsman, and the same could be said for his captaincy, which greatly influenced the young Ian Chappell. In Test cricket Favell's technique led to inconsistent performances and a failure to establish a permanent Test place, his only century being against India in 1959–60. In a long career he toured every cricket country except England. After retirement he became a respected radio commentator. Favell, a much loved figure, died tragically from cancer in 1987.

BATTING	M	Inn	NO	HS	Runs	Ave	100s	50s	C/S
Tests	19	31	3	101	757	27.03	1	5	9
First-class	202	347	9	190	12379	36.62	27	68	110

BOWLING	Runs	Wkts	Ave	BB	5wI	10wM	
First-class	345	5	69.00	1/0	–	–	

FERRIS, John James

NSW, SA, LHB/LM
Born: 21 May 1867
Sydney, New South Wales
Died: 21 November 1900
Durban, South Africa

In the late 1880s Ferris formed a bowling partnership with Charles Turner which made them the most feared combination in the world. He made his debut for New South Wales in 1886–87 and played his first Test that same season, taking, 4/27 and 5/76 in a losing cause, followed by another nine wickets in the next Test a month later. In England the pair caused dismay among the batsman, Ferris taking 220 wickets at 14.10 in 1888 and 215 wickets at 13.20 in 1890, but Australia's weak batting was seldom able to capitalise on the bowling. In 1890 Ferris opted to qualify for Gloucestershire and actually played for England on a tour of South Africa. Somewhere in the 1890's his skill deserted him and he returned to Australia. JJ Ferris died from enteric fever while serving with the Imperial Light Horse during the Boer War.

BATTING	M	Inn	NO	HS	Runs	Ave	100s	50s	C/S
Tests	8	16	4	20*	98	8.16	–	–	4
First-class	198	328	56	106	4264	15.67	1	15	90

BOWLING	Balls	Runs	Wkts	Ave	BB	5wI	10wM
Tests	2030	684	48	14.25	5/26	4	–
First-class	–	14260	813	17.53	8/41	63	11

FINGLETON, John Henry Webb

NSW, RHB
Born: 28 April 1908
Waverley, New South Wales
Died: 22 November 1981
Killara, New South Wales.

Jack Fingleton was a sound opening batsman, who made his first-class debut in 1928–29 and his Test debut against South Africa in 1931–32. Next summer, in the Bodyline series, he played some brave innings against frightening opposition. Fingleton was unlucky to miss the tour of England in 1934, but came back against South Africa in 1935–36 to score three successive Test centuries. He scored another in his next innings, against England in 1936–37. Later, in the third Test, he made 136 in a sixth wicket partnership of 346 with Don Bradman, which turned the series. On his one tour of England in 1938 he made little impact. After his playing days, Fingleton, a journalist by trade, became a popular commentator and wrote some excellent books on the game, one of which, *Cricket Crisis*, is probably the best account of the Bodyline series.

BATTING	M	Inn	NO	HS	Runs	Ave	100s	50s	C/S
Tests	18	29	1	136	1189	42.46	5	3	13
First-class	108	166	13	167	6816	44.54	22	31	81/4

BOWLING	Runs	Wkts	Ave	BB	5wI	10wM	
First-class	54	2	27.00	1/6	–	–	

FLEETWOOD-SMITH, Leslie O'Brien

Vic, RHB/SLC
Born: 30 March 1908
Stawell, Victoria
Died: 16 March 1971
Fitzroy, Victoria

On his day 'Chuck' Fleetwood-Smith could destroy the best batmen in the world with unorthodox left-arm deliveries, which he spun viciously. If he had been more consistent with line and length he would have been the finest spin bowler of his or any age. After some strong performances for Victoria, for whom he made his debut in 1931–32, taking 11 wickets in his first game, he toured England in 1934 without playing a Test, and again in 1938, and he also visited South Africa in 1935–36. In 1936–37 his dismissal of Wally Hammond at Adelaide won a crucial Test which helped retain the Ashes. Fleetwood-Smith would often sing or make birdcalls as he was running in to bowl, and he struggled to see anything serious in cricket. Sadly, his later life assumed the proportions of a tragedy as alcohol led him to the life of a derelict. After a court appearance for vagrancy in 1969, he attempted to make a fresh start before his death just under two years later.

BATTING	M	Inn	NO	HS	Runs	Ave	100s	50s	C/S
Tests	10	11	5	16*	54	9.00	–	–	–
First-class	112	117	33	63	617	7.34	–	1	42

BOWLING	Balls	Runs	Wkts	Ave	BB	5wl	10wM
Tests	3093	1570	42	37.38	6/110	2	1
First-class	–	13519	597	22.64	9/36	57	18

FRANCIS, Bruce Colin

NSW, RHB
Born: 18 February 1948
Sydney, New Wales

Bruce Francis was a solid right-handed opening batsman, whose good performances for New South Wales, following his debut in 1968–69, earned some matches against the Rest of the World XI in 1971–72. Although he did little of note in those games, he was taken to England in 1972 as an opening partner for Keith Stackpole. He had been particularly successful playing for Essex in English county cricket, scoring over 1500 runs in 1971, and much was expected of him. Unfortunately, he could not make the transition to Test cricket and lost his place after three games. In 1985 Francis was in the headlines for organising and then managing the rebel Australian team in South Africa.

BATTING	M	Inn	NO	HS	Runs	Ave	100s	50s	C/S
Tests	3	5	0	27	52	10.40	–	–	1
First-class	109	192	10	210	6183	33.97	13	31	42

BOWLING	Runs	Wkts	Ave	BB	5wI	10wM		
First-class	15	1	15.00	1/10	–	–		

FREEMAN, Eric Walter

SA, RHB/RFM
Born: 13 July 1944
Largs Bay, South Australia

Eric Freeman was a talented all-rounder who forced his way into the Test team against India in 1967–68. While his bowling lacked the yard of pace needed to make him a threat at the highest level, he was a strong man with the bat, capable of hitting enormous sixes. His first scoring shot in Test cricket went over the fence. Freeman made the first century of the 1968 tour of England, but could not cement a place in the Test side. He went on the tour to India and South Africa in 1969–70 and it was the awesome power of the Springbok batting which ended his Test career. Eric Freeman was also a fine Australian Rules footballer. These days he is still a well-known figure through his perceptive commentaries on ABC radio.

BATTING	M	Inn	NO	HS	Runs	Ave	100s	50s	C/S
Tests	11	18	0	76	345	19.16	–	2	5
First-class	83	123	6	116	2244	19.17	1	9	60

BOWLING	Balls	Runs	Wkts	Ave	BB	5wI	10wM
Tests	2183	1128	34	33.17	4/42	–	–
First-class	–	6690	241	27.75	8/47	7	2

FREER, Frederick William

Vic, RHB/RFM
Born: 4 December 1915
North Carlton, Victoria

All-rounder Fred Freer was unlucky to play just one Test, against England at Sydney in 1946–47. He was by no means a failure, but the presence of Lindwall, who he replaced for the game, Miller, and Bill Johnston restricted the Victorian's chances. Like many fringe Test players at that time, Freer took his talents to English league cricket, where he was a successful professional. In addition to his bowling, he was also a fine batsman, scoring three centuries in India with a Commonwealth team in 1949–50. When he retired in 1953, Freer must have wished that he had played in a less powerful period in Australia's Test history, when he may have had a career that would have done justice to his obvious all-round talents. Certainly he would have played in more Tests.

BATTING	M	Inn	NO	HS	Runs	Ave	100s	50s	C/S
Tests	1	1	1	28*	28	–	–	–	–
First-class	40	51	11	132	1284	32.10	3	5	25

BOWLING	Balls	Runs	Wkts	Ave	BB	5wI	10wM
Tests	160	74	3	24.66	2/49	–	–
First-class	–	2886	104	27.75	7/29	4	–

G

GANNON, John Bryant

WA, RHB/LFM
Born: 8 February, 1947
Subiaco, Western Australia

'Sam' Gannon played his three Tests against India in 1977–78, the first season of World Series Cricket. The left-arm, fast-medium bowler made his first-class debut in 1966–67 and recorded his best figures, 6/107 against South Australia, in that season. It took Gannon a number of years to establish a place in the Western Australian side, but he provided useful support for the likes of Lillee and Massie. In his Test appearances he bowled steadily, without threatening to run through a side. His best performance was 4/77 at Perth on debut.

BATTING	M	Inn	NO	HS	Runs	Ave	100s	50s	C/S
Tests	3	5	4	3*	3	3.00	–	–	3
First-class	40	43	21	20	141	6.40	–	–	19

BOWLING	Balls	Runs	Wkts	Ave	BB	5wl	10wM
Tests	726	361	11	32.81	4/77	–	–
First-class	–	3565	117	30.47	6/107	2	–

GARRETT, Thomas William

NSW, RHB/RFM
Born: 26 July 1858
Wollongong, New South Wales
Died: 6 August 1943
Warrawee, New South Wales

Tom Garrett was a notable player in the early years of Test cricket. Although he was a useful batsman, Garrett was better known for his fast-medium bowling. Alongside players like Boyle and Palmer, he provided excellent support for the 'Demon' Spofforth, the country's premier bowler. Garrett played in the first Test in 1877, and at 18 years, 232 days is still the youngest Australian to play against England. He toured England in 1878, 1882 and 1886, taking over 100 wickets on each of the last two occasions. A tall man, Garrett could move the ball either way, and was particularly good at exploiting any help in the pitch. While he was a fine performer in England, he was no less successful at home, his best figures of 6/78 coming at Sydney in 1881–82. Later he became an excellent captain of New South Wales in a fitting end to a successful career.

BATTING	M	Inn	NO	HS	Runs	Ave	100s	50s	C/S
Tests	19	33	6	51*	339	12.55	–	1	7
First-class	160	256	29	163	3673	16.18	2	10	80

BOWLING	Balls	Runs	Wkts	Ave	BB	5wl	10wM
Tests	2708	970	36	26.94	6/78	2	–
First-class	–	8353	445	18.77	7/38	29	5

GAUNT, Ronald Arthur

WA, Vic, LHB/RF
Born: 26 February 1934
Yarloop, Western Australia

Ron Gaunt made his first-class debut for Western Australia in 1955–56, and in 1957–58 he was chosen as a mid-tour replacement for the injured John Drennan in South Africa, where he made his Test debut at Durban, taking 2/87. He moved to Victoria for the 1960–61 season and earned a place in the side to tour England in 1961, where he played only in the fifth Test. A further Test against South Africa at Adelaide in 1963–64 ended a disjointed career. Dragging when delivering, and a tendency to no ball, may have been the reason Gaunt was not selected on a more regular basis. His first-class career certainly suggests that he was a more than useful fast bowler. His best figures of 7/104 were taken against the strong New South Wales side in Sydney.

BATTING	M	Inn	NO	HS	Runs	Ave	100s	50s	C/S
Tests	3	4	2	3	6	3.00	–	–	1
First-class	85	92	33	32*	616	10.44	–	–	31

BOWLING	Balls	Runs	Wkts	Ave	BB	5wI	10wM
Tests	716	310	7	44.28	3/53	–	–
First-class	–	7143	266	26.85	7/104	10	–

GEHRS, Donald Raeburn Algernon

SA, RHB/LB/WK
Born: 29 November 1880
Port Victor now Victor Harbour, South Australia
Died: 25 June 1953
Kings Park, South Australia

Although 'Algie' Gehrs had a long and distinguished career for South Australia, his Test appearances were disappointing for a batsman of such ability. He made his Test debut against England in 1903–04, and, despite his failure, he was chosen to tour England in 1905. He was not a success, averaging just over 20 in scoring only 600 runs. Gehrs' best performances in Tests were against South Africa in 1910–11, when he made his two fifties. For South Australia it was a different matter; his hard-hitting style posed a constant threat to bowlers' figures. Among many fine innings, he was the first South Australian to score a century in each innings of a first-class game; a feat he achieved against Western Australia in 1906. Throughout his career he vied for top billing with his team mate, Clem Hill, and while he could compete at first-class level, the transition to Test cricket was unfortunately beyond him.

BATTING	M	Inn	NO	HS	Runs	Ave	100s	50s	C/S
Tests	6	11	0	67	221	20.09	–	2	6
First-class	83	142	12	170	4377	33.66	13	16	71/4

BOWLING	Balls	Runs	Wkts	Ave	BB	5wI	10wM
Tests	6	4	0	–	–	–	–
First-class	–	416	8	52.00	2/9	–	–

GIFFEN, George

SA, RHB/RM,OB
Born: 27 March 1859
Adelaide, South Australia
Died: 29 November 1927
Parkside, South Australia

George Giffen was Australia's finest all-rounder of the nineteenth century, and arguably its best ever. A right-handed batsman of considerable determination and a bowler of medium pace or off spin, depending on the conditions, Giffen was the first Australian to score 1000 runs and take 100 wickets in Tests. So good a player was he, that he was often called 'Australia's WG', a compliment that his career seems to justify.

Giffen made his debut for South Australia in 1880 and toured England for the first time in 1882. Subsequently he toured there in 1884, 1886, 1893 and 1896, and was unavailable in 1888 and 1890. Although he played well in England, Giffen was a better performer in Australian conditions, and it was there that his best efforts were recorded. His ten-wicket haul won the second Test at Sydney in 1891–92, while his only Test century was recorded against England on the same ground three years later. After Blackham was injured in the first Test of that 1894–95 series, Giffen took over as captain for the remaining four games, winning two and losing two.

At first-class level he was nothing less than astonishing. His top score of 271 came against Victoria in 1891–92, a game in which he also took 16 wickets for 166. His best bowling of 10/66 in an innings was taken for the Australian team against The Rest at Sydney in 1883–84, the first time this had happened in Australia. In 1886 he accumulated 40 wickets in only five innings, and against the English team of 1886–87 he scored 203 and took a hat-trick. At 43 years of age Giffen scored 81 and 97 not out and took 15 wickets for South Australia against Victoria in 1902–03.

There were faults in his character. As captain he was inclined to over-bowl himself, almost heedless of giving others a turn, but the results generally supported his decisions and for much of his career he alone stood between South Australia and defeat. There were also thoughts that he played only when it suited him, but his performances showed that he never shirked an issue or feared an opponent. Towards the end of his career Giffen wrote a book, *With Bat and Ball*, which has become a classic of the game's literature. In over a hundred years of cricket Australia can have produced few better players.

BATTING	M	Inn	NO	HS	Runs	Ave	100s	50s	C/S
Tests	31	53	0	161	1238	23.35	1	6	24
First-class	251	421	23	271	11758	29.54	18	54	195

BOWLING	Balls	Runs	Wkts	Ave	BB	5wI	10wM
Tests	6325	2791	103	27.09	7/117	7	1
First-class	–	21782	1023	21.29	10/66	95	30

GIFFEN, Walter Frank

SA, RHB
Born: 20 September 1861
Adelaide, South Australia
Died: 28 June 1949
North Unley, South Australia

The younger brother of George, Walter Giffen was a useful right-handed batsman and a fine fielder. He made his debut for South Australia in 1882–83 and failed in his first Test against England in 1886–87. His two subsequent Tests in 1891–92 were equally unsuccessful. On form it is difficult to see why he was selected to tour England in 1893. Many experts believe his brother was responsible. Again he was distinctly unsuccessful, averaging only 15.31 on the trip. If Walter Giffen's career was less than satisfying, perhaps his brother must take some of the blame. It must have been difficult playing in such a giant shadow.

BATTING	M	Inn	NO	HS	Runs	Ave	100s	50s	C/S
Tests	3	6	0	3	11	1.83	–	–	1
First-class	47	80	6	89	1178	15.91	–	6	23

BOWLING	Runs	Wkts	Ave	BB	5wI	10wM
First-class	15	0	–	–	–	–

GILBERT, David Robert

NSW, Tas, RHB/RFM
Born: 19 December 1960
Darlinghurst, New South Wales

Dave Gilbert made his Test debut in England in 1985, at a time when Australia's Test side was undergoing a rebuilding process. Although he played nine Tests over the next two years, Gilbert was unable to establish his position. He then had trouble maintaining selection in the New South Wales team, but in 1988–89 he resurrected his first-class career by moving to Tasmania where he was very successful. Producing swing, bounce and pace off a gliding approach to the wicket, Dave Gilbert became one of the most feared opening bowlers in the country. In 1989–90 he equalled the Tasmanian record for the number of wickets in a Sheffield Shield season. In the process of rebuilding his career, Gilbert helped to lift Tasmania out of the cricketing doldrums. He become the State's vice-captain in 1991–92, a fitting accolade for such a likeable and whole-hearted player, before a back injury forced his retirement at the end of that season.

BATTING	M	Inn	NO	HS	Runs	Ave	100s	50s	C/S
Tests	9	12	4	15	57	7.12	–	–	–
First-class	127	149	53	117	1374	14.31	1	1	34

BOWLING	Balls	Runs	Wkts	Ave	BB	5wl	10wM
Tests	1647	843	16	52.68	3/48	–	–
First-class	–	11469	354	32.40	8/55	11	1

GILMOUR, Gary John

NSW, LHB/LFM
Born: 26 June 1951
Waratah, New South Wales

A left-handed all-rounder, Gary Gilmour seemed likely to emulate the feats of Alan Davidson. There were days when he looked capable of almost anything, swinging the ball both ways or playing a devastating innings. Other days were disappointing, but when he was involved there was always the possibility that something might happen. Gilmour made

122 on his debut against South Australia in 1971–72, and two years later was in the Test team. He produced a spell of 6/14 to bowl Australia into the World Cup Final in 1975 and performed well against the West Indies in 1975–76. Gilmour's sole Test century came in New Zealand in 1976–77. After a disappointing game, due to injury, in the Centenary Test, he missed the 1977 tour of England. From there he joined World Series Cricket and after the settlement soon returned to Newcastle.

BATTING	M	Inn	NO	HS	Runs	Ave	100s	50s	C/S
Tests	15	22	1	101	483	23.00	1	3	8
First-class	75	120	18	122	3126	30.64	5	18	68

BOWLING	Balls	Runs	Wkts	Ave	BB	5wl	10wM
Tests	2661	1406	54	26.03	6/85	3	–
First-class	–	7345	233	31.52	6/85	6	–

GLEESON, John William

NSW, RHB/LBG
Born: 14 March 1938
Wiangaree, New South Wales

John Gleeson bowled spin with an unorthodox bent finger grip which made him difficult to 'read'. After a successful country career he was persuaded to try grade cricket in 1965–66, and within two years was in the Test team. He remained a regular member of Australian sides for the next five years, touring England in 1968 and 1972 and India and South Africa in 1969–70. He was also successful against the West Indies at home in 1968–69. Even after batsmen had overcome their initial difficulties with 'reading' his spin, Gleeson was still a good enough bowler to take wickets at the highest level. This set him above an earlier bowler with a similiar grip, Jack Iverson, who quickly dropped out of first-class cricket once his mystery had been solved. In addition to his playing skills, Gleeson possessed an extremely likeable personality and was a very popular cricketer.

BATTING	M	Inn	NO	HS	Runs	Ave	100s	50s	C/S
Tests	29	46	8	45	395	10.39	–	–	17
First-class	116	137	38	59	1095	11.06	–	1	58

BOWLING	Balls	Runs	Wkts	Ave	BB	5wl	10wM
Tests	8857	3367	93	36.20	5/61	3	–
First-class	–	10729	430	24.95	7/52	22	2

GRAHAM, Henry

Vic, RHB/LB
Born: 22 November 1870
Carlton, Victoria
Died: 7 February 1911
Dunedin, New Zealand

Known as 'the Little Dasher', Harry Graham was an aggressive right-handed batsman, who had a meteoric rise to the top. He made his debut in 1892–93 and was so successful that he was chosen to tour England in 1893 where he exceeded 1000 runs and topped the averages. Graham had the honour of scoring a hundred in his first Test, at Lord's. His other century was made against England at Sydney in 1894–95. On his second trip to England he was restricted by ill-health and was far less successful. With his hard hitting and fast running he was a delight to spectators. Throughout his career he strove to the utmost to entertain them, and if he was occasionally inconsistent, there was also much to admire in the way he played the game.

BATTING	M	Inn	NO	HS	Runs	Ave	100s	50s	C/S
Tests	6	10	0	107	301	30.10	2	–	3
First-class	114	201	9	124	5054	26.32	7	23	87

BOWLING	Runs	Wkts	Ave	BB	5wl	10wM	
First-class	235	6	39.16	4/39	–	–	

GREGORY, David William

NSW, RHB/RF(r)
Born: 15 April 1845
Fairy Meadow, New South Wales
Died: 4 August 1919
Turramurra, New South Wales

Dave Gregory was Australia's first Test captain and a member of a distinguished cricketing family. A tall, bearded, right-handed batsman, useful bowler and excellent fieldsman, Gregory was a natural leader, whose handling of New South Wales led to his selection as captain for the match against Lillywhite's English team at Melbourne in 1876–77. His skilful leadership was a major factor in Australia's success. In the second Test he made his highest score and was the unanimous choice to lead the Australian team to England in 1878. This tour helped establish Australia's cricketing reputation and although there were no Tests, a strong MCC side was defeated in a single day. Gregory captained Australia against Lord Harris's team in 1878–79, but declined to tour England again in 1880. He continued to play for New South Wales until 1882–83, retiring with a secure place in Australia's cricket history.

BATTING	M	Inn	NO	HS	Runs	Ave	100s	50s	C/S
Tests	3	5	2	43	60	20.00	–	–	–
First-class	41	68	7	85	889	14.57	–	5	35

BOWLING	Balls	Runs	Wkts	Ave	BB	5wl	10wM
Tests	20	9	0	–	–	–	–
First-class	–	553	29	19.06	5/55	1	–

GREGORY, Edward James

NSW, RHB/RM(r)
Born: 29 May 1839
Waverley, New South Wales
Died: 22 April 1899
Randwick, New South Wales

'Ned' Gregory joined his younger brother, Dave, in the first Test side, although he contributed little to Australia's victory. He had the dubious distinction of making the first duck in Test cricket. Perhaps he was a little past his best, having made his debut as far back as 1862–63. From then, until his retirement in 1877–78, he held his place in the New South Wales side as a useful batsman and outstanding fielder. After his playing days he became a notable curator of the Sydney Cricket Ground. Gregory is credited with designing the first comprehensive scoreboard at the ground, which he did during the 1890s. His son, Sydney, played over 50 Tests for Australia.

BATTING	M	Inn	NO	HS	Runs	Ave	100s	50s	C/S
Tests	1	2	0	11	11	5.50	–	–	1
First-class	16	29	2	65*	470	17.40	–	2	11

BOWLING	Runs	Wkts	Ave	BB	5wl	10wM
First-class	106	5	21.20	2/14	–	–

GREGORY, JACK MORRISON

NSW, LHB/RF
Born: 14 August 1895
North Sydney, New South Wales
Died: 7 August 1973
Bega, New South Wales

A magnificent all-rounder, Jack Gregory was a fast bowler with a huge leap before delivering the ball, an aggressive left-handed batsman who scored a century in 70 minutes against South Africa in 1921, the fastest in Test history, in terms of elapsed time, and the finest of slips fieldsmen. The nephew of Dave and 'Ned', Gregory came to prominence when he was chosen in the AIF side at the end of the World War I. After taking 100 wickets in 1919 he was a certainty for the 1920–21 series against England when he scored 442 runs at 73.66, took 23 wickets at 24.17 and held 15 catches. Towards the end of the series he was paired with Ted McDonald in a devastating fast bowling partnership which destroyed England, in Australia and on tour in 1921. This was the high point of his career. Although he played until 1928–29, when a knee injury forced his retirement, his speed was no longer as fearsome and his wickets gradually increased in cost. On his second trip to England in 1926 he took only five Test wickets. Despite that, in his prime he was a superb player, and one of Australia's finest all-rounders.

BATTING	M	Inn	NO	HS	Runs	Ave	100s	50s	C/S
Tests	24	34	3	119	1146	36.96	2	7	37
First-class	129	173	18	152	5561	36.52	13	27	195

BOWLING	Balls	Runs	Wkts	Ave	BB	5wI	10wM
Tests	5582	2648	85	31.15	7/69	4	–
First-class	–	10580	504	20.99	9/32	33	8

GREGORY, Ross Gerald

Vic, RHB/LB
Born: 28 February 1916
Murchison, Victoria
Died: 10 June 1942
near Ghafargon, Assam, India

When Ross Gregory made a brilliant 80 in the fifth Test of the 1936–37 series against England it seemed to be the start of a glittering career for the dashing Victorian right-handed batsman. Sadly, it was his second, and last, Test, and a potentially great player was lost. Gregory had made his first-class debut in 1933–34 and took little time in establishing himself as a player of the future. After such a fine beginning to his Test career he missed selection on the 1938 trip to England, losing out to the young batsmen Sid Barnes and Lindsay Hassett. There were no other chances to reclaim his Test place before World War II. Gregory joined the RAAF and was killed on active service in India.

BATTING	M	Inn	NO	HS	Runs	Ave	100s	50s	C/S
Tests	2	3	0	80	153	51.00	–	2	1
First-class	33	51	2	128	1874	38.24	1	17	20

BOWLING	Balls	Runs	Wkts	Ave	BB	5wl	10wM
Tests	24	14	0	–	–	–	–
First-class	–	1767	50	35.34	5/69	1	–

GREGORY, Sydney Edward

NSW, RHB
Born: 14 April 1870
Randwick, New South Wales
Died: 1 August 1929
Randwick, New South Wales

The son of 'Ned' Gregory, born at the Sydney Cricket Ground where his father was the curator, Sydney Gregory was an aggressive batsman and an outstanding fieldsman who played 58 Tests between 1890 and 1912. He toured England in 1890, 1893, 1896, 1899, 1902, 1905, 1909 and 1912, a record eight times. His highest score, 201, was made at Sydney in 1894–95 against England, against whom he made all his Test centuries. Wearing only one batting glove, Gregory liked nothing better than taking the attack up to the bowlers with aggressive strokes and quick running between the wickets. Always a crowd pleaser, he retained his skills over a long and distinguished career. On his last trip to England, Gregory was persuaded to lead a weakened side, after six of the country's best cricketers refused to tour because of a dispute over the appointment of a manager. Tactically he was a good skipper, but he lacked the toughness to control some of his players. It was a sad ending to a fine career.

BATTING	M	Inn	NO	HS	Runs	Ave	100s	50s	C/S
Tests	58	100	7	201	2282	24.53	4	8	25
First-class	368	587	55	201	15192	28.55	25	65	174

BOWLING	Balls	Runs	Wkts	Ave	BB		5wI	10wM
Tests	30	33	0	–	–		–	–
First-class	–	394	2	197.00	1/8		–	–

GRIMMETT, Clarence Victor

SA, Vic, RHB/LBG
Born: 25 December 1891
Caversham near Dunedin, New Zealand
Died: 2 May 1980
Kensington Gardens, South Australia

Clarrie Grimmett was one of cricket's great bowlers. A small man, often called 'the Gnome', he delivered his leg spinners, top spinners and googlies with a round-arm action and a straight-faced cunning that would have done credit to the finest of gamblers. He was as much a match-winner with the ball as Don Bradman was with the bat, and his great achievements were made at an age when most had either retired or lost the edge off their skill. Not Grimmett, he continued to experiment, to lay traps that sent even the finest of batsmen to their destruction.

But Grimmett was no overnight success. Born in New Zealand, he made his first-class debut for Wellington in 1911–12, primarily as a batsman, before moving to Sydney in 1914, then to Melbourne in 1917. Unable to secure a regular first-class game he went to South Australia, making his debut for them in 1924–25, and playing his first Test the same season, taking 11 wickets. From that moment until 1936 he was a Test regular, taking 216 wickets in just 37 games. He toured England in 1926, 1930 and 1934, each time capturing over 100 wickets. The 1930 tour was his best, with 142 wickets, including 29 in the Tests, and an innings best of 10/37 against Yorkshire.

In Australia he was just as great a threat, destroying the West Indies and South African sides in successive seasons. On his one trip to South Africa in 1935–36 he took 44 wickets in the Tests. Sadly that was the end of his Test career, as he was not selected for the 1936–37 and 1938 series against England. He may have been over 45, but he was taking plenty of wickets in the Sheffield Shield, something he continued to do until first-class cricket was suspended in 1941. His omission from those games remains one of Australia's greatest selection controversies. It seems unbelievable to think that he would not have outperformed most of the players taken in his place. Grimmett himself thought he was still improving.

He waged constant psychological warfare against batsmen and was meticulous in plotting their downfall. Stories about him are many: his wearing of a hat while bowling to cover his baldness and disguise his age; training his fox terrier to fetch balls for him in the nets; or bowling in his garden, aged over 80, and complaining that his deliveries had lost their 'nip'.

BATTING	M	Inn	NO	HS	Runs	Ave	100s	50s	C/S
Tests	37	50	10	50	557	13.92	–	1	17
First-class	248	321	54	71*	4720	17.67	–	12	139

BOWLING	Balls	Runs	Wkts	Ave	BB	5wI	10wM
Tests	14513	5231	216	24.21	7/40	21	7
First-class	–	31740	1424	22.28	10/37	127	33

GROUBE, Thomas Underwood

Vic, RHB/RM
Born: 2 September 1857
Taranaki, New Zealand
Died: 5 August 1927
Glenferrie, Victoria

Born in New Zealand, but educated in Melbourne, Groube's solitary Test came at The Oval in 1880, when he was chosen for the tour after sickness forced Charles Bannerman to decline. In fact he probably owed his Test selection to an injury suffered by leading bowler, Fred 'Demon' Spofforth. The right-handed Groube was a good grade cricketer, but his first-class record suggests that he was unable to make the transition to the higher levels of the game. His top score of 61 was made on the 1880 tour, against Yorkshire, but other than that, he achieved little of note.

BATTING	M	Inn	NO	HS	Runs	Ave	100s	50s	C/S
Tests	1	2	0	11	11	5.50	–	–	–
First-class	13	23	2	61	179	8.52	–	1	2

GROUT, Arthur Theodore Wallace

Qld, RHB/WK
Born: 20 March 1927
Mackay, Queensland
Died: 9 November 1968
Spring Hill, Queensland

Wally Grout gave his life to cricket, and it certainly contributed to his early death. A highly talented 'keeper and capable batsman, Grout made his first-class debut in 1946–47, but could not gain a regular place in the Queensland side because of the presence of Don Tallon. When Tallon retired in 1953–54, Grout quickly cemented his place, and his selection to tour South Africa in 1957–58 brought him into Test cricket. From then, until he retired in 1965–66, he was Australia's first choice 'keeper, and an integral part of the strong teams led by Richie Benaud. He set an Australian record for dismissals, since surpassed only by Rod Marsh, and a world record, eight in a first-class innings against Western Australia in 1959–60. The depth of Australian batting gave him little chance to display his skills in the Test arena, but he played some useful innings for his country and frequently dug Queensland out of trouble. He batted aggressively and had a particular fondness for the pull and hook.

Grout suffered a heart attack before going to the West Indies in 1964–65, but, despite the risks involved, he continued to play on for a couple more seasons. He had waited a long time for his chance at international cricket and loved it so much that he was prepared to gamble to stay in the side. His death in Brisbane, aged only 41, was greeted with universal dismay. There can have been few players more loved and admired than 'the Griz'.

BATTING	M	Inn	NO	HS	Runs	Ave	100s	50s	C/S
Tests	51	67	8	74	890	15.08	–	3	163/24
First-class	183	253	24	119	5168	22.56	4	25	473/114

BOWLING	Runs	Wkts	Ave	BB	5wl	10wM
First-class	115	3	38.33	1/22	–	–

GUEST, Colin Ernest John

Vic, WA, RHB/RFM
Born: 7 October 1937
Melbourne, Victoria

Colin Guest was a fast-medium bowler who made his first-class debut for Victoria in 1958–59. A series of good performances in 1962–63, saw him selected for the third Test against England. He failed to take a wicket and was never chosen again. That season he produced his best performances: 10 wickets (7/95 and 3/39) against Western Australia and a six-wicket haul against Queensland. In 1966–67 he moved to Western Australia where he played for one season, performing well with the bat, averaging over 30 and making his top score of 74.

BATTING	M	Inn	NO	HS	Runs	Ave	100s	50s	C/S
Tests	1	1	0	11	11	11.00	–	–	–
First-class	36	52	4	74	922	19.20	–	3	13

BOWLING	Balls	Runs	Wkts	Ave	BB	5wI	10wM
Tests	144	59	0	–	–	–	–
First-class	–	3121	115	27.13	7/95	5	1

H

HAMENCE, Ronald Arthur

SA, RHB/RM
Born: 25 November 1915
Hindmarsh, South Australia

Ron Hamence had the misfortune of having his career coincide with a period when Australia's team was at its greatest strength. He made his first-class debut in 1935–36, scoring a century against Tasmania, and continued to perform well until World War II suspended first-class cricket. After the War he made his Test debut against England in the fifth match of the 1946–47 series. Hamence played two Tests against India next season and won selection in the 1948 side to tour England. In possibly the best side to represent Australia, he could not force his way into the Test team. He continued to play for South Australia until he retired after the first match against the MCC in the 1950–51 season, a game in which he scored a century. Had he played at another time, Ron Hamence may have had a long and distinguished Test career.

BATTING	M	Inn	NO	HS	Runs	Ave	100s	50s	C/S
Tests	3	4	1	30*	81	27.00	–	–	1
First-class	99	155	15	173	5285	37.75	11	26	34

BOWLING	Runs	Wkts	Ave	BB	5wl	10wM
First-class	239	8	29.87	2/13	–	–

HAMMOND, Jeffrey Roy

SA, RHB/RFM
Born: 19 April 1950
North Adelaide, South Australia

Jeff Hammond's fast bowling made an instant impression after his debut for South Australia in 1969–70. He was chosen to tour England in 1972, but the presence of Lillee and Massie, plus some injury problems, kept him out of the Test side. In fact, a back injury prevented him from maintaining his Test place, just when it seemed he had broken through. On the West Indies tour of 1972–73, Hammond played all five Tests providing excellent support for Max Walker, taking 15 wickets at 32.53. The two proved a match–winning combination when spearheads Lillee and Massie could play no part in the series. On his return to Australia the injuries which ruined his career set in. He returned to play a few matches for South Australia, but the pace had been taken from his bowling. Hammond was a very promising young player, but his talent never really had the chance to come to fruition.

BATTING	M	Inn	NO	HS	Runs	Ave	100s	50s	C/S
Tests	5	5	2	19	28	9.33	–	–	2
First-class	69	87	31	53	922	16.46	–	1	36

BOWLING	Balls	Runs	Wkts	Ave	BB	5wI	10wM
Tests	1031	488	15	32.53	4/38	–	–
First-class	–	5315	184	28.88	6/15	8	–

HARRY, John

Vic, RHB/OB/WK
Born: 1 August 1857
Ballarat, Victoria
Died: 27 October 1919
Canterbury, Victoria

Harry was a Victorian all-rounder who made his first-class debut in 1883–84. Consistent performances over a period of time, including his career best of 114 against Western Australia in 1892–93, saw him eventually gain Test selection against England at Adelaide in the third Test of the 1894–95 series, but a double failure caused him to be dropped from the side. An injury forced him to withdraw from the 1896 team to England, and he never had the chance to play Test cricket again. Luck and poor selection seemed to conspire against him, as his performances suggest he was well worth a further chance at the highest level. In addition to his batting and bowling Harry was a more than useful wicket-keeper.

BATTING	M	Inn	NO	HS	Runs	Ave	100s	50s	C/S
Tests	1	2	0	6	8	4.00	–	–	1
First-class	32	60	3	114	1466	25.71	2	9	18/3

BOWLING	Runs	Wkts	Ave	BB	5wI	10wM	
First-class	618	26	23.76	4/15	–	–	

HARTIGAN, Roger Joseph

NSW, Qld, RHB
Born: 12 December 1879
Chatswood, New South Wales
Died: 7 June 1958
Brisbane, Queensland

Roger Hartigan made his first-class debut for New South Wales in 1903–04, but it was his move to Queensland which resulted in his selection for the third Test of the 1907–08 series. He was an instant success, making 48 and 116. He missed the fourth Test, but played in the last. Strangely, he did not play Test cricket again, although he did tour England in 1909. Representing Queensland in those pre–Shield days must have been a drawback, but the lack of regular competition did not stop him from playing some fine innings, in addition to captaining the side. After his playing career, Hartigan became an efficient administrator and was instrumental in gaining Queensland's admittance to the Sheffield Shield. He was also a member of the Australian Board of Control for 35 years.

BATTING	M	Inn	NO	HS	Runs	Ave	100s	50s	C/S
Tests	2	4	0	116	170	42.50	1	–	1
First-class	45	80	4	116	1901	25.01	2	14	36

BOWLING	Balls	Runs	Wkts	Ave	BB	5wI	10wM
Tests	12	7	0	–	–	–	–
First-class	–	351	9	39.00	3/27	–	–

HARTKOPF, Albert Ernst Victor

Vic, RHB/LBG
Born: 28 December 1889
North Fitzroy, Victoria
Died: 20 May 1968
Kew, Victoria

Hartkopf was an aggressive right-handed batsman and leg-spin bowler who made his first-class debut in 1911. He played his only Test at Melbourne, in the second game of the 1924–25 series against England. In Australia's first innings of 600 Hartkopf made a rapid 80, adding 100 with 'keeper Bert Oldfield for the ninth wicket. His bowling was not so successful, only capturing the wicket of last man Strudwick in England's first innings. Despite his good performance with the bat, Hartkopf was not chosen again. This must be viewed as a rather strange decision given his success with both bat and ball over a long period of time. It may be that he was past his best at the time of his selection and Australia was looking for a bowler rather than a batsman. Hartkopf's career may have been more substantial had medical duties not forced him to miss a number of games.

BATTING	M	Inn	NO	HS	Runs	Ave	100s	50s	C/S
Tests	1	2	0	80	80	40.00	–	1	–
First-class	41	60	9	126	1758	34.47	2	12	36

BOWLING	Balls	Runs	Wkts	Ave	BB	5wI	10wM
Tests	240	134	1	134.00	1/120	–	–
First-class	–	3726	121	30.79	8/105	7	1

HARVEY, Mervyn Roye

Vic, RHB
Born: 29 April 1918
Broken Hill, New South Wales

The eldest of a famous cricketing family, (four of the six brothers played first-class cricket), Merv Harvey was a right-handed opening

93

batsman who first represented Victoria in 1940–41. Like many others, Harvey lost some important seasons to the Second World War, but emerged after the conflict to win selection for the fourth Test against England in 1946–47. In the second innings, his 31 was made in a partnership of 116 for the first wicket with Arthur Morris. While this could hardly be termed a failure, the presence of so many top-class openers, Sid Barnes, Arthur Morris and Bill Brown to name just three, prevented the aggressive Victorian from being given another chance. Harvey's career ended in 1948–49 after just 22 first-class games, in which he made three centuries.

BATTING	M	Inn	NO	HS	Runs	Ave	100s	50s	C/S
Tests	1	2	0	31	43	21.50	–	–	–
First-class	22	33	3	163	1147	38.23	3	3	11

HARVEY, Robert Neil

NSW, LHB/OB
Born: 8 October 1928
Fitzroy, Victoria

The most talented of the cricketing brotherhood, Neil Harvey made his Test debut against India in the fourth Test of the 1947–48 series and remained an integral part of the Australian team until he retired in 1962–63. He played 79 Tests, surpassing the record set by Syd Gregory, and at the time of his retirement only Don Bradman had made more runs and centuries for Australia.

Harvey was a left-handed batsman, possibly the finest left-hander to represent his country, and a brilliant fieldsman. A small man, he was nimble on his feet and possessed all the strokes, which he played with power and perfect timing. His first-class debut came in 1946–47, and within a year he had made 153 against India, at the age of 19 years and 121 days. He is still the youngest Australian to score a Test century. Harvey toured England in 1948, hitting a century in his first Ashes Test, at Headingley in the fourth game of the series. He toured England again in 1953, 1956 and 1961. On the last tour he captained Australia to a magnificent win in the Lord's Test when Benaud was injured.

While he performed well against all bowling, Harvey seemed to have a particular liking for South Africans. In 1949–50 he scored four Test centuries and made over 1500 runs on tour, and when the Springboks visited Australia in 1952–53 he scored 834 runs in the series. Perhaps Harvey's finest innings was played on that 1949–50 tour. After being bowled out for 75 by off spinner Hugh Tayfield, Australia was required to make 336 to win, and this unlikely target was achieved thanks to 151 not out from Harvey. His highest Test score of 205 came at Melbourne in 1952–53. He also made 204 against the West Indies in Kingston, Jamaica in 1955. Harvey was a member of every Australian touring side between 1948 and 1963, making runs against all opposition under all conditions. His 21 Test centuries were scored on 15 different grounds.

Perhaps Harvey's greatest disappointment was not to be given the Australian captaincy. Vice-captain for many years, he was passed over, first for Ian Craig and then for Richie Benaud. There was never a hint of disloyalty in him as he faithfully gave his all for both, cheerfully serving as vice-captain and leading the side when required. Benaud's injury gave him his one chance to lead Australia in a Test, a task he accomplished with consummate skill.

BATTING	M	Inn	NO	HS	Runs	Ave	100s	50s	C/S
Tests	79	137	10	205	6149	48.41	21	24	64
First-class	306	461	35	231*	21699	50.93	67	94	229

BOWLING	Balls	Runs	Wkts	Ave	BB	5wI	10wM
Tests	414	120	3	40.00	1/8	–	–
First-class	–	1106	30	36.86	4/8	–	–

HASSETT, Arthur Lindsay

Vic, RHB/RM
Born: 28 August 1913
Geelong, Victoria
Died: 16 June 1993
Batehaven, New South Wales

In addition to his great talent as a right-handed batsman, Lindsay Hassett was a much loved figure in Australian cricket. A small, whimsical man with a wonderful sense of humour, he was a very fine cricketer and a successful captain.

Hassett first came to prominence in 1930–31 when as a Geelong schoolboy he was selected to play for a Victorian Country team against the West Indies, and made 147 not out. He played one game for Victoria in 1932, but did not receive another chance until 1935–36 when he was able to cement a place in the side. His promise was obvious, and he was chosen to tour England in 1938, where he averaged over 50 and made his Test debut.

The War halted his progress, but he returned in 1945 to lead the AIF side on its tour of England. The tour was a great success, bringing cricket to a sport–starved country. Hassett was appointed vice-captain to Don Bradman in 1946–47 and became a vital part of Australia's finest team. His batting lacked some of its pre–War dash, but Hassett had become a much sounder player, now capable of adapting his play to the conditions and the needs of his side. On the 1948 tour of England he scored 1563 runs at 74.42, and when Bradman retired he became Australia's captain.

His sense of humour tended to distract attention from his leadership skills, but he was a fine captain. Between 1949 and 1953 he led Australia 24 times, winning 14 games and losing only four. He successfully led Australia to South Africa and was undefeated in three series at home. His only loss of a series came in England in 1953 when his team lost the last Test of a closely fought series to part with the Ashes. Hassett could count himself unlucky, as Australia had good chances to win two of the Tests, despite the fact that the powers of his team were certainly on the decline. He accepted the loss graciously and never complained about the fates which seemed to conspire against him. On that final tour, aged 40, he was Australia's best batsman, stepping into the opening role in order to give his team a better start. Lindsay Hassett retired after that tour, but his involvement with cricket was not finished as he became a radio commentator with the ABC, and for many more years Australians were able to discover just how well the little Victorian understood the game of cricket.

BATTING	M	Inn	NO	HS	Runs	Ave	100s	50s	C/S
Tests	43	69	3	198*	3073	46.56	10	11	30
First-class	216	322	32	232	16890	58.24	59	74	170

BOWLING	Balls	Runs	Wkts	Ave	BB	5wl	10wM
Tests	111	78	0	–	–	–	–
First-class	–	703	18	39.05	2/10	–	–

HAWKE, Neil James Napier

WA, SA, Tas, RHB/RFM
Born: 27 June 1939
Cheltenham, South Australia

A fast-medium bowler from South Australia, Neil Hawke formed an effective new ball partnership with Graham McKenzie during the sixties. Hawke made his first-class debut for Western Australia in 1959–60, but returned to his home state next season. Some good bowling in 1962–63 saw him make his Test debut against England in the fifth Test of that series. He bowled well against South Africa in 1963–64 and earned himself a trip to England in 1964 where he headed the bowling averages. Hawke's finest effort came in the West Indies in 1965 when he took 24 wickets at 21.83 against the best team in the world. Sadly, his Test career ended in 1968, on his second tour of England, when he was dropped after two Tests. A shoulder injury sustained while playing Australian Rules football in 1966 had certainly reduced his effectiveness as a bowler. He played successfully in English League cricket until a serious illness in 1980 almost claimed his life. His incredible fight to stay alive has certainly been his greatest performance.

BATTING	M	Inn	NO	HS	Runs	Ave	100s	50s	C/S
Tests	27	37	15	45*	365	16.59	–	–	9
First-class	145	198	57	141*	3383	23.99	1	11	85

BOWLING	Balls	Runs	Wkts	Ave	BB	5wl	10wM
Tests	6974	2677	91	29.41	7/105	6	1
First-class	–	12088	458	26.39	8/61	23	5

HAZLITT, Gervys Rignold

Vic, NSW, RHB/RFM
Born: 4 September 1888
Enfield, New South Wales
Died: 30 October 1915
Parramatta, New South Wales

Although born in New South Wales, Gerry Hazlitt was educated in Victoria and made his first-class debut there in 1905–06. He was a

97

useful batsman, but a more threatening bowler, able to cut the ball off the wicket with what some considered a suspect action. Hazlitt's Test debut came in the 1907–08 series against England, but he achieved little of note. He returned to New South Wales in 1911–12 and won his Test place back for the last game of the series against England. His efforts earned a tour to England for the Triangular Series of 1912, where he produced his best performance of 7/25 against England at Lord's. Hazlitt's career was played under the handicap of a weak heart which claimed his life at the age of just 27.

BATTING	M	Inn	NO	HS	Runs	Ave	100s	50s	C/S
Tests	9	12	4	34*	89	11.12	–	–	4
First-class	57	83	14	82*	876	12.69	–	5	31

BOWLING	Balls	Runs	Wkts	Ave	BB	5wI	10wM
Tests	1563	623	23	27.08	7/25	1	–
First-class	–	4906	188	26.09	7/25	8	–

HEALY, Ian Andrew

Qld, RHB/WK
Born: 30 April 1964
Spring Hill, Queensland

Ian Healy's sudden rise into the Test team astounded many of the game's followers. Selected as a replacement for injured Queensland 'keeper, Peter Anderson, towards the end of the 1987–88 season, Healy made such an impression on the selectors that he was chosen in the side to tour Pakistan in 1988. He made a rather unimpressive debut in difficult conditions, but the selectors maintained their faith in him, and he has repaid them with a series of steadily improving performances with both bat and gloves. As a keeper he is generally neat and unobtrusive, his glovework ensuring that he misses few chances. With the bat he is an aggressive striker of the ball, and if he is prone to bouts of compulsive hooking he also scores many runs with the stroke and has played a number of valuable innings for both Queensland and Australia. Healy finally passed the century mark when he made 102 not out at Old Trafford in the first Test of the 1993 Ashes series. In addition to his batting, his keeping to the spin of Warne and May played a major part in Australia's triumph. His batting has been particularly effective in limited-overs cricket, where he scores at nearly a run a ball, giving a strong impetus towards the end of an innings.

Healy was appointed captain of Queensland for season 1992–93, suggesting that he may have a leadership role to play at the highest level.

BATTING	M	Inn	NO	HS	Runs	Ave	100s	50s	C/S
Tests	53	78	7	102*	1730	24.37	1	9	167/12
First-class	114	164	33	102*	3987	30.44	1	21	343/30

BOWLING	Runs	Wkts	Ave	BB	5wi	10wM
First-class	1	0	–	–	–	–

HENDRY, Hunter Scott Thomas Laurie

NSW, Vic, RHB/RFM
Born: 24 May 1895
Double Bay, New South Wales
Died: 16 December 1988
Rose Bay, New South Wales

A useful all-rounder and a wonderful character, 'Stork' Hendry, so–called because of his long legs, represented Australia in 11 Tests between 1921 and 1928–29. He made his first-class debut in 1918–19 for New South Wales and did enough to earn selection for the 1921 tour of England, where he played in the first four Tests. In 1924 he moved to Victoria, for whom he made his highest score of 325 not out against New Zealand at Melbourne in 1926–27. He toured England again in 1926, but illness restricted his chances. Hendry's last Test series was against England in 1928–29 when he made his only century, in the second Test. He continued to be a force at first-class level and his final tour was to India in 1935–36 with an unofficial Australian team. In later life he was unafraid to express strong opinions or tell superb stories of the past. At the time of his death he was the oldest living Test cricketer.

BATTING	M	Inn	NO	HS	Runs	Ave	100s	50s	C/S
Tests	11	18	2	112	335	20.93	1	–	10
First-class	140	206	25	325*	6799	37.56	14	34	152

BOWLING	Balls	Runs	Wkts	Ave	BB	5wi	10wM
Tests	1706	640	16	40.00	3/36	–	–
First-class	–	6647	229	29.02	8/33	6	1

HIBBERT, Paul Anthony

Vic, LHB/LM
Born: 23 July 1952
Brunswick, Victoria

Paul Hibbert made his first-class debut for Victoria in 1974–75, and played his only Test against India at Brisbane in the first game of the 1977–78 series. Opening in both innings, he had little success and was not chosen again. He probably deserved another chance, as he was a talented left-handed batsman who gave good service to Victoria throughout a long first-class career. After a loss of form in the opening position, he returned as a middle order batsman in the eighties and played some of his best cricket. After retirement he became part of the ABC's radio commentary team and later a State selector.

BATTING	M	Inn	NO	HS	Runs	Ave	100s	50s	C/S
Tests	1	2	0	13	15	7.50	–	–	1
First-class	78	134	10	163	4790	38.62	9	25	38

BOWLING	Runs	Wkts	Ave	BB	5wI	10wM
First-class	285	15	19.00	4/28	–	–

HIGGS, James Donald

Vic, RHB/LBG
Born: 11 July 1950
Kyabram, Victoria

Jim Higgs was a very talented leg-spin bowler who, despite playing 22 Tests, was never given an extended run in the side. Although he made his first-class debut in 1970–71, and toured England in 1975, it took World Series Cricket to give him his Test chance. He made his debut in the West Indies on the 1977–78 tour, where he bowled particularly well to take 15 wickets. He took a further 19 against England in 1978–79. His best bowling was a superb 7/143 off 41.3 overs in the sauna–

like conditions of Madras in 1979–80. After the World Series settlement he could never be sure of a Test place, but he was certainly unlucky to miss a second trip to England in 1981. As a batsman, he had little pretentions to skill, being one of those rare souls who took more first-class wickets than they made runs. He set some kind of dubious record on that 1975 tour when he failed to make a run. Although he was certainly a character, he was also a very fine bowler, and given the chance, could have made much more of a contribution to Australian Test cricket. These days he is still associated with the game as a national selector.

BATTING	M	Inn	NO	HS	Runs	Ave	100s	50s	C/S
Tests	22	36	16	16	111	5.55	–	–	3
First-class	122	131	60	21	384	5.40	–	–	43

BOWLING	Balls	Runs	Wkts	Ave	BB	5wl	10wM
Tests	4752	2057	66	31.16	7/143	2	–
First-class	–	11838	399	29.66	8/66	19	3

HILDITCH, Andrew Mark Jefferson

NSW, SA, RHB
Born: 20 May 1956
North Adelaide, South Australia

A right–handed opening batsman, Andrew Hilditch had a most unusual career. He captained New South Wales at the age of 21 and made his Test debut against England in the last game of the 1978–79 series. In his third Test he was made Australian vice-captain and had the dubious distinction of being given out Handled the Ball, on appeal from Pakistani paceman Sarfraz Nawaz. After the World Series settlement Hilditch found himself out of both the Australian and New South Wales sides. He moved to South Australia and eventually won a recall to the Australian team for the fourth Test against the West Indies in 1984–85. With 70 and 113 he helped end a depressing series of losses. Hilditch regained the Test vice-captaincy for the 1985 tour of England, but after a century in the first Test his compulsion for the hook shot became a serious weakness. One more failure in the first Test against New Zealand in 1985–86, both times out hooking, saw him lose his place. Hilditch continued to make runs at first-class level, and in 1990–91 replaced David Hookes as South Australian captain, only to lose the job to Jamie Siddons after just one year. He retired after the 1991–92 season, a considerable player to the very end.

BATTING	M	Inn	NO	HS	Runs	Ave	100s	50s	C/S
Tests	18	34	0	119	1073	31.55	2	6	13
First-class	156	276	13	230	9962	37.88	20	55	101

BOWLING	Runs	Wkts	Ave	BB	5wl	10wM
First-class	197	4	49.25	1/5	–	–

HILL, Clement

SA, LHB
Born: 18 March 1877
Adelaide, South Australia
Died: 5 September 1945
Melbourne, Victoria

Clem Hill was Australia's best left-handed batsman in the period before World War I, and one of its finest ever. He was a member of an exceptional cricketing family (six of his brothers also played first-class cricket) and an outstanding schoolboy batsman, a fact which led to his first-class debut in 1892–93 as a wicketkeeper-batsman. In 1895–96 he headed the South Australian batting averages and was considered unlucky not to be selected in the team to tour England. A double century against New South Wales shortly afterwards saw him added to the side. From that moment until 1912 he was an automatic selection in Australian teams, touring England in 1896, 1899, 1902 and 1905. Next to Trumper, Hill was the team's best batsman, always looking to push the scoring along and with a special liking for the pull and cut. He was also an outstanding fielder.

While his Test record is an extremely good one, it could have been much better—he was dismissed in the nineties five times in Tests against England, three in succession in the 1901–02 series. He did, however, often overcome those problems in the nineties to make seven Test and 45 first-class centuries, under varying conditions and the best bowling that could be pitted against him. His highest Test score of 191 was made against South Africa at Sydney in 1910–11, one of three hundreds taken off the Springbok bowlers. Among his 24 centuries for South Australia was a monumental 365 not out against New South Wales in Adelaide during the 1900–01 season, a total exceeded by only one left-hander, New Zealand's Bert Sutcliffe.

When Monty Noble retired in 1909, Hill took over the Australian captaincy, winning five and losing five of his 10 Tests in charge. His captaincy ended in sensation, when he was involved in a fist fight with another selector, Peter McAlister, over the choice of players for a coming Test against England. Shortly afterwards another dispute over the appointment of a manager saw Hill and five of his team mates refuse to tour England in 1912.

An involvement with the Adelaide Racing Club restricted his later playing career, but he remained a revered figure in Australian cricket circles until his death from injuries sustained in a Melbourne traffic accident.

BATTING	M	Inn	NO	HS	Runs	Ave	100s	50s	C/S
Tests	49	89	2	191	3412	39.21	7	19	33
First-class	252	416	21	365*	17213	43.57	45	83	168/1

BOWLING	Runs	Wkts	Ave	BB	5wI	10wM
First-class	323	10	32.30	2/6	–	–

HILL, John Charles

Vic, RHB/LBG
Born: 25 June 1923
Murrumbeena, Victoria
Died: 11 August 1974
Caulfield, Victoria

John Hill bowled his leg spin at a brisk pace for Victoria and in three Tests for Australia. Making his debut in 1945–46, he took a wicket with his first ball. Hill held his place at first-class level for the next decade, producing some excellent performances and a very good record. His speed of delivery could create some uncomfortable bounce and he could be quite a handful if there was anything in the wicket. He gained selection in the 1953 team to England where he played in two Tests. Hill's other Test came on the 1955 tour of the West Indies, where he finished on top of the bowling averages. The emerging presence of Richie Benaud, a far better all-round cricketer, certainly restricted Hill's chance to establish a place in the Test side.

BATTING	M	Inn	NO	HS	Runs	Ave	100s	50s	C/S
Tests	3	6	3	8*	21	7.00	–	–	2
First-class	69	78	24	51*	867	16.05	–	1	63

BOWLING	Balls	Runs	Wkts	Ave	BB	5wI	10wM
Tests	606	273	8	34.12	3/35	–	–
First-class	–	5040	218	23.11	7/51	9	1

HOARE, Desmond Edward

WA, RHB/RFM
Born: 19 October 1934
Perth, Western Australia

A big Western Australian fast bowler, Des Hoare played his only Test at Adelaide against the West Indies in 1960–61. In a match which ended in a gripping draw, he performed better with the bat than the ball and was never given another chance. At first-class level Hoare was much more of a handful, able to swing the ball disconcertingly and gain plenty of lift from his high action. His first-class career lasted from 1955–56 to 1965–66 and his best figures of 8/98 were recorded against the strong New South Wales side at Perth in 1964–65. Hoare also had claims to some skill with the bat, his only century being made as an opener for Western Australia against the Australian XI at Perth in 1960–61. In recent times he has been a prominent administrator at the WACA Ground.

BATTING	M	Inn	NO	HS	Runs	Ave	100s	50s	C/S
Tests	1	2	0	35	35	17.50	–	–	2
First-class	63	90	21	133	1276	18.49	1	3	30

BOWLING	Balls	Runs	Wkts	Ave	BB	5wl	10wM
Tests	232	156	2	78.00	2/68	–	–
First-class	–	6055	225	26.91	8/98	12	1

HODGES, John Robart

Vic, LHB/LFM(r)
Born: 11 August 1855
Knightsbridge, London, England
Died: Death details unknown at present.

John Hodges is a shadowy figure from Australia's early Test days, even his date and place of death remain unknown. He had the unusual distinction of making his first-class debut in a Test match. Following some good performances in club cricket for Richmond he was selected to play in the first Test in 1876–77 to replace Frank Allan, before he had played for his home state Victoria. A left-arm bowler, he played well enough to hold his place for the second Test. In fact an umpiring error prevented him obtaining a wicket with his first delivery. The next season he played two games for Victoria against New South Wales before drifting out of first-class cricket. The term meteoric could certainly have been applied to Hodges' career, as he made his senior club, intercolonial and international debuts in the same season. In 1884 he appeared in Richmond Court charged with indecent exposure. The charges were later dismissed, but little else is known of the man.

BATTING	M	Inn	NO	HS	Runs	Ave	100s	50s	C/S
Tests	2	4	1	8	10	3.33	–	–	–
First-class	4	8	2	22	75	12.50	–	–	1

BOWLING	Balls	Runs	Wkts	Ave	BB	5wl	10wM
Tests	136	84	6	14.00	2/7	–	–
First-class	–	198	12	16.50	3/11	–	–

HOGAN, Tom George

WA, RHB/SLA
Born: 23 September 1956
Merredin, Western Australia

Tom Hogan was a left-arm orthodox slow bowler and useful batsman, who represented Australia in seven Tests between 1982 and 1984. He made his first-class debut for Western Australia in 1981–82 and achieved Test selection on the Australian tour of Sri Lanka, where his second innings 5/66 helped give his side an innings victory. The early promise was not fulfilled as Hogan found wickets difficult to come by in subsequent games at home and in the West Indies, where he played the last of his Tests. Accepting an invitation to tour South Africa in 1985 cost him any further chance in Test cricket. He returned from the two 'rebel' tours to resume his cricket with Western Australia, and although he produced some useful performances he was unable to claim a regular place in the side.

BATTING	M	Inn	NO	HS	Runs	Ave	100s	50s	C/S
Tests	7	12	1	42*	205	18.63	–	–	2
First-class	80	104	17	115*	1756	20.18	1	6	52

BOWLING	Balls	Runs	Wkts	Ave	BB	5wI	10wM
Tests	1436	706	15	47.06	5/66	1	–
First-class	–	7497	209	35.87	8/86	9	–

HOGG, Rodney Malcolm

Vic, SA, RHB/RF
Born: 5 March 1951
Richmond, Victoria

Fast bowler Rodney Hogg had a sensational start to his Test career when he took 41 wickets in his first series, against England in 1978–79, and 10 more in two Tests against Pakistan. His best figures of 6/74 were taken on debut at Brisbane. At a time when his country's fast bowling stocks had been decimated due to World Series Cricket, Hogg formed an excellent attacking partnership with Victorian Alan Hurst. All this was achieved with apparently little liking for his captain Graham Yallop. After World Series Cricket ended Hogg held his place in the Australian side, touring England in 1981, but breaking down with a back injury. He successfully returned to the Test side and was Australia's vice-captain in 1984–85. He gave up the chance of another English tour by opting to go to South Africa, where despite his years, he continued to bowl fast and accurately, giving the batsman no room for error.

BATTING	M	Inn	NO	HS	Runs	Ave	100s	50s	C/S
Tests	38	58	13	52	439	9.75	–	1	7
First-class	107	141	28	52	1185	10.48	–	1	25

BOWLING	Balls	Runs	Wkts	Ave	BB	5wI	10wM
Tests	7633	3499	123	28.24	6/74	6	2
First-class	–	9211	378	24.36	7/53	20	4

HOHNS, Trevor Victor

Qld, LHB/LBG
Born: 23 January 1954
Nundah, Queensland

Trevor Hohns made his first-class debut for Queensland in 1972 and for over a decade was a useful all-rounder, more likely to make runs than dismiss a side with his leg spin. There seemed little consternation when he chose to tour South Africa in 1985, but two seasons there greatly improved his bowling and he returned to Australia a far better player. With the selectors seeking to unleash some leg spin on the West Indies, Hohns was chosen for the last two Tests of the 1988–89 series. He bowled well enough to earn a trip to England in 1989, where he provided excellent support for the fast bowlers. On his return Hohns announced his retirement. However, in 1990–91 he was persuaded to return to captain Queensland. Much to the selectors' disappointment he declared himself unavailable for Test cricket, and retired again after just one season.

BATTING	M	Inn	NO	HS	Runs	Ave	100s	50s	C/S
Tests	7	7	1	40	136	22.66	–	–	3
First-class	152	232	40	103	5210	27.13	2	30	86

BOWLING	Balls	Runs	Wkts	Ave	BB	5wI	10wM
Tests	1528	580	17	34.11	3/59	–	–
First-class	–	10701	288	37.15	6/56	11	1

HOLE, Graeme Blake

NSW, SA, RHB/OB
Born: 6 January 1931
Concord West, New South Wales
Died: 14 February 1990
Kensington Gardens, South Australia

Graeme Hole made his first-class debut for New South Wales in 1949–50 and quickly established himself as a potential Test batsman. He soon moved to Adelaide and was chosen for the fifth Test of the 1950–51 season. Between then and 1954–55 he was given a number of chances at Test level, but he seemed unable to produce the batting which typified his first-class play. Too often he would get out when he appeared to have the bowling at his mercy. He played against the West Indies and South Africa, and toured England in 1953, before his Test career ended against England in 1954–55. He continued to play until 1957–58, when his career was ended by a fielding accident which ruptured his spleen. He survived a life-threatening situation, but his chances at further representative cricket were over. Hole's death from cancer in 1990 was greeted with deep regret by all who knew the likeable and talented batsman.

BATTING	M	Inn	NO	HS	Runs	Ave	100s	50s	C/S
Tests	18	33	2	66	789	25.45	–	6	21
First-class	98	166	12	226	5647	36.66	11	31	82

BOWLING	Balls	Runs	Wkts	Ave	BB	5wl	10wM
Tests	398	126	3	42.00	1/9	–	–
First-class	–	2686	61	44.03	5/109	1	–

HOLLAND, Robert George

NSW, RHB/LBG
Born: 19 October 1946
Camperdown, New South Wales

Bob Holland arrived on the Test scene at a time when most would have given the game away for a more relaxing pursuit. He made his first-class debut for New South Wales in 1978–79, and for the next few seasons made good use of the turning Sydney pitch. He was selected for Australia in 1984–85, aged 38, in the hope that his leg spin would upset the West Indians at Sydney. The selectors' judgement was vindicated when he took 6/54 and 4/90 in the Sydney Test, (his second) with Australia winning by an innings. Holland toured England in 1985 and had his moment of glory at Lord's, where his 5/68 helped produce a four-wicket win. For the remainder of that series he was less effective, being cast in too defensive a role. He produced another 10-wicket haul against New Zealand at Sydney in 1985–86, before slipping out of Test cricket. A popular and gentlemanly player, Holland's moments of triumph were enjoyed by all, except perhaps the opposing batsmen.

BATTING	M	Inn	NO	HS	Runs	Ave	100s	50s	C/S
Tests	11	15	4	10	35	3.18	–	–	5
First-class	95	95	22	53	706	9.67	–	1	54

BOWLING	Balls	Runs	Wkts	Ave	BB	5wI	10wM
Tests	2889	1352	34	39.76	6/54	3	2
First-class	–	9857	316	31.16	9/83	14	3

HOOKES, David William

SA, LHB/LM, SLC
Born: 3 May 1955
Mile End, South Australia

A controversial, but immensely talented left-handed batsman, David Hookes' Test record is by no means a true reflection of his skill. In 1976–77 he made four successive centuries to force his way into the Centenary Test team. In the second innings of that match he made a half-century, striking Tony Greig for five successive boundaries. He toured England in 1977, then joined World Series Cricket. After 1979 he was never able to command a secure place in the Test side. His only Test century came on tour in Sri Lanka in 1983. At first-class level he was capable of awesome displays: a triple century against Tasmania and a hundred in 44 minutes, to name just two. Before being sensationally stripped of the job for the 1990–91 season, he had been a bold and imaginative captain of South Australia. Hookes retired at the end of the 1991–92 season as the leading run scorer in Shield cricket, but his inability to successfully adapt his temperament and talent to Test cricket was the great tragedy of his career.

BATTING	M	Inn	NO	HS	Runs	Ave	100s	50s	C/S
Tests	23	41	3	143*	1306	34.36	1	8	12
First-class	178	304	16	306*	12671	44.00	32	65	167

BOWLING	Balls	Runs	Wkts	Ave	BB	5wI	10wM
Tests	96	41	1	41.00	1/4	–	–
First-class	–	2379	41	58.02	3/58	–	–

HOPKINS, Albert John Young

NSW, RHB/RFM
Born: 3 May 1876
Sydney, New South Wales
Died: 25 April 1931
North Sydney, New South Wales

Bert Hopkins was a capable all-rounder who represented Australia in 20 Tests in the early years of this century. He made his first-class debut for New South Wales in 1896–97 and played his first Test in 1901–02 when he was chosen to play against England in the final two Tests of that season's series. Hopkins toured England in 1902, 1905 and 1909 providing useful support, rather than outstanding performances. His last English tour was a disappointment and he did not play for Australia again, although he continued to represent New South Wales until 1914–15. His top score of 218 was made against South Australia in 1908–09, while his 7/10 was taken against Cambridge University, on tour in 1902.

BATTING	M	Inn	NO	HS	Runs	Ave	100s	50s	C/S
Tests	20	33	2	43	509	16.42	–	–	11
First-class	162	240	21	218	5563	25.40	8	22	87

BOWLING	Balls	Runs	Wkts	Ave	BB	5wl	10wM
Tests	1327	696	26	26.76	4/81	–	–
First-class	–	6613	271	24.40	7/10	10	–

HORAN, Thomas Patrick

Vic, RHB/RFM(r)
Born: 8 March 1854
Middleton, County Cork, Ireland
Died: 16 April 1916
Malvern, Victoria

Tom Horan was an aggressive right-handed batsman and useful bowler in the early days of Test cricket. He came to Australia as a child and made his first-class debut for Victoria against New South Wales in 1874–75. Future Test stars Jack Blackham and Fred Spofforth also began their careers in the same match. Horan played in the first-ever Test in Melbourne and took part in the 1878 tour of England under Dave Gregory's captaincy. Returning to England in 1882, he played in the historic Ashes match at The Oval. Horan scored his only Test century against England at Melbourne in 1881–82, and he led Australia in the second and fifth Tests of the 1884–85 series, losing both. Horan's selection for the first of these was part of a controversy which saw the entire team from the first Test removed after they demanded fifty per cent of the gate money for the match. His career ended in 1891 and his figures are comparable with the best players of the time. Retirement didn't end his involvement, however, and for many years he wrote brilliantly on the game as 'Felix' of *The Australasian*, becoming Australia's first great cricket writer. Two sons, Thomas and James, both represented Victoria.

BATTING	M	Inn	NO	HS	Runs	Ave	100s	50s	C/S
Tests	15	27	2	124	471	18.84	1	1	6
First-class	106	187	14	141*	4027	23.27	8	12	39

BOWLING	Balls	Runs	Wkts	Ave	BB	5wI	10wM
Tests	373	143	11	13.00	6/40	1	–
First-class	–	829	35	23.68	6/40	2	–

HORDERN, Herbert Vivian

NSW, RHB/LBG
Born: 10 February 1883
North Sydney, New South Wales
Died: 17 June 1938
Darlinghurst, New South Wales

'Ranji' Hordern was the first Australian to employ the newly developed googly, which he did successfully in seven Tests between 1910 and 1912. He first played for New South Wales in 1905–06, then spent some years studying dentistry in America, an occupation which saw him lost to cricket all too soon. After touring England with the Gentlemen of Philadelphia in 1907 he returned to Australia. He played in the last two Tests of the 1910–11 series against South Africa, taking 14 wickets, and so was an automatic choice for the next summer's series against England. Taking 12 wickets in the first Test and 10 in the fifth, he emerged with 32 wickets in a losing side. That was Hordern's last opportunity, as his dentistry career claimed his time, but in a short period he left a record fit to rank him with the finest leg spinners ever produced by Australia.

BATTING	M	Inn	NO	HS	Runs	Ave	100s	50s	C/S
Tests	7	13	2	50	254	23.09	–	1	6
First-class	33	53	9	64	721	16.38	–	3	39

BOWLING	Balls	Runs	Wkts	Ave	BB	5wI	10wM
Tests	2148	1075	46	23.36	7/90	5	2
First-class	–	3644	217	16.79	8/31	23	9

HORNIBROOK, Percival Mitchell

Qld, LHB/LM, SLA
Born: 27 July 1899
Obi Obi, Queensland
Died: 25 August 1976
Spring Hill, Queensland

A left-arm orthodox spin bowler, Percy Hornibrook made his first-class debut for Queensland in 1919, but had to play for a decade before receiving Test selection, in the fifth match of the 1928–29 series against England. He had certainly been on the fringe of selection for some time, and many thought him unlucky not to have been chosen earlier. Hornibrook's dental profession often caused him to miss matches away from Brisbane and this must have hindered his chances. When the opportunity came, he did well enough on debut to earn a trip to England in 1930 where he took 93 wickets, second only to Grimmett. The highlight of his tour was a return of 7/92 in the second innings of the fifth Test, which helped win the game and bring home the Ashes. For the greater part of his career, Hornibrook was the mainstay of the Queensland attack, seeing them into the Sheffield Shield and through their first seasons in that competition. Australia may have benefited much more had he been chosen earlier, rather than towards the end of his career.

BATTING	M	Inn	NO	HS	Runs	Ave	100s	50s	C/S
Tests	6	7	1	26	60	10.00	–	–	7
First-class	71	91	21	59*	754	10.77	–	1	66

BOWLING	Balls	Runs	Wkts	Ave	BB	5wI	10wM
Tests	1579	664	17	39.05	7/92	1	–
First-class	–	6648	279	23.82	8/60	17	6

HOWELL, William Peter

NSW, LHB/RM
Born: 29 December 1869
Penrith, New South Wales
Died: 14 July 1940
Castlereagh near Penrith, New South Wales

'Farmer Bill' Howell did not make his first-class debut for New South Wales, until 1894–95, when he was 25 years old, but he quickly became an integral part of the side and remained so for the next decade. He was a big bowler of quickish cutters and seamers, and a useful batsman. He made his Test debut against England at Adelaide in the third Test of the 1897–98 series. He was chosen to tour England in 1899, took 10/28 against Surrey in his first bowl, and ended with 117 wickets. He visited England again in 1902 and 1905. While his batting was not a success at Test level, in first-class cricket he was always capable of producing a fast-scoring innings, swinging a game with a few huge blows. Howell was the nephew of former Test player Edwin Evans.

BATTING	M	Inn	NO	HS	Runs	Ave	100s	50s	C/S
Tests	18	27	6	35	158	7.52	–	–	12
First-class	141	201	51	128	2228	14.85	1	6	124

BOWLING	Balls	Runs	Wkts	Ave	BB	5wI	10wM
Tests	3892	1407	49	28.71	5/81	1	–
First-class	–	11157	520	21.45	10/28	30	5

HUGHES, Kimberley John

WA, RHB
Born: 26 January 1954
Margaret River, Western Australia

On his day, the fair–haired Kim Hughes could exhibit a batting talent to rival anyone who ever played the game, but his genius was an erratic one and many innings were terminated by a 'rush of blood', usually at the most inopportune moment or when he had the bowling at his mercy. He also seemed to have a flair for controversy, in which he became involved on far too many occasions, though not always of his own making. Hughes made a century on his first-class debut for Western Australia in 1975–76 and was chosen to tour New Zealand in 1976–77 and England in 1977 where he made his Test debut. One of the few Australians on that trip not to sign for World Series Cricket, Hughes came to prominence in the official Test team. He toured the West Indies without success, but a century in the first Test against England at Brisbane in 1978–79 secured his place in the side. When Graham Yallop was injured Hughes took over as skipper for the last Test against Pakistan, and led the inexperienced Australians to a victory. He maintained the captaincy for the 1979 tour of India, where he scored 594 Test runs.

When the World Series players returned Hughes lost the Australian captaincy to Greg Chappell, but retained the Western Australian leadership ahead of Rod Marsh. This certainly created some animosity, which was not helped by the Australian selectors, who shuffled the captaincy between Hughes and Chappell until the latter retired in 1983–84. In this period luck was not always on his side, as in England in 1981, and he sometimes did not help his own cause by making ill–conceived remarks to the media. This further undermined his relationships with some of his senior players. As a batsman he was still erratic, but capable of dazzling innings such as his 117 and 84 which lit up the 1980 Centenary Test at Lord's, or his Test highest score of 213 against India at Adelaide in 1980–81. In 1984–85, after suffering two heavy defeats to the West Indies, he tearfully resigned the captaincy. A run of poor form then saw him dropped from the Australian side. In response, he accepted the leadership of the rebel Australian team to South Africa. He fought and won a court case, costing in excess of $350 000, against the Western Australian Cricket Association, played a few more games for his home state and then returned to play first-class cricket in South Africa before retiring in 1991.

BATTING	M	Inn	NO	HS	Runs	Ave	100s	50s	C/S
Tests	70	124	6	213	4415	37.41	9	22	50
First-class	216	368	20	213	12711	36.52	26	69	155

BOWLING	Balls	Runs	Wkts	Ave	BB	5wl	10wM
Tests	85	28	0	–	–	–	–
First-class	–	97	3	32.33	1/0	–	–

HUGHES, Mervyn Gregory

Vic, RHB/RF
Born: 23 November 1961
Euroa, Victoria

When the moustachioed Victorian pace man made his Test debut against India in 1985–86, he looked a player out of his depth, and further Tests against England confirmed the impression. However, Hughes showed immense dedication to improve, and in doing so has made himself a vital part of the Australian team. His transformation came with 5/72 and 8/87, including a hat-trick, against the West Indies at Perth in 1988–89. At Adelaide he made 72 not out against them to confirm his vast improvement with the bat. In England on the 1989 tour he was an important part of the attack which decimated the home side's batting, as well as contributing useful runs in the lower order. In subsequent seasons he has been one of Australia's leading bowlers, despite battling injuries and a tendency to put on weight. Hughes' great value to the side is that despite the problems, he keeps going. Over the years he has successfully completed whatever tasks have been set, whether it be making some runs, holding an end up, making a breakthrough or bowling a containing spell. When Australia's bowlers were struggling against the West Indies in 1992–93 it was Hughes, with 20 wickets, including 5/64 at Adelaide, who led the way. With the loss of Craig McDermott early in the 1993 Ashes series, Hughes manfully led an inexperienced attack. His work in conjunction with the spin of Warne and May dominated the English batting, and in the process he captured his 200th Test wicket. His constant desire to improve, his ability to drag some life from the deadest of pitches and his determination make Merv Hughes much more than an outrageous cricketing character.

BATTING	M	Inn	NO	HS	Runs	Ave	100s	50s	C/S
Tests	51	67	7	72*	999	16.65	–	2	22
First-class	153	181	41	72*	2488	17.77	–	7	52

BOWLING	Balls	Runs	Wkts	Ave	BB	5wl	10wM
Tests	11865	5780	208	27.79	8/87	7	1
First-class	–	15894	557	28.54	8/87	20	3

HUNT, William Alfred

NSW, LHB/LM,SLA
Born: 26 August 1908
Balmain, New South Wales
Died: 30 December 1983
Balmain, New South Wales

Bill Hunt bowled left-arm medium pace for New South Wales, making his first-class debut in 1929–30 and playing his only Test against South Africa in the fourth match of the 1931–32 series. Something of an aggressive player, he did not get on well with Australia's captain Bill Woodfull, who stood for no nonsense. This led Hunt to the Lancashire League, convinced he had no future in Australia. The decision was a tragedy, as Hunt was a gifted player, a fact which he continued to show for a number of years in league and grade cricket. He took 11 hat tricks in his career, five of them in 1933. In later life the rebel from Balmain mellowed, and Bill Hunt spent much of his time establishing the SCG Cricket Museum.

BATTING	M	Inn	NO	HS	Runs	Ave	100s	50s	C/S
Tests	1	1	0	0	0	0.00	–	–	1
First-class	18	25	4	45	301	14.33	–	–	12

BOWLING	Balls	Runs	Wkts	Ave	BB	5wl	10wM
Tests	96	39	0	–	–	–	–
First-class	–	1426	62	23.00	5/36	2	–

HURST, Alan George

Vic, RHB/RF
Born: 15 July 1950
Altona, Victoria

A tall fast bowler, capable of plenty of pace and movement, Alan Hurst made his first-class debut for Victoria in 1972 and his Test debut, against New Zealand, in 1973–74. Although he achieved little there he was chosen to tour England in 1975, but failed to appear in a Test. Hurst's form was indifferent and affected by injury for the next few seasons, but the highpoint in his career came when he partnered Rodney Hogg in the 1978–79 summer. After declining an offer to join World Series Cricket it was some reward to take 40 wickets in the summer's eight Tests. His best figures of 5/28 were taken against England at Sydney in the fourth Test. Together with Hogg, he gave Australia an excellent opening attack which the batsmen generally couldn't capitalise on. After the 1979 World Cup a back injury cost him his place in the side and he retired from first-class cricket in 1980. Hurst occasionally appears on ABC radio giving expert comments on games played in Victoria.

BATTING	M	Inn	NO	HS	Runs	Ave	100s	50s	C/S
Tests	12	20	3	26	102	6.00	–	–	3
First-class	77	88	30	27*	504	8.68	–	–	26

BOWLING	Balls	Runs	Wkts	Ave	BB	5wl	10wM
Tests	3054	1200	43	27.90	5/28	2	–
First-class	–	7360	280	26.28	8/84	11	1

HURWOOD, Alexander

Qld, RHB/RM, OB
Born: 17 June 1902
Kangaroo Point, Queensland
Died: 26 September 1982
Coffs Harbour, New South Wales

Alex Hurwood was a medium pace bowler, who could successfully switch to off spin if the need arose. From his debut in 1925 until his retirement in 1931, Hurwood was a key member of the Queensland team. He was chosen to tour England in 1930, and although he bowled well he was not chosen in any of the Tests. Hurwood was, however, selected in the first two Tests of the 1930–31 series against the West Indies, bowling particularly well in both games and providing Clarrie Grimmett with plenty of support. According to reports, he was unavailable for the third Test and was never selected again. A talented performer, his career at the highest level should have been much longer.

BATTING	M	Inn	NO	HS	Runs	Ave	100s	50s	C/S
Tests	2	2	0	5	5	2.50	–	–	2
First-class	43	56	5	89	575	11.27	–	3	29

BOWLING	Balls	Runs	Wkts	Ave	BB	5wl	10wM
Tests	517	170	11	15.45	4/22	–	–
First-class	–	3132	113	27.71	6/80	5	1

INVERARITY, Robert John

WA, SA, RHB/SLA
Born: 31 January 1944
Subiaco, Western Australia

Although he played only six Tests, John Inverarity exerted considerable influence on Australian cricket. He made his first-class debut for Western Australia in 1962–63 as a solid right-handed batsman. Chosen to tour England in 1968, Inverarity made his highest score of 56 when he opened the batting and was last man out in the second innings of the fifth Test. He inherited the WA captaincy after Tony Lock retired and proved himself an excellent leader, establishing his state as a real power in Australian cricket. He toured England again in 1972, but was more useful as a left-arm slow bowler, a skill he continued developing throughout his career. Inverarity played no more Test cricket, but many thought he was the man to tackle Mike Brearley in 1978–79. In 1979–80 he moved to South Australia, where he had much to do with the leadership of David Hookes. It is that influence on players, as much as his considerable cricketing ability (he also held the Shield run–scoring record), that makes Inverarity's career such an important one.

BATTING	M	Inn	NO	HS	Runs	Ave	100s	50s	C/S
Tests	6	11	1	56	174	17.40	–	1	4
First-class	223	377	49	187	11777	35.90	26	60	250

BOWLING	Balls	Runs	Wkts	Ave	BB	5wI	10wM
Tests	372	94	4	23.25	3/26	–	–
First-class	–	6780	221	30.67	7/86	7	–

IREDALE, Francis Adams

NSW, RHB
Born: 19 June 1867
Surry Hills, New South Wales
Died: 15 April 1926
North Sydney, New South Wales

Frank Iredale was a talented right-handed batsman who gave New South Wales excellent service in a career that lasted from 1888 until 1902. He made his Test debut against England at Sydney in 1894–95, scoring 81, and in the third Test at Adelaide he made his highest score of 140. Iredale toured England in 1896, making his other century at Manchester in the second Test, and heading the averages. He toured England again in 1899. Despite being a nervous starter, Iredale's record compares favourably with the best of the time, and he possessed a good defence to go with his attractive attacking strokes. He was also an excellent fieldsman.

BATTING	M	Inn	NO	HS	Runs	Ave	100s	50s	C/S
Tests	14	23	1	140	807	36.68	2	4	16
First-class	133	214	12	196	6794	33.63	12	36	111

BOWLING	Balls	Runs	Wkts	Ave	BB	5wI	10wM
Tests	12	3	0	–	–	–	–
First-class	–	211	6	35.16	3/1	–	–

IRONMONGER, Herbert

Vic, Qld, LHB/SLA
Born: 7 April 1882
Pine Mountain, Queensland
Died: 31 May 1971
St Kilda, Victoria

Bert Ironmonger is probably the best Australian player never to tour England. He was a quite outstanding left-arm slow bowler, despite

119

missing a finger joint on his bowling hand, and his Test average is one of the best ever recorded by an Australian. A tall, ungainly man, he was an extremely accurate bowler who could extract spin from the most unresponsive of pitches. On a wet or helpful wicket he was unplayable.

Ironmonger's first-class career began in 1909 in Queensland. He eventually moved to Victoria, representing both that state and Queensland in 1913–14, but it was not until 1927–28 that he became a permanent member of the side, forming an unusual partnership with the equally elderly Don Blackie. Next season he made his Test debut against England at Brisbane, aged 45, not 41 as he claimed. Although he bowled well, he failed to gain a place on the 1930 tour of England, but returned to destroy the West Indies and South Africa in the next two Australian seasons, taking 22 and 31 wickets respectively. This was despite the fact that he played only four Tests in each series. Ironmonger's best efforts were 11/79 in the fourth Test against the West Indies and 11/24 in the fifth Test against South Africa, bowling the hapless Springboks out for 36 and 45. He also took 15 wickets in the last four Tests of the 1932–33 Bodyline series.

As a batsman and fieldsman he held no claims to skill and was nicknamed 'Dainty' because he wasn't. Some suggested his action was suspect, giving this as the reason why he never toured England, but most, including Sir Donald Bradman, had no doubts that it was fair. Former team mates Len Darling and Harry Alexander were unstinting in their praise of his skill and the fairness of his action. It is a pity the Australian selectors were not prepared to risk him, as he could have been devastating in English conditions.

In addition to his playing skills, Ironmonger was something of a character. His wife is reported to have rung the dressing-room to speak to him. On being told her husband was on his way out to bat, she replied, 'I'll wait'. According to Ironmonger's daughter, his finger was lost in a chaff cutter, but all sorts of stories have circulated, including those in which he is supposed to have lost two fingers instead of one. Former team mate Harry Alexander maintained that Ironmonger had only one finger missing. Regardless of the handicap he was a magnificent bowler. Although he played no more Tests after 1932–33, Ironmonger's first-class career ended in 1935–36, when he toured India with Frank Tarrant's Australian team.

BATTING	M	Inn	NO	HS	Runs	Ave	100s	50s	C/S
Tests	14	21	5	12	42	2.62	–	–	3
First-class	96	127	47	36*	476	5.95	–	–	30

BOWLING	Balls	Runs	Wkts	Ave	BB	5wl	10wM
Tests	4695	1330	74	17.97	7/23	4	2
First-class	–	9980	464	21.50	8/31	36	10

IVERSON, John Brian

Vic, RHB/OB
Born: 27 July 1915
Melbourne, Victoria
Died: 24 October 1974
Brighton, Victoria

Jack Iverson's unusual folded-finger grip, a forerunner of that used by John Gleeson, gave him a season of triumph against England in 1950–51. He came late into the game, making his first-class debut in 1949–50, and as no batsman was confident in picking him, Iverson was rapidly elevated to the Test team. The English batsmen were completely bemused by his mixture of off and top spin, and he took 21 wickets at 15.23 in the series, with a best of 6/27 at Sydney in the third Test. Iverson's career was not a long one. Once batsmen began to pick him, he did not know how to adapt and declared himself unavailable for first-class cricket. He played his final game in 1953. Jack Iverson ended his life with an overdose of sleeping pills at the age of 59.

BATTING	M	Inn	NO	HS	Runs	Ave	100s	50s	C/S
Tests	5	7	3	1*	3	0.75	–	–	2
First-class	34	46	27	31*	277	14.57	–	–	13

BOWLING	Balls	Runs	Wkts	Ave	BB	5wI	10wM
Tests	1108	320	21	15.23	6/27	1	–
First-class	–	3019	157	19.22	7/77	9	1

JACKSON, Archibald

NSW, RHB/OB
Born: 5 September 1909
Rutherglen, Scotland.
Died: 16 February 1933
Albion, Queensland

Archie Jackson was an Australian sporting tragedy whose cricket and life were cut short by tuberculosis. He was a gifted right-handed batsman, some thought as good a player as Bradman. Throughout his career he was never fully fit. He made his first-class debut in 1926–27, averaging 50. He continued scoring runs, which led to his selection for the fourth Test of the 1928–29 series against England. He opened the batting and made 164 in his first innings. Jackson toured England in 1930, and although he scored 1000 runs he did little in the Tests, apart from 73 in partnership with Bradman in the final game. The last of Jackson's Tests came against the West Indies in 1930–31. In fact his final appearance on a first-class ground was as twelfth man in the fifth Test of that series. His health deteriorated rapidly, and despite making some brave efforts to continue playing, the young man was doomed. When he died, aged 23, there was universal sadness for the loss of a batsman who could have been one of the finest ever.

BATTING	M	Inn	NO	HS	Runs	Ave	100s	50s	C/S
Tests	8	11	1	164	474	47.40	1	2	7
First-class	70	107	11	182	4383	45.65	11	23	26

BOWLING	Runs	Wkts	Ave	BB	5wl	10wM		
First-class	49	0	–	–	–	–		

JARMAN, Barrington Noel

SA, RHB/WK
Born: 17 February 1936
Hindmarsh, South Australia

For much of his career, Barry Jarman was Australia's second-string wicket-keeper behind Wally Grout. In fact he toured England twice, South Africa, the West Indies and the subcontinent as Grout's deputy, gaining only the occasional Test when the Queensland 'keeper was injured. Although he made his first-class debut in 1955–56, it was not until 1967–68 that he became Australia's number one 'keeper. He was vice-captain to Bill Lawry on the 1968 tour of England, captaining the side in the fourth Test, and against the West Indies in 1968–69 until he lost his place to Brian Taber. Despite his solid build he was agile behind the stumps and missed few chances. He was also a capable batsman, and he led South Australia for a number of seasons. But for the presence of Grout, Jarman would cetainly have played many more Tests.

BATTING	M	Inn	NO	HS	Runs	Ave	100s	50s	C/S
Tests	19	30	3	78	400	14.81	–	2	50/4
First-class	191	284	37	196	5615	22.73	5	26	431/129

BOWLING	Runs	Wkts	Ave	BB	5wl	10wM
First-class	98	3	32.66	1/17	–	–

JARVIS, Arthur Harwood

SA, RHB/WK
Born: 19 October 1860
Hindmarsh, South Australia
Died: 15 November 1933
Hindmarsh, South Australia

'Affi' Jarvis was a wicket-keeper who, like Jarman, suffered by being the second best. In his case it was to Jack Blackham, and he toured England in 1880, 1886, 1888 and 1893 as Blackham's deputy. Making his debut in 1877–78, Jarvis quickly established a strong reputation behind the stumps, as well as contributing useful runs with the bat. He made his Test debut against England in 1884–85 at Melbourne and scored 82. Despite this, he played only 11 Tests spread over the next decade. When Blackham retired after the first game of the 1894–95 series, Jarvis kept in the remaining four games, but missed another trip to England in 1896. He continued playing for South Australia until 1900–01, and throughout the last part of his career his work in taking the speed of Ernie Jones and the spin of George Giffen was exceptional.

BATTING	M	Inn	NO	HS	Runs	Ave	100s	50s	C/S
Tests	11	21	3	82	303	16.83	–	1	9/9
First-class	141	226	23	98*	3161	15.57	–	13	114/82

BOWLING	Runs	Wkts	Ave	BB	5wl	10wM
First-class	63	1	63.00	1/9	–	–

JENNER, Terrence James

WA, SA, RHB/LBG
Born: 8 September 1944
Mt Lawley, Western Australia

A talented leg-spin bowler and useful batsman, Terry Jenner began his first-class career with Western Australia in 1963–64, but moved to South Australia in 1967–68 where he formed a strong bowling partnership with off spinner Ashley Mallett. He made his Test debut against England in 1970–71 and in the final Test was struck on the head by a delivery from fast bowler John Snow, an event which ultimately led to an England walk-off following disruption of the game by the crowd. Although he toured the West Indies in 1972–73, where he took 5/90 in the fifth Test at Port–of–Spain, Trinidad, Jenner was never sure of a regular place. He ended his Test career against England in 1974–75, a series in which he made a fine 74 in Adelaide on a difficult pitch against Derek Underwood. An addiction to gambling led to his being gaoled for fraud, but on his release Jenner has made a concerted and successful attempt to rebuild his life through coaching and some radio broadcasting.

BATTING	M	Inn	NO	HS	Runs	Ave	100s	50s	C/S
Tests	9	14	5	74	208	23.11	–	1	5
First-class	131	199	38	86	3580	22.23	–	10	87

BOWLING	Balls	Runs	Wkts	Ave	BB	5wI	10wM
Tests	1881	749	24	31.20	5/90	1	–
First-class	–	12520	389	32.18	7/84	14	1

JENNINGS, Claude Barrows

SA, Qld, RHB
Born: 5 June 1884
East St Kilda, Victoria
Died: 20 June 1950
Adelaide, South Australia

Claude Jennings owed his place in the 1912 Australian team to a dispute which saw six of the leading players refuse to tour. He made his first-class debut for South Australia in 1902–03, but moved to Queensland in 1910–11, for which he made his only century, 123 against New South Wales, an innings that almost certainly clinched his place in the touring team. Although he scored 1000 runs on the tour, he found English conditions difficult to cope with and did little of note in the Tests. AG 'Johnny' Moyes believed he was not up to Test standard. Jennings returned to South Australia after the tour and later was a member of the Australian Board of Control.

BATTING	M	Inn	NO	HS	Runs	Ave	100s	50s	C/S
Tests	6	8	2	32	107	17.83	–	–	5
First-class	60	103	7	123	2453	25.55	1	16	38/3

BOWLING	Runs	Wkts	Ave	BB	5wI	10wM
First-class	17	0	–	–	–	–

JOHNSON, Ian William

Vic, RHB/OB
Born: 8 December 1918
North Melbourne, Victoria

Ian Johnson was an off-spin bowler and useful batsman, who played 45 Tests between 1945–46 and 1956. He captained Australia in the last 17, winning seven games, but losing two series to England in 1954–55 and 1956. As a bowler he was quite slow through the air and relied on bounce and turn in the pitches to make his control and use of flight a danger. Good performances in Australia against England and India saw him selected to tour England in 1948 ahead of some talented opposition. He was never successful in England because the pitches were too soft and slow for him. In fact, many thought he was not worth his place on the 1956 tour. Despite that, over the years he produced some good performances, particularly in South Africa in 1949–50, where he was the leading wicket–taker on tour, and in the West Indies, where his 7/44 helped win the third Test at Georgetown. After retirement he served as Secretary of the Melbourne Cricket Club for many years.

BATTING	M	Inn	NO	HS	Runs	Ave	100s	50s	C/S
Tests	45	66	12	77	1000	18.51	–	6	30
First-class	189	243	29	132*	4905	22.92	2	21	137

BOWLING	Balls	Runs	Wkts	Ave	BB	5wI	10wM
Tests	8780	3182	109	29.19	7/44	3	–
First-class	–	14423	619	23.30	7/42	27	4

JOHNSON, Leonard Joseph

Qld, RHB/RFM
Born: 18 March 1919
Ipswich, Queensland
Died: 20 April 1977
Ipswich, Queensland

Despite some fine performances for Queensland, Len Johnson's fast-medium bowling could not win a place in the Australian side due to

126

the presence of Lindwall, Miller and Bill Johnston. Making his first-class debut in 1946–47, Johnson's only Test came against India at Melbourne in 1947–48, and it could hardly be said that he failed. However, the competition for places was such that he never played again, although he did tour New Zealand with a B team in 1949–50, taking 41 wickets at 9.68 in all games. Until his retirement in 1952–53 he was the leading bowler in the Queensland attack, and his figures show just how well he coped with that particular task.

BATTING	M	Inn	NO	HS	Runs	Ave	100s	50s	C/S
Tests	1	1	1	25*	25	–	–	–	2
First-class	56	87	19	75	1139	16.75	–	3	35

BOWLING	Balls	Runs	Wkts	Ave	BB	5wl	10wM
Tests	282	74	6	12.33	3/8	–	–
First-class	–	5052	218	23.17	7/43	16	1

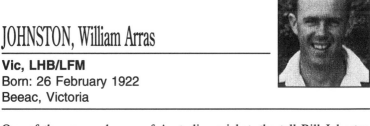

JOHNSTON, William Arras

Vic, LHB/LFM
Born: 26 February 1922
Beeac, Victoria

One of the unsung heroes of Australian cricket, the tall Bill Johnston could bowl left-arm fast-medium, medium pace or spin, and provided a perfect foil for the better known Miller and Lindwall. Although he played first-class cricket from the end of the War, he did not make his Test debut until 1947–48, against India. His four Tests produced 16 wickets and he was chosen to tour England in 1948. He took 102 wickets on the tour, 27 in the Tests, and emerged a key member of the side, a position he continued to hold until 1953 when knee trouble reduced his effectiveness. On that 1953 tour he created a statistical oddity, recording a batting average of 102, being dismissed only once. He came back to tour the West Indies in 1954–55. Johnston performed well under all conditions and in all countries; his best Test figures were recorded in South Africa in 1949–50, and 160 wickets in 40 Tests is a superb testimony to his skill. In addition to his cricketing ability, he was an engaging and popular character.

BATTING	M	Inn	NO	HS	Runs	Ave	100s	50s	C/S
Tests	40	49	25	29	273	11.37	–	–	16
First-class	142	162	73	38	1129	12.68	–	–	52

BOWLING	Balls	Runs	Wkts	Ave	BB	5wl	10wM
Tests	11048	3826	160	23.91	6/44	7	–
First-class	–	12936	554	23.35	8/52	29	6

JONES, Dean Mervyn

Vic, RHB/OB
Born: 24 March 1961
Coburg, Victoria

Despite a slow start to his international career, Dean Jones developed into a superbly aggressive right-handed batsman, particularly devastating in limited-overs cricket. His first taste of international cricket came when he toured the West Indies in 1983–84, where he made his Test debut at Port–of–Spain, but it was not until the Tied Test in Madras in 1986–87 that he established himself with an heroic innings of 210. Following that knock, which must be one of the bravest ever played, he was hospitalised suffering from exhaustion and placed on a saline drip. Jones made another double century in 1988–89 against the West Indies, and on the 1989 England tour he played a series of attacking innings, highlighted by some electrifying running between the wickets. Jones' frequent limited-overs onslaughts helped Australia become a force in this form of cricket.

A tendency towards being a nervous starter has caused him to struggle in recent series. Jones batted well on tour in Sri Lanka at the start of the 1992–93 season, but on his return to Australia he could not find sufficient form to retain his place in the Test side. He played in the limited-overs games and was flown out to New Zealand for the one-day series there, but was unable to make the runs necessary to secure a place in the 1993 team to tour England.

Dean Jones is a very determined character who will fight to reclaim his place in the side. Spectators, too, will be hoping they have not seen the last of a player capable of destroying any bowling under any conditions.

BATTING	M	Inn	NO	HS	Runs	Ave	100s	50s	C/S
Tests	52	89	11	216	3631	46.55	11	14	34
First-class	169	277	30	248	12468	50.48	35	57	128

BOWLING	Balls	Runs	Wkts	Ave	BB	5wI	10wM
Tests	174	64	1	64.00	1/5	–	–
First-class	–	1010	16	63.12	1/0	–	–

JONES, Ernest

SA, WA, RHB/RF
Born: 30 September 1869
Auburn, South Australia
Died: 23 November 1943
Adelaide, South Australia

South Australian Ernie Jones is enshrined in legend as the fast bowler who fired a ball through WG Grace's beard, (this supposedly occurred during his first tour of England in 1896), and as a 'character'. When asked if he had attended Prince Alfred College, the decidedly working class Jones is said to have replied, 'Yes, sir. Each week to collect the garbage.' But in addition to being a character, 'Jonah' was a fine pace bowler, possessing great stamina, who developed considerable variation as the years progressed. He made his Test debut in 1894–95 and toured England in 1896, 1899 and 1902, taking more than a hundred wickets on the first two occasions. In his early days some considered his action suspect, and he was no–balled for throwing in 1897–98. His best bowling of 7/88 (10 wickets in the match) was taken at Lord's in 1899. In a first-class career that lasted until 1907–08, the rough and ready, former miner gave great service at all levels of the game.

BATTING	M	Inn	NO	HS	Runs	Ave	100s	50s	C/S
Tests	19	26	1	20	126	5.04	–	–	21
First-class	144	209	27	82	2390	13.13	–	7	107

BOWLING	Balls	Runs	Wkts	Ave	BB	5wI	10wM
Tests	3748	1857	64	29.01	7/88	3	1
First-class	–	14638	641	22.83	8/39	47	9

JONES, Samuel Percy

NSW, Qld, RHB/RFM
Born: 1 August 1861
Sydney, New South Wales
Died: 14 July 1951
Auckland, New Zealand

Sammy Jones was a sound right-handed batsman, who made his Test debut against England at Sydney in 1881–82. He then gained selection for the 1882 tour of England, playing in the famous Ashes Test, where he was controversially run out by WG Grace while patting down a spot on the wicket. Jones toured England again in 1886, 1888 and 1890, his best effort being on the first of those trips when he scored nearly 1500 runs and made his highest Test score of 87 at Old Trafford. On his final tour he was stricken with smallpox and remained dangerously ill for some weeks. Over the years he developed a reputation for playing well on bad wickets, of which there were plenty at the time, and his performances at Test and first-class level were comparable with most of the period's best players. Jones had a long first-class career, which ended in 1909 following a few seasons in Auckland, where he had moved in 1904, and where he remained until his death.

BATTING	M	Inn	NO	HS	Runs	Ave	100s	50s	C/S
Tests	12	24	4	87	432	21.60	–	1	12
First-class	151	259	13	151	5193	21.10	5	24	82

BOWLING	Balls	Runs	Wkts	Ave	BB	5wI	10wM
Tests	262	112	6	18.66	4/47	–	–
First-class	–	1844	55	33.52	5/54	1	–

JOSLIN, Leslie Ronald

Vic, LHB/LM
Born: 13 December 1947
Yarraville, Victoria

Les Joslin was a left-handed batsman who made his debut for Victoria in 1966–67. A number of good innings in the next season, including 121 not out against New South Wales, saw Joslin selected for the fourth

Test against India. Although he made only seven and two, he was chosen to tour England in 1968 on the basis of the promise he undoubtedly possessed. However, he failed to come to terms with the conditions, averaging barely 20. Joslin's first-class career was a short one, ending in 1968–69, and leaving the distinct impression of what might have been.

BATTING	M	Inn	NO	HS	Runs	Ave	100s	50s	C/S
Tests	1	2	0	7	9	4.50	–	–	–
First-class	44	67	6	126	1816	29.77	2	12	27

BOWLING	Runs	Wkts	Ave	BB	5wl	10wM
First-class	73	1	73.00	1/14	–	–

JULIAN, Brendon Paul

WA, RHB/LFM
Born: 10 August 1970
Hamilton, New Zealand

A promising young all-rounder, Brendon Julian made his first-class debut in 1989–90. He missed all of the next season with a stress fracture of the back, but returned to the Western Australian side in 1991–92; when he was more successful with his left arm fast medium bowling than his batting. In 1992–93 the tall, part Polynesian Julian advanced in both areas of the game. Using his height to gain lift and showing the capacity to swing the ball, he was a regular wicket-taker. At the same time he scored valuable runs in the lower order, and it came as no surprise when he was selected to tour England in 1993. Julian played in the first and third Tests before a groin injury cost him his place in the side. While he took some valuable wickets, he tended to bowl too many loose deliveries, but he did make an undefeated 56 in the second innings of the third Test to save his side from possible defeat. Young and with plenty of promise, Julian should have a part to play in Australia's cricket future.

BATTING	M	Inn	NO	HS	Runs	Ave	100s	50s	C/S
Tests	2	3	1	56*	61	30.50	–	1	2
First-class	37	54	13	87	875	21.24	–	6	14

BOWLING	Balls	Runs	Wkts	Ave	BB	5wl	10wM
Tests	492	291	5	58.20	2/30	–	–
First-class	–	3359	99	33.93	5/26	5	–

KELLEWAY, Charles

NSW, RHB/RFM
Born: 25 April 1886
Lismore, New South Wales
Died: 16 November 1944
Lindfield, New South Wales

Kelleway was a useful all-rounder for New South Wales and Australia before and after the First World War. A dour batsman, (one Test century took nearly seven hours) and fast-medium bowler with a high action, he had made his first-class debut in 1907–08 and his first Test was against South Africa in 1910–11. Kelleway had a successful tour of England in 1912, averaging 60 in the Tests. Following the War he was selected to captain the AIF side, but was replaced by Herbie Collins after only a handful of games, an event which probably cost him the job at Test level. Unavailable for the 1921 tour, Kelleway had a successful series with bat and ball against England in 1924–25, but was not chosen for the 1926 tour. His last Test was against England at Brisbane in 1928–29, when he became ill and took little part in the match.

BATTING	M	Inn	NO	HS	Runs	Ave	100s	50s	C/S
Tests	26	42	4	147	1422	37.42	3	6	24
First-class	132	205	23	168	6389	35.10	15	28	103

BOWLING	Balls	Runs	Wkts	Ave	BB	5wI	10wM
Tests	4363	1683	52	32.36	5/33	1	–
First-class	–	8925	339	26.32	7/35	10	1

KELLY, James Joseph

NSW, RHB/WK
Born: 10 May 1867
Port Melbourne, Victoria
Died: 14 August 1938
Bellevue Hill, New South Wales

The presence of Australian wicket-keeper Jack Blackham in his home state of Victoria caused JJ Kelly to move to Sydney in the hope of playing first-class cricket. He achieved this in 1894–95, and made his Test debut at Lord's in 1896. Kelly toured England again in 1899, 1902 and 1905 remaining Australia's first-choice keeper until the end of that last tour. He was safe and sure, being the first to take eight catches in a match, a feat he performed at Sydney in the fourth Test of the 1901–02 series. Also at Sydney, in 1897–98, he became the first not to concede a bye in an innings of over 500 (England had accumulated 551). As a batsman Kelly was a stubborn player who made the bowlers earn his wicket, and over the years he proved to be a good man in a crisis.

BATTING	M	Inn	NO	HS	Runs	Ave	100s	50s	C/S
Tests	36	56	17	46*	664	17.02	–	–	43/20
First-class	185	266	60	108	4108	19.94	3	16	243/112

BOWLING	Runs	Wkts	Ave	BB	5wl	10wM
First-class	16	0	–	–	–	–

KELLY, Thomas Joseph Dart

RHB/RaB
Born: 3 May 1844
County Waterford, Ireland
Died: 20 July 1893
Melbourne, Victoria

Born in Ireland, Thomas Kelly came to Australia as a young man and made his debut for Victoria in 1865–66. He was a useful right-handed batsman and a fine fieldsman at point. He learned his cricket in Gloucestershire, the home of the Grace family. Kelly played in the second Test in 1876–77, when he made 35 in the second innings, including eight fours. His only other Test was against England at Melbourne in 1878–79, when he batted at number ten and made 10. His highest score was 86 against New South Wales and he was, according to Fred Spofforth, the first Australian cricketer to wear a blazer. Kelly was also involved in the administration of the Victorian Cricket Association.

BATTING	M	Inn	NO	HS	Runs	Ave	100s	50s	C/S
Tests	2	3	0	35	64	21.33	–	–	1
First-class	16	28	1	86	543	20.11	–	5	20

BOWLING	Runs	Wkts	Ave	BB	5wI	10wM
First-class	2	0	–	–	–	–

KENDALL, Thomas Kingston

Vic, Tas, LHB/LM,SLA
Born: 24 August 1851
Bedford, England
Died: 17 August 1924
Hobart, Tasmania

Tom Kendall was a left-arm spinner of outstanding talent, who bowled Australia to a 45-run victory in the very first Test in 1876–77 with second innings figures of 7/55. In the second Test he took a further six wickets. He was to tour England in 1878, but was sent home from Perth; his liking for a drink was probably the reason. Kendall accepted a coaching appointment in Tasmania, making his debut there in 1881. He remained a top-line performer for the next decade. In 1883–84 he took 150 wickets at 7.01 in all cricket, and no side which visited Tasmania could afford to take him lightly. That year he had turned down the offer of a Test trial to stay in Tasmania. In 1891–92, at the end of his career, he took 7/79 against Lord Sheffield's Englishmen, including WG Grace, whom he bowled for 27, after betting that he would do so. In addition to his playing skills, Kendall provided excellent coaching and practice for players like Charlie Eady and Kenny Burn. After his retirement he looked after the visitors' rooms at Hobart's TCA Ground.

BATTING	M	Inn	NO	HS	Runs	Ave	100s	50s	C/S
Tests	2	4	1	17*	39	13.00	–	–	2
First-class	8	15	4	43	141	12.81	–	–	6

BOWLING	Balls	Runs	Wkts	Ave	BB	5wI	10wM
Tests	563	215	14	15.35	7/55	1	–
First-class	–	666	40	16.65	7/24	3	–

KENT, Martin Francis

Qld, RHB
Born: 23 November 1953
Mossman, Queensland

Martin Kent was a highly talented Queensland batsman whose career was tragically ended by a serious back injury. A batsman who played aggressively, striking the ball with great power, he scored 140 on his first-class debut against New South Wales in 1974–75. Later he toured South Africa with an International Wanderers side and then joined World Series Cricket. Kent's chance at Test cricket finally came when he was chosen to tour England in 1981. He played in the last three Tests, scoring 46, 54 and 52 in three of his six innings. However, the favourable impression he created in those games was given no further chance to develop as the back injury ended his career in the next Australian season. He has kept an involvement in cricket by becoming an expert commentator on ABC radio broadcasts from Brisbane and in a managerial role with the Queensland team.

BATTING	M	Inn	NO	HS	Runs	Ave	100s	50s	C/S
Tests	3	6	0	54	171	28.50	–	2	6
First-class	64	110	11	171	3567	36.03	7	20	60

BOWLING	Runs	Wkts	Ave	BB	5wI	10wM
First-class	3	0	–	–	–	–

KERR, Robert Byers

Qld, RHB
Born: 16 June 1961
Herston, Queensland

Robbie Kerr had a successful career for Queensland, mostly in the opening role and occasionally at number three, but made little impression in his two Tests, against New Zealand in 1985–86. Making his debut in 1980–81, Kerr formed a strong partnership with South African born Kepler Wessels, with whom he shared a record stand of 388 against Victoria at St Kilda in 1982–83. Kerr's performances in Shield cricket certainly warranted a chance at Test level, but he could make no headway against the Kiwi bowlers, his best effort in four innings being only 17. As vice-captain of Queensland he led the side capably in the absence of Allan Border. Kerr's retirement, announced in 1990, was unfortunately hastened by a neck injury received in a car accident. At only 29 years of age, it seemed that he still had the chance to add to the 16 first-class centuries he made for Queensland.

BATTING	M	Inn	NO	HS	Runs	Ave	100s	50s	C/S
Tests	2	4	0	17	31	7.75	–	–	1
First-class	93	161	8	201*	5709	37.31	16	28	90

BOWLING	Runs	Wkts	Ave	BB	5wl	10wM			
First-class	16	1	16.00	1/12	–	–			

KIPPAX, Alan Falconer

NSW, RHB/LBG
Born: 25 May 1897
Paddington, New South Wales
Died: 5 September 1972
Bellevue Hill, New South Wales

One of cricket's most stylish players, Alan Kippax entranced spectators with his play in a career which lasted from 1918 to 1936. He possessed all the strokes and could play them with power and exquisite timing: his best was cricket's most difficult, the late cut. Kippax made his Test debut against England in 1924–25, and in 1925–26 he averaged 112 in the Sheffield Shield, but was not picked to tour England in 1926. This was an almost unbelievable selection error which rivals, and probably exceeds, the non–selection of Grimmett in 1938.

He was eventually chosen to tour in 1930 and 1934, but had been a far better player in the twenties. On that first trip, aged 33, only Bradman made more runs, and Kippax played some fine innings in the Tests.

He displayed great tactical skill in leading New South Wales, and at first-class level he was a dominating player. His highest score, 315 not out, was made against Queensland in 1926–27. In 1928–29 he finally established his Test place and in first-class cricket he set a record which may never be beaten. New South Wales were 9/113 when the last man, Hooker, joined Kippax. A day later Hooker was dismissed for 62, Kippax was 260 not out, and the two had added 307 for the last wicket.

Against the West Indies in 1930–31 he made his highest Test score (146), but the next season his confidence was severely dented when he was twice struck in the head while batting. Once a glorious exponent of the hook, he never again played the stroke with the same confidence. Like many of his colleagues, Kippax had no counter to Bodyline, but was taken to England again in 1934. Although he failed to score a thousand runs, he did average 50, an excellent effort for a 37-year-old.

In a long first-class career Kippax made plenty of runs, but it was the manner as much as the quantity which left a lasting impression, frequently causing old timers to think of the immortal skills of Victor Trumper.

BATTING	M	Inn	NO	HS	Runs	Ave	100s	50s	C/S
Tests	22	34	1	146	1192	36.12	2	8	13
First-class	175	256	33	315*	12762	57.22	43	45	73

BOWLING	Balls	Runs	Wkts	Ave	BB	5wI	10wM
Tests	72	19	0	–	–	–	–
First-class	–	1099	21	52.33	4/66	–	–

KLINE, Lindsay Francis

Vic, LHB/SLC
Born: 29 September 1934
Camberwell, Victoria

A left-arm 'chinaman' bowler, Victorian Lindsay Kline must have three amazing memories of Test cricket. Against South Africa in 1957–58 at Cape Town he took a hat-trick on his way to finishing on top of the Test averages with 15 wickets at 16.33. At Brisbane in 1960–61 it was Kline who hit the ball, only to see Ian Meckiff run out and the match end in Test cricket's first tie. At Adelaide in the same series, Kline,

137

with no pretensions to batting, held out for just under two hours with Ken Mackay to deny the West Indies a win. Despite bowling in a style prone to inaccuracy, Kline took his wickets at a very acceptable average, particularly in Test cricket. He toured South Africa, India, Pakistan and England, bowling well under varying conditions. His Test best of 7/75 was taken against Pakistan at Lahore in 1959–60. For Victoria he produced many fine efforts in a career which lasted from 1955 to 1961.

BATTING	M	Inn	NO	HS	Runs	Ave	100s	50s	C/S
Tests	13	16	9	15*	58	8.28	–	–	9
First-class	88	96	31	37*	559	8.60	–	–	55

BOWLING	Balls	Runs	Wkts	Ave	BB	5wI	10wM
Tests	2373	776	34	22.82	7/75	1	–
First-class	–	7562	276	27.39	7/75	11	–

L

LAIRD, Bruce Malcolm

WA, RHB
Born: 21 November 1950
Mt. Lawley, Western Australia

Bruce Laird was a tough little opening batsman from Western Australia, who played some brave innings in his 21 Tests, particularly against the West Indies pace attack. He made his first-class debut in 1972–73 and toured England in 1975 without playing a Test. Joining World Series Cricket undoubtedly delayed his Test debut, which finally took place in 1979–80 against the West Indies at Brisbane, when he batted superbly to make 92, his highest Test score, and 75. Although he passed fifty on eleven occasions in Tests he never reached three figures; his only century for Australia was a brilliant effort in a One-day International against the West Indies. Laird toured England in 1980, New Zealand in 1981–82 and Pakistan in 1982–83. Injury caused him to miss the 1981 tour of England, where his determined batting would have been very useful in shoring up a weak top order.

BATTING	M	Inn	NO	HS	Runs	Ave	100s	50s	C/S
Tests	21	40	2	92	1341	35.28	–	11	16
First-class	103	186	14	171	6085	35.37	8	41	86

BOWLING	Balls	Runs	Wkts	Ave	BB	5wI	10wM
Tests	18	12	0	–	–	–	–
First-class	–	69	0	–	–	–	–

LANGER, Justin Lee

WA, LHB
Born: 21 November 1970
Perth, Western Australia

Few players can have faced a more fiery Test baptism than left handed Justin Langer. Selected as a last-minute replacement for the injured Damien Martyn in the fourth Test of the 1992–93 series against the West Indies, he faced the full might of a Curtly Ambrose–led attack. Displaying great temperament as well as courage, he batted in the difficult number three position. His innings of 20 and 54 made under great pressure marked him as a Test player of the future. He had less luck as an opening batsman in the fifth Test, although he was unlucky to be given out in the second innings. Langer's selection for the New Zealand tour gave him another opportunity to press for a regular place. He made his highest score in the first Test, but failed in the others, collecting a pair in the final game. Langer returned to Australia before the one-day series and missed a place in the 1993 Ashes team. The youngster had come to notice with some defiant innings in 1991–92, principally an innings of 149 in the Sheffield Shield Final, a knock which ensured his state would win the trophy. A player of grit and determination, Langer may have a place in Australia's cricket future. He is the nephew of former Western Australian batsman Robbie Langer.

BATTING	M	Inn	NO	HS	Runs	Ave	100s	50s	C/S
Tests	5	8	0	63	172	21.50	–	2	2
First-class	21	37	1	149	1498	41.61	3	8	21

BOWLING	Runs	Wkts	Ave	BB	5wI	10wM	
First-class	4	0	–	–	–	–	

LANGLEY, Gilbert Roche Andrews

SA, RHB/WK
Born: 14 September 1919
North Adelaide, South Australia

Gil Langley's bulky build tended to disguise his agility and safety behind the stumps. He made his first-class debut as a batsman in 1945–46, but became his state's wicket-keeper in 1947–48. The unavailability of Don Tallon gave Langley the second 'keeping position on the South African tour of 1949–50. He made his Test debut in 1951–52 against the West Indies at Brisbane, and was generally the first choice 'keeper until he retired after the 1956 tour of England. An excellent average of four dismissals per Test shows just how capable he was. In 1956 at Lord's he became the first 'keeper to dismiss nine batsmen in a Test. With the bat, he played a number of fine innings at first-class level, but was not the same threat in the Test side. Langley turned to politics in later life, becoming the Speaker in the South Australian Parliament, of which he was a member for many years.

BATTING	M	Inn	NO	HS	Runs	Ave	100s	50s	C/S
Tests	26	37	12	53	374	14.96	–	1	83/15
First-class	122	165	39	160*	3236	25.68	4	12	292/77

BOWLING	Runs	Wkts	Ave	BB	5wl	10wM
First-class	2	0	–	–	–	–

LAUGHLIN, Trevor John

Vic, LHB/RM
Born: 30 January 1951
Nyah West, Victoria

A big-hitting, left-handed batsman and right-arm medium pacer, Trevor Laughlin produced some useful performances for Victoria at first-class level, but with one exception seemed unable to translate his ability to Test cricket. Laughlin made his debut for Victoria in 1974–75, and played his three Tests during the period of World Series Cricket. He toured the West Indies in 1977–78, making his debut in the third Test at Georgetown, Guyana. In the fifth Test he had his moment of glory, taking 5/101 in a match ended by a riot. Laughlin played the first Test of the 1978–79 series against England, failed, and was not chosen again, although he did play in Australia's 1979 World Cup side. A loss of form saw him dropped from the Victorian side in 1980–81.

BATTING	M	Inn	NO	HS	Runs	Ave	100s	50s	C/S
Tests	3	5	0	35	87	17.40	–	–	3
First-class	58	94	9	113	2770	32.58	1	19	40

BOWLING	Balls	Runs	Wkts	Ave	BB	5wl	10wM
Tests	516	262	6	43.66	5/101	1	–
First-class	–	3161	99	31.92	5/38	3	–

LAVER, Frank Jonas

Vic, RHB/RFM
Born: 7 December 1869
Castlemaine, Victoria
Died: 24 September 1919
East Melbourne, Victoria

A right-handed batsman with more determination than style and an effective fast-medium bowler, Laver made his first-class debut in 1891. Despite some good performances he did not tour England until 1899 when he made his debut in the first Test. He played against England in 1901–02, missed the 1902 tour, but won back his Test place in 1903–04. He was chosen as player–manager for the 1905 tour and bowled well, taking over a hundred wickets, including 7/64 in the first Test. Retained as player–manager for the 1909 tour, he topped the bowling averages and produced his best analysis of 8/31 in the Manchester Test. The players were keen to have him do the same job in 1912, but the Australian Board would not agree. As a result, six of the country's finest players refused to tour. In Tests his bowling proved more damaging than his batting, but he was a useful all-rounder, and gained fame as an outstanding coach.

BATTING	M	Inn	NO	HS	Runs	Ave	100s	50s	C/S
Tests	15	23	6	45	196	11.52	–	–	8
First-class	163	255	38	164	5431	25.02	6	18	148

BOWLING	Balls	Runs	Wkts	Ave	BB	5wI	10wM
Tests	2361	964	37	27.58	8/31	2	–
First-class	–	9987	404	24.72	8/31	19	5

LAWRY, William Morris

Vic, LHB
Born: 11 February 1937
Thornbury, Victoria

Unkind critics called him 'a corpse with pads on', but to see Victorian left-handed opening batsman Bill Lawry purely as a stonewaller would be to overlook an outstanding contribution to Australian Test cricket over a 10-year period. Lawry made his debut for Victoria in 1955, took a number of years to establish himself, and did not receive a chance at Test level until chosen for the 1961 tour of England. He topped the averages with 2019 runs at 61.18 and scored two centuries in the Tests, in which he averaged over 50. In his early days he was a free–scoring, attractive batsman, but over the years he tailored his game to suit the needs of his side, and became a far more defensive player.

Throughout the sixties he formed one of Australia's finest opening partnerships with Bob Simpson. Their best effort was a stand of 382 against the West Indies at Barbados in 1965 when both made double centuries. Their quick running between the wickets and their capacity to make big scores created a firm foundation for stroke players like O'Neill and Burge to capitalise on.

Lawry had another successful tour of England in 1964, and in 1965–66 he wore the English bowlers into the ground, making 979 runs against them in all matches and batting for over 41 hours. When Simpson retired in 1967–68, Lawry took over the captaincy. He drew the 1968 series in England, then defeated the West Indies 3–1 in Australia. He led from the front, making 205, 151 and 105 in the series. In 1969–70 the Australians won a tough contest in India, but immediately afterwards were swamped by a strong South African team. This, plus his inability to defeat England in 1970–71, saw Lawry removed from the captaincy and the side for the final Test of that series. His replacement,

Ian Chappell, is adamant that Australia would have won that game had Lawry been in the team. His presence in England in 1972 may have shifted a drawn series in Australia's favour. While a change in the captaincy was probably due, Lawry the batsman was still worth a place in the Australian team. When he failed to make that 1972 tour Lawry retired from first-class cricket, leaving behind an enviable record.

Through his frenetic commentaries on television, the Victorian pigeon fancier has now become well known to a whole new generation of cricket followers.

BATTING	M	Inn	NO	HS	Runs	Ave	100s	50s	C/S
Tests	67	123	12	210	5234	47.15	13	27	30
First-class	249	417	49	266	18734	50.90	50	100	121

BOWLING	Balls	Runs	Wkts	Ave	BB	5wl	10wM
Tests	14	6	0	–	–	–	–
First-class	_	188	5	37.60	1/3	–	–

LAWSON, Geoffrey Francis

NSW, RHB/RF
Born: 7 December 1957
Wagga Wagga, New South Wales

Geoff Lawson gave Australia great service in 46 Tests. Beginning his first-class career in 1977–78, he made his Test debut against New Zealand at Brisbane in 1980–81 and was chosen to tour England in 1981. Although he took 7/81 at Lord's, injury ruined the rest of his trip. He bowled well without luck in Pakistan on the 1982 tour, then established himself with 34 wickets against England in 1982–83. Following the retirement of Dennis Lillee, Lawson became Australia's number one pace bowler, taking his best figures of 8/112 against the West Indies at Adelaide in 1984–85 and capturing 22 wickets in a losing cause on the 1985 tour of England. After a period of injury and poor form, he fought his way back to tour England again in 1989, providing Terry Alderman with excellent support. Unfortunately the recall was short–lived, and he returned to Shield cricket after two Tests in 1989–90. A useful tailender with the bat, he played a number of important innings in the lower part of the order. Lawson captained New South Wales with skill and determination in his last few seasons, retiring at the end of the 1991–92 season. He has since moved into the commentary box with the ABC radio team and has done some television work.

BATTING	M	Inn	NO	HS	Runs	Ave	100s	50s	C/S
Tests	46	68	12	74	894	15.96	–	4	10
First-class	191	225	44	74	2683	14.82	–	8	75

BOWLING	Balls	Runs	Wkts	Ave	BB	5wl	10wM
Tests	11118	5501	180	30.56	8/112	11	2
First-class	–	16564	666	24.87	8/112	28	2

LEE, Phillip Keith

SA, RHB/RM, OB
Born: 15 September 1904
Gladstone, South Australia
Died: 9 August 1980
Adelaide, South Australia

'Perka' Lee was probably South Australia's best all-rounder in the period between the two World Wars. Although he made his debut in 1925–26, it was not until the 1930–31 season, when he made 106 and took 5/57 against the West Indies, that he really began to push for Test selection. He played in the second Test against South Africa in 1931–32, when he took one wicket and failed to score. His other Test was against England at Sydney in the fifth Test of the 1932–33 Bodyline series. He was more successful here with 42 and 15, and 4/111 with his off spin. Lee missed the 1934 tour of England and retired at the end of the next Australian season.

BATTING	M	Inn	NO	HS	Runs	Ave	100s	50s	C/S
Tests	2	3	0	42	57	19.00	–	–	1
First-class	55	95	5	106	1669	18.54	2	6	23

BOWLING	Balls	Runs	Wkts	Ave	BB	5wl	10wM
Tests	436	212	5	42.40	4/111	–	–
First-class	–	4583	152	30.15	5/23	6	–

LILLEE, Dennis Keith

WA, Tas, RHB/RF
Born: 18 July, 1949
Subiaco, Western Australia

One of the finest of all fast bowlers, Western Australian Dennis Lillee holds the record for the most wickets taken by an Australian in Test cricket. Starting out as a tearaway quick, he overcame a devastating back injury to return a better bowler, adding subtlety and variation to blistering speed.

Lillee made his first-class debut in 1969–70 and bowled so well he was chosen for an Australian B tour at the end of that season. He continued to improve, and played in the last two Tests against England in 1970–71, taking 5/84 on debut. At Perth in 1971–72 he destroyed a strong World XI with 8/29. In England in 1972 he took 31 wickets in the series, but at the end of the 1972–73 season stress fractures in his spine looked like ending his career. Showing typical courage, he fought back to partner Jeff Thomson in the 1974–75 destruction of England. The pair did the same to the West Indies next season, and when Thomson's shoulder was injured in 1976–77, Lillee continued on, taking 11 wickets in the Centenary Test.

Injury prevented him from touring England in 1977, and then he was lost to Tests for two seasons when he joined World Series Cricket, for whom he was a major drawcard. He returned to Tests in 1979–80, the complete fast bowler. If he lacked the speed of earlier days, he possessed, swing, changes of pace and a lethal leg cutter. He took 39 wickets in a losing 1981 tour of England, despite a bout of pneumonia at the start of the series, and his best effort of 7/83 was taken against the West Indies at Melbourne in 1981–82. His dismissal of Larry Gomes in that innings made him the leading Test wicket–taker. Injury restricted him again in 1982–83, but he fought back next season to lead the Australian attack to victory against Pakistan. Lillee retired after that series, taking a wicket with his final delivery in Test cricket.

In 1987–88 he returned to first-class cricket with Tasmania, took a wicket with his first ball, and showed that he was still a bowler to be feared. Despite his fiery temper, the aluminium bat incident and the Javed Miandad confrontation being the two most infamous manifestations, the abiding memories of Dennis Lillee are of the magnificent flowing run-up, copybook action, and a determination to extract the smallest vestige of life from the deadest of tracks and to remove any batsman unfortunate enough to get in his way.

BATTING	M	Inn	NO	HS	Runs	Ave	100s	50s	C/S
Tests	70	90	24	73*	905	13.71	–	1	23
First-class	198	241	70	73*	2377	13.90	–	2	67

BOWLING	Balls	Runs	Wkts	Ave	BB	5wI	10wM
Tests	18467	8493	355	23.92	7/83	23	7
First-class	–	20695	882	23.46	8/29	50	13

LINDWALL, Raymond Russell

NSW, Qld, RHB/RF
Born: 3 October 1921
Mascot, New South Wales

Ray Lindwall is Lillee's only serious rival as Australia's finest fast bowler. Born in New South Wales, Lindwall lost a number of seasons to the Second World War. Although he bowled at great pace, the speed was allied with cunning and variation, and his smooth action enabled him to maintain his Test place until he was 38 years old.

Lindwall made his first-class debut in 1941–42, but had to wait until 1945–46 to play his first Test, against New Zealand at Wellington. His partnership with Keith Miller gave Australia an attacking edge which carried all before it in the period after the War. The two became firm friends, and on the field the classical fast bowling of Lindwall was beautifully complemented by the unpredictable genius of Miller.

Lindwall took 7/63 in the fifth Test of the 1946–47 series against England, and next season achieved his best figures of 7/38 against India in Adelaide. On the 1948 tour he captured 6/20 at The Oval, to bowl England out for 52, ending the series with 27 wickets. He toured England again in 1953 and 1956, but was less successful than on his first visit. He also toured South Africa, the West Indies, India and Pakistan and bowled well in all conditions. In 1956 he led Australia to a draw against India at Bombay, his only chance at the Test captaincy.

Lindwall moved to Queensland in 1954–55, captaining them for five seasons. When his Test career looked over, he emerged to bowl well against England in 1958–59 and earned himself a second trip to India and Pakistan in 1959–60, where he ended his career with 228 wickets in 61 Tests. Although he secured five wickets in an innings 12 times, he never took 10 in a match, something he achieved only twice in his entire first-class career.

In addition to his bowling, Lindwall was a very talented batsman, scoring Test centuries against England in 1946–47 and the West Indies in 1954–55. He made five first-class centuries in all and would have made many more if he had not been required to do so much bowling.

BATTING	M	Inn	NO	HS	Runs	Ave	100s	50s	C/S
Tests	61	84	13	118	1502	21.15	2	5	26
First-class	228	270	39	134*	5042	21.82	5	19	123

BOWLING	Balls	Runs	Wkts	Ave	BB	5wl	10wM
Tests	13650	5251	228	23.03	7/38	12	–
First-class	–	16956	794	21.35	7/20	34	2

LOVE, Hampden Stanley Bray

NSW, Vic, RHB/WK
Born: 10 August 1895
Balmain, New South Wales
Died: 22 July 1969
Mosman, New South Wales

'Hammy' Love had the misfortune to have his career coincide with that of Bert Oldfield, a fact which undoubtedly cost him many games and forced him to move to Victoria in an effort to establish himself. Love made his first-class debut against Queensland for New South Wales in 1920–21, but was in the Victorian side by 1922–23. Restricted there by Jack Ellis he returned to New South Wales, playing when Oldfield was unavailable or injured. When the Australian 'keeper suffered a fractured skull at Adelaide in 1932–33, Love kept in the fourth Test of the Bodyline series. In addition to his 'keeping skills, his figures show he was an extremely capable batsman, six of his seven centuries being made for Victoria. His first-class career ended with a tour to India with an Australian side in 1935–36.

BATTING	M	Inn	NO	HS	Runs	Ave	100s	50s	C/S
Tests	1	2	0	5	8	4.00	–	–	3
First-class	54	90	7	192	2906	35.01	7	11	73/29

BOWLING	Runs	Wkts	Ave	BB	5wl	10wM
First-class	19	0	–	–	–	–

LOXTON, Samuel John Everett

Vic, RHB/RFM
Born: 29 March 1921
Albert Park, Victoria

Sam Loxton was a useful all-rounder for Victoria and Australia in the period following the Second World War. He was an extremely aggressive batsman, a good fast-medium bowler and an outstanding fieldsman. Loxton had a sensational debut for Victoria in 1946–47, scoring 232 not out against Queensland. He made his Test debut against India next season and scored 80. On the 1948 tour of England he made 93 in the fourth Test, with five sixes, and scored 973 runs at 57.23 in all. His only Test century came in the first Test of the 1949–50 tour of South Africa. In Test cricket his batting was reasonably successful but he struggled as a bowler, and this probably prevented him from playing more often. Loxton became a prominent administrator and was a member of Victoria's state parliament for many years.

BATTING	M	Inn	NO	HS	Runs	Ave	100s	50s	C/S
Tests	12	15	0	101	554	36.93	1	3	7
First-class	140	192	23	232*	6249	36.97	13	32	83

BOWLING	Balls	Runs	Wkts	Ave	BB	5wI	10wM
Tests	906	349	8	43.62	3/55	–	–
First-class	–	5971	232	25.73	6/49	3	–

LYONS, John James

SA, RHB/RM
Born: 21 May 1863
Gawler, South Australia
Died: 21 July 1927
Adelaide, South Australia

JJ Lyons was a South Australian big hitter, capable of turning a match with strokes of awesome power, played to all parts of the ground. He

149

made his debut in 1884–85 and his first Test came against England at Sydney in 1887–88. He toured England in 1888, played only in the third Test, and made few runs. His return visits in 1890 and 1893 were more successful, and he passed 1000 runs on each occasion. His only Test century helped produce a victory. At Sydney in 1891–92, with his side 162 runs behind, he made 134 out of an opening stand of 174 and Australia went on to win by 72 runs. That was Lyons' value as a cricketer. Although he might fail, there was always the chance that the chances he took would pay off and give his side a victory. Despite the risky nature of his batting, his average at Test and first-class level stands comparison with his contemporaries.

BATTING	M	Inn	NO	HS	Runs	Ave	100s	50s	C/S
Tests	14	27	0	134	731	27.07	1	3	3
First-class	153	275	11	149	6752	25.57	11	28	60

BOWLING	Balls	Runs	Wkts	Ave	BB	5wI	10wM
Tests	316	149	6	24.83	5/30	1	–
First-class	–	3225	107	30.14	6/38	5	–

Mc

McALISTER, Peter Alexander

Vic, RHB
Born: 11 July 1869
Williamstown, Victoria
Died: 10 May 1938
Richmond, Victoria

Peter McAlister was a right-handed opening batsman who became more famous as the administrator at the centre of the 1912 dispute. Making his first-class debut in 1898–99, he made a strong impression with 224 against New Zealand in his first season. Although he did well for Victoria, McAlister made little impact in eight Tests between 1903–04 and 1909, his best effort being 41 in the first Test of the 1907–08 series. Despite his poor form, he was appointed vice-captain and treasurer for the 1909 tour of England. At 40 years of age he was well past his best and his results were disappointing. Throughout his playing career McAlister had been establishing himself as an administrator, and in 1911–12 his opposition to Frank Laver's appointment as manager for the 1912 tour of England and arguments over selection led to a fist fight between himself and Australian captain, Clem Hill. Laver's non–appointment saw six of the country's best players, including Hill, refuse to make the tour.

BATTING	M	Inn	NO	HS	Runs	Ave	100s	50s	C/S
Tests	8	16	1	41	252	16.80	–	–	10
First-class	85	148	9	224	4552	32.74	9	22	91

BOWLING	Runs	Wkts	Ave	BB	5wI	10wM
First-class	56	3	18.66	1/0	–	–

MACARTNEY, Charles George

NSW, RHB/SLA
Born: 27 June 1886
West Maitland, New South Wales
Died: 9 September 1958
Little Bay, New South Wales

Charlie Macartney was a supremely talented right-handed batsman and a useful left-arm slow bowler, who represented Australia in 35 Tests either side of the First World War. A short, stocky man with immense strength, Macartney possessed all the strokes in the book, along with the ability to improvise others when necessary. Such was his air of dominance at the crease that he was called 'the Governor–General'. Bowlers existed only to be destroyed. Australian batsman Jack Fingleton once opened with Macartney after the latter had retired from first-class cricket. He was warned to look out for the first ball, which was driven head–high back past the stunned bowler. When the two batsmen met in mid–pitch, Macartney said, 'Bowlers don't like that son, it rattles them.'

Macartney made his first-class debut in 1905–06, and despite some inconsistent performances he was chosen to tour England in 1909, after playing in all five Tests of the 1907–08 series. Although his batting had limited success, he did take 71 wickets, including his career best 7/58 in the Leeds Test. In 1912 he batted in what was to become his customary number three position, came second in the batting averages with 2207 runs at 45.04, and first in the bowling with 43 wickets at 16.34.

Having lost a number of valuable seasons, Macartney returned to Test cricket against England in 1920–21. He played only two Tests, but scored 170 in one of them. As his bowling declined, his batting seemed to became more dominant, and no better example of his stroke-play exists than his 345 in less than four hours, against Nottinghamshire on the 1921 tour of England. He struck an amazing 47 fours and four sixes.

On his final tour of England in 1926, at the age of 40, he played his most famous innings. At Leeds, with Bardsley out first ball, Macartney survived an early chance in the slips, went on to score a hundred before lunch and finished with 151. He made two other centuries in his last Test series, to show that the advancing years had dimmed none of his skills. In fact, his final first-class match came in 1935–36, when he

152

was nearing fifty, on a tour of India with an Australian team. Even then he was able to show flashes of brilliance that thrilled the crowds.

BATTING	M	Inn	NO	HS	Runs	Ave	100s	50s	C/S
Tests	35	55	4	170	2131	41.78	7	9	17
First-class	249	360	32	345	15019	45.78	49	53	102

BOWLING	Balls	Runs	Wkts	Ave	BB	5wI	10wM
Tests	3561	1240	45	27.55	7/58	2	1
First-class	–	8781	419	20.95	7/58	17	1

McCABE, Stanley Joseph

NSW, RHB/RM
Born: 16 July 1910
Grenfell, New South Wales
Died: 25 August 1968
Mosman, New South Wales

Stan McCabe's cricket career coincided with that of Don Bradman in the decade before the Second World War, and to some extent his skills never received the acclaim they deserved. However, it fell to McCabe to play three of the greatest innings ever seen in Test cricket. On his day, the New South Wales right-hander was unstoppable, and if he had possessed the killer instinct of a Bradman he would certainly have scored many more runs.

Born in the New South Wales country town of Grenfell, McCabe was educated in Sydney and made his first-class debut in 1928–29. At the age of 20 he was taken to England in 1930. The move was a success as he scored over 1000 runs and played in all five Tests. Good performances against the West Indies and South Africa followed in the next two Australian summers. Then the first of his great innings came at Sydney in the first Test of the 1932–33 Bodyline series. Coming in at 3/82, he hooked Larwood's first ball to the fence and continued to attack while wickets fell around him. He ended with 187 not out, in four hours, including 49 out of a last wicket partnership of 55 with Tim Wall.

He had a successful tour of England in 1934, and in 1935–36 Australia toured South Africa, without Bradman. Following a century in the first Test, McCabe came in at Johannesburg, at 1/17, on a wearing pitch with his side needing 399 to win the second Test. He went on the attack, thrashing the bowling in appalling light as storm clouds gathered. At with 2/274, McCabe 189 not out, Springbok skipper Herbert Wade appealed against the light as McCabe's shots were endangering his fieldsmen. The match ended in a draw as rain washed out further play.

McCabe became Australia's vice-captain to Bradman in 1936–37, and in England on the 1938 tour he played the third of his epic innings. In the first Test at Trent Bridge, chasing 8/658, Australia were struggling at 6/194. McCabe tore into the bowling, making 232 out of 300. With Fleetwood–Smith he made 72 out of 77 for the last wicket in 28 minutes. This innings, which Bradman said was the greatest he ever saw, saved the game for his side. Unfortunately, trouble with his feet ended McCabe's career in 1941–42, but on at least three accounts, his place in cricket history is secure.

BATTING	M	Inn	NO	HS	Runs	Ave	100s	50s	C/S
Tests	39	62	5	232	2748	48.21	6	13	41
First-class	182	262	20	240	11951	49.38	29	68	139

BOWLING	Balls	Runs	Wkts	Ave	BB	5wI	10wM
Tests	3746	1543	36	42.86	4/13	–	–
First-class	–	5362	159	33.72	5/36	1	–

McCOOL, Colin Leslie

NSW, Qld, RHB/LBG
Born: 9 December 1915
Paddington, New South Wales
Died: 5 April 1986
Concord, New South Wales

Colin McCool was a leg-spinning all-rounder, who suffered from the wealth of cricketing talent possessed by Australia after the Second World War. He delivered the ball with a round-arm action which reminded some of Clarrie Grimmett, and he certainly should have played more than 14 Tests. McCool made his first-class debut in 1939–40, but had to wait until 1945–46 to play Test cricket. Against England in 1946–47 he scored 272 runs at 54.50, including a century in the third Test, and took 18 wickets at 27.27. He played three times against India in 1947–48, then toured England in 1948 without playing a Test.

His best bowling figures of 5/41 were recorded against South Africa at Cape Town in 1949–50. In the early fifties McCool moved to England to play League cricket, and in 1956, aged 40, he played county cricket for Somerset. In each of his five seasons in England he passed 1000 runs, after which he returned to Australia.

BATTING	M	Inn	NO	HS	Runs	Ave	100s	50s	C/S
Tests	14	17	4	104*	459	35.30	1	1	14
First-class	251	412	34	172	12420	32.85	18	66	262/2

BOWLING	Balls	Runs	Wkts	Ave	BB	5wI	10wM
Tests	2504	958	36	26.61	5/41	3	–
First-class	–	16542	602	27.47	8/74	34	2

McCORMICK, Ernest Leslie

Vic, LHB/RF
Born: 16 May 1906
North Carlton, Victoria
Died: 28 June 1991
Tweed Heads, New South Wales

Victorian Ernie McCormick was Australia's fastest bowler of the thirties. Off a long run, the tall McCormick could generate great pace, making the ball lift alarmingly, but when the rhythm was missing he could be disappointing. He was no-balled 35 times during his first match of the 1938 English tour. McCormick made his first-class debut in 1929–30, but did not play Test cricket until the 1935–36 tour of South Africa, where he took 15 wickets in the series. Despite back problems, McCormick was Australia's first-choice opening bowler against England in 1936–37 and 1938, often managing to take an early wicket for his side. In addition to his fast bowling, McCormick possessed a delightful sense of humour. Those who toured with him are adamant that he was one of the funniest men they ever met.

BATTING	M	Inn	NO	HS	Runs	Ave	100s	50s	C/S
Tests	12	14	5	17*	54	6.00	–	–	8
First-class	85	98	31	77*	582	8.68	–	1	46

BOWLING	Balls	Runs	Wkts	Ave	BB	5wI	10wM
Tests	2107	1079	36	29.97	4/101	–	–
First-class	–	6686	231	27.74	9/40	6	1

McCOSKER, Richard Bede

NSW, RHB
Born: 11 December 1946
Inverell, New South Wales

Rick McCosker was a capable right-handed batsman who gave excellent service to New South Wales and Australia, despite not entering first-class cricket until he was 26. A good run of form in 1974–75 saw him chosen to open the batting with Ian Redpath in the fourth Test against England. He made a fine 80 and earned a trip to England in 1975, where he scored over 1000 runs and made 127 in the fourth Test, following 95 not out in the third. In the 1977 Centenary Test, he batted with a broken jaw in the second innings, made 25, and helped his side to a historic victory. McCosker toured England again in 1977, then joined World Series Cricket. In 1979–80 he returned to captain New South Wales, and although he played no further Tests, McCosker continued to score heavily at first-class level until he retired in 1982.

BATTING	M	Inn	NO	HS	Runs	Ave	100s	50s	C/S
Tests	25	46	5	127	1622	39.56	4	9	21
First-class	116	209	24	168	8260	44.64	26	43	129

BOWLING	Runs	Wkts	Ave	BB	5wI	10wM			
First-class	119	2	59.50	2/28	–	–			

McDERMOTT, Craig John

Qld, RHB/RF
Born: 14 April 1965
Ipswich, Queensland

The red-haired Queensland fast bowler has had a rollercoaster ride in cricket, before establishing himself as Australia's spearhead. McDermott had a meteoric rise when he was selected to play against the

156

West Indies in 1984–85, aged 19. He earned a trip to England in 1985 where he took 30 wickets in the series, including 8/141 at Old Trafford and 6/70 at Lord's. From there he seemed to lose his way. He was in and out of the side, and at one time even lost his place in the Queensland team.

To McDermott's credit, he fought back, going on a rigid training schedule and shortening his approach to the wicket. The hard work paid off in 1990–91 when his outstanding Shield bowling earned him a recall for the fourth Test against England. He bowled superbly, taking 5/97. In the fifth Test he did even better, with 8/97 and 11 wickets in the match. His good form continued with 24 wickets against the West Indies on tour, giving the world's most feared pace attack a little of its own medicine. McDermott's 31 wickets against India in 1991–92 won him the International Cricketer of the Year Award and established his place as one of the world's best fast bowlers.

McDermott seemed to lack a little rhythm in the 1992–93 series against the West Indies and then in New Zealand. The hoped for recovery did not materialise in England when illness cut short his 1993 tour. With his dedication and desire to succeed this must be only a momentary lapse in what should become an outstanding career.

BATTING	M	Inn	NO	HS	Runs	Ave	100s	50s	C/S
Tests	47	66	8	42*	691	11.91	–	–	11
First-class	135	172	29	74	2350	16.43	–	5	37

BOWLING	Balls	Runs	Wkts	Ave	BB	5wl	10wM
Tests	10853	5612	198	28.34	8/97	9	2
First-class	–	14703	542	27.13	8/44	30	4

McDONALD, Colin Campbell

Vic, RHB
Born: 17 November 1928
Glen Iris, Victoria

Colin McDonald was a determined right-handed batsman who opened the innings for Australia in 47 Tests between 1951–52 and 1961. He made his first-class debut for Victoria in 1947–48 and played his first Test against the West Indies. From then until his retirement he was almost a permanent fixture at the top of the Australian order. His best series was against England in 1958–59 when he scored 519 runs at 64.87, and he also displayed great courage against the West Indians in 1960–61. When Jim Laker took 19 wickets at Old Trafford in 1956, McDonald was the batsman who played him best, with innings of 32 and 89. He toured England in 1953, 1956 and 1961, India and Pakistan in 1956 and 1959–60, the West Indies in 1955 and South Africa in 1957–58. At first-class level, he captained Victoria for five seasons until he retired in 1963.

BATTING	M	Inn	NO	HS	Runs	Ave	100s	50s	C/S
Tests	47	83	4	170	3107	39.32	5	17	14
First-class	192	307	26	229	11375	40.48	24	57	53/2

BOWLING	Balls	Runs	Wkts	Ave	BB	5wl	10wM
Tests	8	3	0	–	–	–	–
First-class	–	192	3	64.00	1/10	–	–

McDONALD, Edgar Arthur

Tas, Vic, RHB/RF
Born: 6 January 1891
Launceston, Tasmania
Died: 22 July 1937
Blackrod, Lancashire, England.

Ted McDonald was a right-handed fast bowler with a superb action. He played the majority of his cricket in England, representing Australia in only 11 Tests. Born in Tasmania, McDonald made his debut for that state in 1909–10, but it was not until he moved to Victoria just before the First World War that he really began to make an impression. In the third Test of the 1920–21 series against England, McDonald was paired with Jack Gregory to create Test cricket's first dual speed attack. They carried all before them there and in England on the 1921 tour, where he was the leading wicket taker. The two provided an interesting contrast. Gregory made a huge leap before delivering the ball, while McDonald possessed a copybook action, gliding almost silently to the crease. After the 1921–22 season McDonald moved to England, at first to League cricket. In 1924 he qualified for Lancashire and took over 1000 wickets for them before he retired in 1931. Despite the advancing years he remained one of the most feared bowlers in England. McDonald was killed in a road accident when he stopped to help another motorist.

BATTING	M	Inn	NO	HS	Runs	Ave	100s	50s	C/S
Tests	11	12	5	36	116	16.57	–	–	3
First-class	281	302	47	100*	2663	10.44	1	2	98

BOWLING	Balls	Runs	Wkts	Ave	BB	5wI	10wM
Tests	2885	1431	43	33.27	5/32	2	–
First-class	–	28966	1395	20.76	8/41	119	31

McDONNELL, Percy Stanislaus

Vic, NSW, Qld, RHB
Born: 13 November 1858
Kennington, England
Died: 24 September 1896
South Brisbane, Queensland

Percy McDonnell was a right-handed batsman, born in England, who made his debut for Victoria in 1877–78. He toured England in 1880, where he played his first Test and again in 1882 and 1884. While studies restricted his appearances (he was a medical student with a liking for ancient Greece), McDonnell gained the Australian captaincy in 1886–87 and led the side to England in 1888. Unfortunately, England was at peak form in this period and his captaincy was largely unsuccessful, principally due to the batsmen's failure to capitalise on the fine bowling of Turner and Ferris. He lost five and won only one of his six games in charge. As a batsman he was top class, his sound technique being particularly valuable on wet wickets. His top score of 147 was made against England at Sydney in 1881–82, and his average is excellent considering the conditions he played under.

BATTING	M	Inn	NO	HS	Runs	Ave	100s	50s	C/S
Tests	19	34	1	147	950	28.78	3	2	6
First-class	166	285	10	239	6470	23.52	7	24	99

BOWLING	Balls	Runs	Wkts	Ave	BB	5wI	10wM
Tests	52	53	0	–	–	–	–
First-class	–	247	2	123.50	1/7	–	–

McILWRAITH, John

Vic, RHB
Born: 7 September 1857
Collingwood, Victoria
Died: 5 July 1938
Camberwell, Victoria

John McIlwriath was an aggressive right-handed batsman who made his first-class debut in 1884–85 following some large scores in grade cricket. He earned a place on the 1886 tour of England following two centuries in 1885–86, 133 against NSW and 125 for the Australian XI against Victoria, the only ones he scored in first-class cricket. McIlwraith's trip to England was unsuccessful: 532 runs at 16.62. He played his only Test at The Oval in the third game of the series. Although he continued to play for Victoria until 1889, McIlwraith was never again a serious contender for a Test place. AG 'Johnny' Moyes described McIlwraith as 'a player whose promise was never fulfilled.'

BATTING	M	Inn	NO	HS	Runs	Ave	100s	50s	C/S
Tests	1	2	0	7	9	4.50	–	–	1
First-class	44	68	7	133	1468	24.06	2	6	24

MACKAY, Kenneth Donald

Qld, LHB/RM
Born: 24 October 1925
Windsor, Queensland
Died: 13 June 1982
Point Lookout, Stradbroke Island, Queensland

An extremely valuable all-rounder and lovable character, Ken 'Slasher' Mackay gum-chewed his way through 37 Tests between 1956 and 1963, scoring runs when they were most needed, occupying the crease for interminable periods when necessary, and bowling medium pace with all the generosity of a scrooge. All of this drove opponents to distraction, but certainly made him the man for a crisis. Although he made his debut for Queensland in 1946–47, it was not until the 1956 tour of England that he established a place in Test cricket. The South

Africans could find no counter to him in 1957–58, but he performed his greatest rescue act at Adelaide against the West Indies in 1960–61. He batted out the last 100 minutes with number eleven Lindsay Kline to earn a draw, taking the final delivery from Wes Hall on the body rather than risk giving a chance. At Manchester in 1961 when Richie Benaud bowled Australia to victory, it was Mackay who tied down the other end with his medium pace. The 'Slasher' retired in 1963. It is something of a tragedy that he never made a Test century, despite passing 50 on 13 occasions. For Queensland he was more successful, making 23 centuries, the highest of which was 223 (in just under 10 hours) against Victoria in 1953–54.

BATTING	M	Inn	NO	HS	Runs	Ave	100s	50s	C/S
Tests	37	52	7	89	1507	33.48	–	13	16
First-class	201	294	46	223	10823	43.64	23	59	84

BOWLING	Balls	Runs	Wkts	Ave	BB	5wI	10wM
Tests	5792	1721	50	34.42	6/42	2	–
First-class	–	8363	251	33.31	6/42	7	–

McKENZIE, Graham Douglas

WA, RHB/RF
Born: 24 June 1941
Cottesloe, Western Australia

Western Australian fast bowler Graham McKenzie led the Test attack for a decade. His superb physique and high action enabled him to generate considerable pace without noticeable change in his delivery. Despite the ability to produce a viciously quick ball, it was the out-swinger which accounted for most batsmen. A man of placid temper-ament, McKenzie sometimes lacked 'the devil' necessary to stir up an opposing batsman, but that is a minor criticism in what was an out-standing career.

Coming from a cricketing background (his father and uncle both played for Western Australia), McKenzie received his chance when chosen for the 1961 tour of England. He formed a strong partnership with Alan Davidson, and after the left-hander retired in 1963 McKenzie became the country's premier fast bowler. He did so well that he achieved 100 Test wickets for Australia in the shortest time, three years and 165 days, and at the youngest age, just 23.

161

McKenzie also toured England in 1964 and 1968, the West Indies in 1965, India and Pakistan in 1964, India again in 1969–70, and South Africa in 1966–67 and 1969–70. Probably his best effort was against the West Indies in 1968–69 when he took 30 wickets in the series, including his best bowling of 8/71 at Melbourne. After a successful trip to India in 1969–70, the huge workload seemed to catch up with him as he struggled against South Africa and then England in 1970–71. When he was omitted from the team to tour England in 1972, his Test career ended. Undoubtedly he still had the skills, as he continued to play county cricket for Leicestershire until 1975.

As a batsman McKenzie was capable of playing some useful innings, the highest of which was 76 against South Africa in 1963–64. However, the most valuable was probably a 32 made against England at Manchester in 1961, in a last-wicket partnership of 98 with Alan Davidson, which gave Australia enough runs to win.

McKenzie should have ended his career as Australia's highest Test wicket taker. Apart from not choosing him for England in 1972, the selectors left him out of two Tests against India in 1967–68, on the rather lame excuse that they wanted to try a few other players. He finished his career just two wickets short of Richie Benaud's record tally.

BATTING	M	Inn	NO	HS	Runs	Ave	100s	50s	C/S
Tests	60	89	12	76	945	12.27	–	2	34
First-class	383	471	109	76	5662	15.64	–	18	201

BOWLING	Balls	Runs	Wkts	Ave	BB	5wI	10wM
Tests	17681	7328	246	29.78	8/71	16	3
First-class	–	32868	1219	26.96	8/71	49	5

McKIBBIN, Thomas Robert

NSW, LHB/RM, OB
Born: 10 December 1870
Raglan near Bathurst, New South Wales
Died: 15 December 1939
Bathurst, New South Wales

Tom McKibbin came from the New South Wales country near the town of Bathurst. Bowling a mixture of medium pacers and off breaks, he had a sudden rise to the top, making his Test debut in 1894–95, the same season he began in first-class cricket. McKibbin toured England in 1896, taking over a hundred wickets on the trip. Unfortunately, his Test record did not match his performances in first-class cricket, where he was a consistent matchwinner, taking 10 wickets in a match on no less than 11 occasions. McKibbin's Test career was given no chance to flourish, possibly because many believed he delivered the ball with a suspect action. When the administrators went to work to clean up this aspect of the game, the likeable Bathurst bowler was one of those to suffer.

BATTING	M	Inn	NO	HS	Runs	Ave	100s	50s	C/S
Tests	5	8	2	28	88	14.66	–	–	4
First-class	57	92	24	75	683	10.04	–	1	46

BOWLING	Balls	Runs	Wkts	Ave	BB	5wI	10wM
Tests	1032	496	17	29.17	3/35	–	–
First-class	–	6297	319	19.73	9/68	28	11

McLAREN, John William

Qld, RHB/RF
Born: 22 December 1886
Toowong, Queensland
Died: 17 November 1921
Highgate Hill, Queensland

John McLaren's only Test came in the last match of the 1911–12 series against England. While he was not a success in that game he achieved a small piece of fame by becoming the first player born in Queensland to represent Australia. Despite his performance in this game, McLaren won a trip to England in 1912, but did not play in any of the Tests. Over the years he bowled very well for Queensland, usually against overwhelming opposition in the days before that state was admitted to the Sheffield Shield. McLaren was the centre of an interesting incident in 1911–12 when the Brisbane waterside workers urged their Melbourne counterparts to boycott the fourth Test of the series if the Queenslander played. They alleged that he had acted as a special constable in a strike–breaking campaign during a prolonged dispute on the

Brisbane wharves early in 1912. The issue never came to a head as he was not chosen for the game. McLaren died from diabetes a month short of his 35th birthday.

BATTING	M	Inn	NO	HS	Runs	Ave	100s	50s	C/S
Tests	1	2	2	0*	0	–	–	–	–
First-class	34	59	14	43*	564	12.53	–	–	8

BOWLING	Balls	Runs	Wkts	Ave	BB	5wI	10wM
Tests	144	70	1	70.00	1/23	–	–
First-class	–	2862	107	26.74	5/55	3	–

MACLEAN, John Alexander

Qld, RHB/WK
Born: 27 April 1946
Brisbane, Queensland

John Maclean had enjoyed a long and successful career for Queensland before he was selected as Australia's 'keeper for the first four Tests of the 1978–79 series against England. Greatly weakened by World Series Cricket, the inexperienced Australians had no answer to a strong visiting side. Maclean 'kept well, but could not reproduce his first-class batting form at Test level. He was discarded after four games and retired at the end of the season. After a decade's work for Queensland he finished with a record number of dismissals for the state. In addition to his solid batting in the lower order, Maclean captained the side with skill in the latter part of his career.

BATTING	M	Inn	NO	HS	Runs	Ave	100s	50s	C/S
Tests	4	8	1	33*	79	11.28	–	–	18/-
First-class	108	184	25	156	3888	24.45	2	14	354/31

BOWLING	Runs	Wkts	Ave	BB	5wI	10wM
First-class	4	0	–	–	–	–

McLEOD, Charles Edward

Vic, RHB/RM
Born: 24 October 1869
Port Melbourne, Victoria
Died: 26 November 1918
Toorak, Victoria

Charlie McLeod was a useful all-rounder for Victoria and Australia at the turn of the century. From a cricketing family (one brother, Robert, played for Australia, another, Daniel, played for Victoria and four others played for Melbourne) McLeod made his first-class debut in 1893–94 and his Test debut against England in the next season. His best series was in 1897–98 when he played in all five Tests. He scored his only century, 112, in the second Test at Melbourne, when he opened the batting, and also scored two half centuries in the series. At Adelaide in the third Test he produced his best bowling of 5/65. Such form earned him a trip to England in 1899, where he played steady rather than spectacular cricket, something which could be said of his entire career. He toured England again in 1905, but he was certainly a better player under Australian conditions.

BATTING	M	Inn	NO	HS	Runs	Ave	100s	50s	C/S
Tests	17	29	5	112	573	23.87	1	4	9
First-class	114	179	22	112	3321	21.15	2	17	63

BOWLING	Balls	Runs	Wkts	Ave	BB	5wI	10wM
Tests	3374	1325	33	40.15	5/65	2	–
First-class	–	8123	334	24.32	7/34	22	4

McLEOD, Robert William

Vic, LHB/RM
Born: 19 January 1868
Port Melbourne, Victoria
Died: 14 June 1907
Middle Park, Victoria

The first of the McLeod brothers to play Test cricket, Robert was a left-handed batsman and a right-arm medium pacer who made his first-class debut in 1889–90 and would probably have gone to England in

1890 had he been available. McLeod's first Test was delayed until the 1891–92 series against England, when he played in all three games, taking 5/55 on debut in Melbourne. He did tour England in 1893 where he played his other three Tests. By the time the next English team visited Australia in 1894–95, McLeod had been replaced in the Test team by his younger brother, Charlie, who proved more capable at both Test and first-class level. Robert McLeod continued playing for Victoria until 1899. His only century came against South Australia in Adelaide during the 1892–93 season.

BATTING	M	Inn	NO	HS	Runs	Ave	100s	50s	C/S
Tests	6	11	0	31	146	13.27	–	–	3
First-class	57	95	19	101	1701	22.38	1	6	39

BOWLING	Balls	Runs	Wkts	Ave	BB	5wI	10wM
Tests	1089	384	12	32.00	5/55	1	–
First-class	–	3206	141	22.73	7/24	7	2

McSHANE, Patrick George

Vic, LHB/LM
Born: 18 April 1858
Keilor, Victoria
Died: 11 December 1903
Kew, Victoria

Commonly known as 'Paddy', McShane was a left-handed all-rounder who made his first-class debut for Victoria in 1880–81. He can claim something unique in Test cricket, when in the 1884–85 series against England he umpired the fourth Test and played in the fifth. His other two Tests were also against England, in 1886–87 and 1887–88. While his Test figures are unimpressive, he was a useful player at first-class level, probably more proficient as a bowler than a batsman. His best figures, an excellent 9/45, were taken for The Rest against The Australian XI at Sydney in 1880–81. Shortly after his appearances for Australia, McShane began to suffer bouts of mental illness and was admitted to an institution, where he died at the age of 45.

BATTING	M	Inn	NO	HS	Runs	Ave	100s	50s	C/S
Tests	3	6	1	12*	26	5.20	–	–	2
First-class	36	65	4	88	1117	18.31	–	5	24

BOWLING	Balls	Runs	Wkts	Ave	BB	5wI	10wM
Tests	108	48	1	48.00	1/39	–	–
First-class	–	1827	72	25.37	9/45	4	1

M

MADDOCKS, Leonard Victor

Vic, Tas, RHB/WK
Born: 24 May 1926
Beaconsfield, Victoria

Len Maddocks was a wicketkeeper-batsman who made his first-class debut for Victoria in 1946, but had his Test career restricted to seven games by the presence of players like Tallon, Langley and Grout. Maddocks toured the West Indies in 1955 and England and India in 1956 as Langley's deputy. He made his Test debut against England in the 1954–55 series and played some brave innings against the speed of Tyson and Statham, including his highest score of 69. Despite such a promising beginning, he was unable to maintain a regular Test place. In 1962–63 he moved to Tasmania, captaining them for some seasons. After retirement, Maddocks became an administrator, managing the 1977 team to England, a difficult task with World Series Cricket impending.

BATTING	M	Inn	NO	HS	Runs	Ave	100s	50s	C/S
Tests	7	12	2	69	177	17.70	–	1	18/1
First-class	112	158	33	122*	4106	32.84	6	20	209/68

BOWLING	Runs	Wkts	Ave	BB	5wl	10wM
First-class	4	1	4.00	1/4	–	–

MAGUIRE, John Norman

Qld, RHB/RFM
Born: 15 September 1956
Murwillumbah, New South Wales

An honest, right-arm fast-medium bowler, John Maguire played three Tests for Australia in 1983–84. Before his selection to play against Pakistan in the fourth Test of that season, he had bowled well for Queensland, proving a useful foil for fast bowlers like Jeff Thomson and Carl Rackemann. Three wickets in that match earned Maguire a trip to the West Indies, where he played in the last two Tests. His best bowling of 4/57 came in the fifth Test at Sabina Park, Jamaica. A decision to join the rebel tour of South Africa in 1985 prevented Maguire from playing any further Tests. After the two tours he returned to Queensland. In 1989–90 he opted to play first-class cricket in South Africa, where he was a notable success, taking 60 wickets at 15.05 for Eastern Province in his first season. Maguire also played for Leicestershire in the English County Championship.

BATTING	M	Inn	NO	HS	Runs	Ave	100s	50s	C/S
Tests	3	5	1	15*	28	7.00	–	–	2
First-class	134	152	46	65*	1162	10.96	–	2	43

BOWLING	Balls	Runs	Wkts	Ave	BB	5wI	10wM
Tests	616	323	10	32.30	4/57	–	–
First-class	–	12851	463	27.75	7/46	26	3

MAILEY, Arthur Alfred

NSW, RHB/LBG
Born: 3 January 1886
Waterloo, New South Wales
Died: 31 December 1967
Kirrawee, New South Wales

Arthur Mailey was a leg-spin and googly bowler of enormous talent. Because he spun the ball so much he could be inaccurate, but he was just as likely to remove any batsman with an unplayable delivery. Although he made his first-class debut in 1913–14, Mailey had to wait until 1920–21 to play Test cricket. He wasted no time when given the chance, taking 36 wickets in the series, including 9/121 at Melbourne, still the best bowling by an Australian in Tests. On the 1921 tour of England, he provided support for Gregory and McDonald, taking 146 wickets, including 10/66 against Gloucestershire. On his last tour in 1926 he took 141 wickets at 18.70. Although no batsman, Mailey shares the Australian last-wicket record of 127 with Johnny Taylor, against England at Sydney in the first Test of the 1924–25 series. In addition to his cricketing skills, Mailey was a renowned artist, cartoonist and commentator on the game; certainly one of cricket's unique characters.

BATTING	M	Inn	NO	HS	Runs	Ave	100s	50s	C/S
Tests	21	29	9	46*	222	11.10	–	–	14
First-class	158	186	62	66	1529	12.33	–	3	157

BOWLING	Balls	Runs	Wkts	Ave	BB	5wI	10wM
Tests	6119	3358	99	33.91	9/121	6	2
First-class	–	18778	779	24.10	10/66	61	16

MALLETT, Ashley Alexander

SA, RHB/OB
Born: 13 July 1945
Chatswood, New South Wales

A tall off-spin bowler and brilliant gully fieldsman, Ashley Mallett moved to South Australia, after once being twelfth man for Western Australia, in an effort to break into first-class cricket, which he did in 1967–68. He was so successful that he was chosen to tour England in 1968 where he made his Test debut at The Oval. Under Bill Lawry's captaincy he was in and out of the side, despite some good performances, particularly in India in 1969–70 where he took 28 wickets, including 5/91 and 5/53 in the fifth Test. He took 5/126 in the first Test of the South African tour, but did not play again in the series. Mallett eventually gained a regular Test place during Ian Chappell's captaincy, which he justified with skilful bowling in support of the pace attack led by Lillee and Thomson, and some of the finest close catching ever seen. His best bowling of 8/59 was taken against Pakistan at Adelaide in 1972–73. Mallett retired in 1976, but returned to join World Series Cricket. He remained in top cricket, even regaining his Test place, until 1980–81 when he finally retired. These days Mallett devotes much of his time to coaching, hoping to re-establish spin bowling as a force in Test cricket.

BATTING	M	Inn	NO	HS	Runs	Ave	100s	50s	C/S
Tests	38	50	13	43*	430	11.62	–	–	30
First-class	183	230	59	92	2326	13.60	–	2	105

BOWLING	Balls	Runs	Wkts	Ave	BB	5wI	10wM
Tests	9990	3940	132	29.84	8/59	6	1
First-class	–	18208	693	26.27	8/59	33	5

MALONE, Michael Francis

WA, RHB/RFM
Born: 9 October 1950
Perth, Western Australia

Mick Malone was a fine fast-medium bowler who was unlucky not to play in more than one Test. He made his first-class debut for Western Australia in 1974–75 and showed great skill in support of Dennis Lillee. He thoroughly earned his trip to England in 1977, where he played his only Test at The Oval. He made it a game to remember, taking 5/63 and scoring 46 in his only innings. He joined World Series Cricket and played for Lancashire, for whom he took his best figures, 7/88 against Nottinghamshire in 1979. Malone played a few one-day internationals for Australia and toured Pakistan in 1980, but he never had another chance at Test level. It was something this talented player certainly deserved before he retired in 1981–82.

BATTING	M	Inn	NO	HS	Runs	Ave	100s	50s	C/S
Tests	1	1	0	46	46	46.00	–	–	–
First-class	73	79	22	46	914	16.03	–	–	30

BOWLING	Balls	Runs	Wkts	Ave	BB	5wI	10wM
Tests	342	77	6	12.83	5/63	1	–
First-class	–	6441	260	24.77	7/88	13	1

MANN, Anthony Longford

WA, LHB/LBG
Born: 8 November 1945
Middle Swan, Western Australia

An aggressive left-handed batsman who also bowled leg spin, Tony Mann was a valuable all-rounder for Western Australia in a first-class career which lasted 20 years. Although he made his debut in 1963–64, it was not until the late sixties that he established a permanent place in the side. Mann's four Tests were played in Australia against India in 1977–78, the first season of World Series Cricket. His bowling proved ineffective, but at Perth in the second Test, he went in as night-watchman and scored 105 in a game Australia won by two wickets. There were no further opportunities at Test level, but Mann continued to give valuable service to Western Australia. His best figures of 6/94 were taken against South Australia in 1974–75, while his other century, 110, was made against England in 1970–71.

BATTING	M	Inn	NO	HS	Runs	Ave	100s	50s	C/S
Tests	4	8	0	105	189	23.62	1	–	2
First-class	80	122	17	110	2544	24.22	2	11	47

BOWLING	Balls	Runs	Wkts	Ave	BB	5wl	10wM
Tests	552	316	4	79.00	3/12	–	–
First-class	–	6908	200	34.54	6/94	5	–

MARR, Alfred Percy

NSW, RHB/RM
Born: 28 March 1862
Pyrmont, New South Wales
Died: 15 March 1940
Arncliffe, New South Wales

Marr was a right-handed bat and medium pace bowler who owed his single Test to the fact that the entire Australian team went on strike over a demand for increased pay after the first Test of the 1884–85 series against England. As a result the selectors had to make eleven changes for the second game. Not surprisingly the match was lost, with Marr himself achieving very little. He was not chosen again, and in fact did little at first-class level, although he was a very good grade player. This possibly accounts for the invitations he received to tour England, but which he was forced to decline. His record suggests that he would not have been a success on English pitches, although he once did take 8/28 in a non-first-class game against Queensland.

BATTING	M	Inn	NO	HS	Runs	Ave	100s	50s	C/S
Tests	1	2	0	5	5	2.50	–	–	–
First-class	14	27	0	69	304	11.25	–	1	8

BOWLING	Balls	Runs	Wkts	Ave	BB	5wI	10wM
Tests	48	14	0	–	–	–	–
First-class	–	454	14	32.42	3/50	–	–

MARSH, Geoffrey Robert

WA, RHB
Born: 31 December 1958
Northam, Western Australia

Geoff Marsh was an important member of the Test team from his debut against India in 1985–86. Initially selected for Western Australia in 1977–78, Marsh played the early part of his career as a middle-order batsman, but soon moved up the order to open. His place in the Test side was secured when the selectors paired him with Tasmanian David Boon and the two established themselves as the country's best opening pair since Simpson and Lawry. When Mark Taylor arrived on the Test scene in 1989, he and Marsh broke the Ashes Test record with an opening stand of 329 at Trent Bridge. In that innings the Western Australian made his highest Test score, 138. Marsh set himself to play the anchor role in many Test innings, but he has plenty of attacking strokes as shown by his 355 not out against South Australia in 1989–90. In one-day cricket Marsh produced many fine displays, his ability to bat through an innings allowed the strokemakers to attack at the other end. Some problems with his technique meant that he found runs hard to come by at Test level in recent seasons. Captain of Western Australia and vice-captain of Australia, a run of poor form cost him his Test place for the last game of the 1991–92 series against India. Although he has continued to make runs at first-class level, the Test recall has not come.

BATTING	M	Inn	NO	HS	Runs	Ave	100s	50s	C/S
Tests	50	93	7	138	2854	33.19	4	15	38
First-class	173	304	23	355*	11145	39.66	32	43	131

BOWLING	Runs	Wkts	Ave	BB	5wl	10wM
First-class	9	1	9.00	1/1	–	–

MARSH, Rodney William

WA, LHB/WK
Born: 11 November 1947
Armadale, Western Australia

Rod Marsh is Australia's most successful wicketkeeper-batsman. An aggressive left-hander who loved to attack the bowling, Marsh played many important innings at number seven, and his 'keeping improved from very ordinary beginnings to a point where he was recognised as one of the world's best. He was also a fine leader, and one of the disappointments of his career must be that he was never chosen to captain his country.

Selected against the West Indies in 1968–69 as a batsman, he made 104 on his first-class debut. In 1970–71 he made an ordinary Test debut against England, his unconvincing display behind the stumps earning him the tag of 'Iron Gloves'. Never one to give in, Marsh worked on his game and his fitness, and within two years had improved almost beyond recognition. He struck the ball hard and often in the middle order, while his solid build belied an incredible agility behind the stumps. He never missed a game from the time he was selected until he joined World Series Cricket in 1977, and his 'keeping to his friend Dennis Lillee and to the speed of Jeff Thomson often had to be seen to be believed.

After World Series, Marsh returned to Test cricket until his retirement in 1983–84. During this second stage of his career his batting was not as effective, but his 'keeping continued to improve. When his career ended no-one had as many Test dismissals. It should also be remembered that Marsh played this last part of his career with knee problems, which made 'keeping extremely painful. He still never missed a game.

There were many highlights in his long career. Against Pakistan in 1972–73 he became the first Australian 'keeper to make a Test century. His highest score, 132, was made against New Zealand in 1973–74, but probably his best innings was 110 not out in the Melbourne Centenary Test of 1977. Behind the stumps he holds the record number of dismissals in an Ashes series, and he also claimed 26 victims in the 1975–76 West Indies series. His ability as a 'keeper made all the bowling just that little bit more dangerous, but it is his work to Lillee that stays in the mind, and it is fitting that a grandstand at the WACA ground is named after them.

In 1991 Marsh was appointed Director of the national Cricket Academy, where he will develop the cream of Australia's cricketing talent. They could have no better example to follow.

BATTING	M	Inn	NO	HS	Runs	Ave	100s	50s	C/S
Tests	96	150	12	132	3633	26.51	3	16	343/12
First-class	244	379	37	236	10607	31.01	11	55	749/61

BOWLING	Balls	Runs	Wkts	Ave	BB	5wl	10wM
Tests	72	54	0	–	–	–	–
First-class	–	74	1	74.00	1/0	–	–

MARTIN, John Wesley

NSW, SA, LHB/SLC
Born: 28 July 1931
Wingham, New South Wales
Died: 16 July 1992
Burrell Creek, New South Wales

It is doubtful if New South Wales has produced a more popular player than Johnny Martin, who was known to all as 'the little favourite'. He was an all-rounder whose batting was typified by some of the biggest hits ever seen in Australia and whose left-arm wrist spin could defeat the finest of players. Coming from the small New South Wales town of Burrell Creek, Martin travelled to Sydney by train each week to play. He made his first-class debut in 1956–57, but moved to Adelaide in 1958–59 for one season. Martin made his Test debut against the West Indies at Melbourne in 1960–61, making 55 and taking three wickets in four balls; Kanhai, Sobers and Worrell. Despite this he was never sure of a Test place, although he toured England in 1964 and South Africa in 1966–67, before retiring to Burrell Creek at the end of the 1967–68 season. In later years he suffered from heart problems, and it was a heart attack which claimed his life a few days short of his sixty–first birthday.

BATTING	M	Inn	NO	HS	Runs	Ave	100s	50s	C/S
Tests	8	13	1	55	214	17.83	–	1	5
First-class	135	193	26	101	3970	23.77	1	21	114

BOWLING	Balls	Runs	Wkts	Ave	BB	5wI	10wM
Tests	1846	832	17	48.94	3/56	–	–
First-class	–	13872	445	31.17	8/97	17	1

MARTYN, Damien Richard

WA, RHB/OB
Born: 21 October 1971
Darwin, Northern Territory

A right-handed batsman of outstanding talent, Damien Martyn moved from a successful junior career into the WA team in 1990–91. He followed up a promising beginning with 822 runs at 51.37 in 1991–92. A century in each innings against Queensland began the next season, and ensured a place in the Test side for the West Indies series. After a promising 36 in his first innings, Martyn made a vital 67 not out in the second innings of the Melbourne Test to ensure an Australian victory. An eye injury, courtesy of an accidental knock from coach Bob Simpson, caused him to miss the fourth Test, but he returned to the side for the final match. Although the West Indies restricted his normal fluency, it is difficult not to imagine the youngster developing into a fine Test batsman as the years progress. His initial efforts were rewarded with a tour to New Zealand at the end of the 1992–93 Australian season. He responded well when called in for the third Test to replace the out of form Mark Waugh, making 74, an innings which helped ensure a trip to England in 1993. The batting power of the

Australians denied Martyn a Test in the Ashes series, but his time will surely come.

BATTING	M	Inn	NO	HS	Runs	Ave	100s	50s	C/S
Tests	5	9	1	74	244	30.50	–	2	1
First-class	43	70	12	139	3092	53.31	10	16	27/2

BOWLING	Balls	Runs	Wkts	Ave	BB	5wl	10wM
Tests	6	0	0	–	–	–	–
First-class	–	285	3	95.00	1/10	–	–

MASSIE, Hugh Hamon

NSW, RHB
Born: 11 April 1854
near Belfast (Port Fairy), Victoria
Died: 12 October 1938
Point Piper, New South Wales

HH Massie was a tall, big-hitting opening batsman who played nine Tests between 1881 and 1885. He made his first-class debut in 1877–78, was unavailable to tour England in 1880, but was a member of the 1882 team. He started the trip in sensational fashion, scoring 206 against Oxford University in his first innings. Massie passed 50 only once in Test cricket, in the second innings of the famous Ashes Test at The Oval. Opening the batting, he attacked on a difficult pitch and gave his side enough runs to win an immortal victory. Massie captained Australia in the third Test of the 1884–85 series and won a thrilling game by just six runs. Although he played many fine innings at first-class level, he failed to translate his obvious ability into Test cricket. His son, RJA Massie, an outstanding fast left-arm bowler, had his career destroyed when he was wounded in the First World War.

BATTING	M	Inn	NO	HS	Runs	Ave	100s	50s	C/S
Tests	9	16	0	55	249	15.56	–	1	5
First-class	64	113	5	206	2485	23.00	1	13	35

BOWLING	Runs	Wkts	Ave	BB	5wl	10wM
First-class	60	2	30.00	2/39	–	–

MASSIE, Robert Arnold Lockyer

WA, LHB/RFM
Born: 14 April 1947
Subiaco, Western Australia

Bob Massie, a right-arm fast-medium bowler from Western Australia, had the most sensational debut of any bowler in Test history. At Lord's in 1972 he took 8/84 and 8/53 to give Australia victory by eight wickets. Massie had made his first-class debut in 1965–66, but it was some good bowling against the Rest of the World XI in 1971–72, principally 7/76 at Sydney, which earned a trip to England. His swing bowling proved the perfect foil to Dennis Lillee's speed, and Australia seemed to have discovered a devastating bowling combination. However, Massie played only five more Tests in which he took 15 wickets. He toured the West Indies in 1973, but did not play in a Test. Suddenly the ability to swing the ball late, and the control that went with it, seemed to vanish and he faded quickly from the scene. These days he can be heard giving special comments on the ABC radio broadcast team.

BATTING	M	Inn	NO	HS	Runs	Ave	100s	50s	C/S
Tests	6	8	1	42	78	11.14	–	–	1
First-class	52	54	14	42	385	9.62	–	–	8

BOWLING	Balls	Runs	Wkts	Ave	BB	5wI	10wM
Tests	1739	647	31	20.87	8/53	2	1
First-class	–	4446	179	24.83	8/53	6	2

MATTHEWS, Christopher Darrell

WA, Tas, LHB/LFM
Born: 22 September 1962
Cunderdin, Western Australia

A big, left-arm fast bowler with an ungainly action, and a useful batsman, Chris Matthews has produced some outstanding performances in

177

first-class cricket, but has been unable to reproduce the same form at Test level. He played in two Tests against England in 1986–87 and one against the West Indies in 1988–89. In those games, the last one in particular, his bowling was so lacking in control that he appeared out of his depth. For Western Australia he proved to be a consistent wicket–taker, although injuries caused him to miss more games than he or the state would have liked. In 1991–92 he moved to Tasmania where he took over 50 wickets in his first season, breaking the island state's record. It seems unlikely that Matthews will play Test cricket again, but he remains one of the most feared bowlers in the Sheffield Shield, capable of producing the unplayable delivery when the batsman leasts expects it.

BATTING	M	Inn	NO	HS	Runs	Ave	100s	50s	C/S
Tests	3	5	0	32	54	10.80	–	–	1
First-class	83	106	16	71	1884	20.93	–	8	27

BOWLING	Balls	Runs	Wkts	Ave	BB	5wl	10wM
Tests	570	313	6	52.16	3/95	–	–
First-class	–	8623	348	24.78	8/101	22	–

MATTHEWS, Gregory Richard John

NSW, LHB/OB
Born: 15 December 1959
Newcastle, New South Wales

Greg Matthews, a determined left-handed batsman and off-spin bowler, appeared to have ended his Test career before making a dramatic come-back against England in 1990–91. Matthews made his Test debut against Pakistan at Melbourne in 1983–84, scoring 75. He toured the West Indies in 1983–84 and England in 1985 with little success, but 1985–86 was a golden year. At Madras he took 10 wickets in the match, including the vital final one off the second–last ball to tie the game. Before the season ended he scored three Test centuries, but within a year he was out of the side; lack of wickets and some disquiet with his rather unusual character were probably to blame. Australia's search for a spinner brought about his recall in 1990–91. He triumphed with the bat, averaging over 50 and saving his side on numerous occa-sions, but the wickets still proved elusive. He could not hold his place on the West Indies tour, but returned again to tour Sri Lanka in 1992. Again he batted well, saving the side's fragile top order with five half centuries in the three Tests. His bowling, too, looked a little more penetrative. Unfortunately, the West Indies' batsmen exposed his bowling weakness, and his place was again lost. With the emergence of Shane Warne and the return of Tim May it seems that Matthews' Test career may finally be at an end. His batting average remains a figure to be proud of, but his bowling at the highest level has been disappointing, considering his success for New South Wales.

BATTING	M	Inn	NO	HS	Runs	Ave	100s	50s	C/S
Tests	33	53	8	130	1849	41.09	4	12	17
First-class	156	228	39	184	7405	39.18	12	41	122

BOWLING	Balls	Runs	Wkts	Ave	BB	5wI	10wM
Tests	6271	2942	61	48.23	5/103	2	1
First-class	–	13197	413	31.95	8/52	18	4

MATTHEWS, Thomas James

Vic, RHB/LBG
Born: 3 April 1884
Williamstown, Victoria
Died: 14 October 1943
Caulfield, Victoria

Tommy Matthews was a Victorian leg-spin bowler who produced one amazing feat in Test cricket. Although he made his first-class debut in 1906–07, Matthews did not play his first Test until 1911–12 at Adelaide against England, where he made 53. Chosen to tour England for the 1912 Triangular Tournament, his moment came in the first Test against South Africa. After making 49 not out he ended the Springboks' first innings with a hat-trick, and when they followed on he took another in the second innings. Two hat-tricks in a day remains a unique achievement in Test cricket. At first-class level he was a very useful player for Victoria.

BATTING	M	Inn	NO	HS	Runs	Ave	100s	50s	C/S
Tests	8	10	1	53	153	17.00	–	1	7
First-class	67	99	13	93	2149	24.98	–	14	56

BOWLING	Balls	Runs	Wkts	Ave	BB	5wI	10wM
Tests	1081	419	16	26.18	4/29	–	–
First-class	–	4507	177	25.46	7/46	8	1

MAY, Timothy Brian Alexander

SA, RHB/OB
Born: 26 January 1962
North Adelaide, South Australia

A South Australian off spinner, Tim May seemed to have had his chances of a Test career ruined by injury. Overcoming the handicap of playing most of his cricket on a 'batsmen's paradise' at Adelaide, May bowled so well that he became the key member of the South Australian attack. With Australia searching for a quality slow bowler it was obvious that May would have his chance. Between 1987 and 1989 he played seven Tests, producing steady rather than spectacular results. However, just when it seemed a career was there for the taking, injury stepped in. First, his 1989 tour of England was ruined by a broken finger; then on a short tour of India in 1989–90 he suffered a serious knee injury which required an operation. On his return to Shield cricket, his movement was restricted and it seemed unlikely the selectors would risk him again. Poor form in 1991–92 even looked like removing him from the South Australian team. However, in 1992–93 May made a remarkable comeback, first to the one-day side and then to the Test team for the dramatic Adelaide Test against the West Indies. With 2/41 and an amazing 5/9 he gave Australia a winning chance, and when that looked lost at 7/74, chasing 186 to win, he stepped in and made a courageous 42 not out to get within a single run of victory. A finger injury sustained in that innings again removed him from the Test team, but he now has a chance to create what could still be an impressive career. A finger injury sustained in that innings again removed him from the team for the final Test, and for the short tour of New Zealand. May returned to the side for the second Test of the 1993 Ashes series. His bowling partnership with Shane Warne destroyed the English batsmen, and his strong performances suggest a dazzling career lies ahead of him.

BATTING	M	Inn	NO	HS	Runs	Ave	100s	50s	C/S
Tests	13	16	7	42*	161	17.89	–	–	3
First-class	106	127	37	128	1489	16.54	1	1	32

BOWLING	Balls	Runs	Wkts	Ave	BB	5wl	10wM
Tests	3790	537n	53	29.00n	5/9	2n	–
First-class	–	11548	331	34.89	7/93	12	–

MAYNE, Richard Edgar

SA, Vic, RHB
Born: 4 July 1882
Jamestown, South Australia
Died: 26 October 1961
Carrum, Victoria

Edgar Mayne was a capable right-handed batsman who did not show his true talent at Test level. He began his first-class career with South Australia in 1906–07. In 1912 he was chosen to tour England where he played his four Tests. After the First World War, Mayne moved to Victoria. He gained a place on the 1921 tour of England, but did not play in any of the Tests. There were no further opportunities at Test level, but against Queensland at Melbourne in 1923–24 Mayne scored 209 in a partnership of 456 with Bill Ponsford, at the time a record for all first-class cricket played in Australia. Mayne captained Victoria in his last season, 1924–25. During his career the competition for Test places was intense; in another period he may have played far more often.

BATTING	M	Inn	NO	HS	Runs	Ave	100s	50s	C/S
Tests	4	4	1	25*	64	21.33	–	–	2
First-class	141	243	10	209	7620	32.70	14	39	80

BOWLING	Balls	Runs	Wkts	Ave	BB	5wl	10wM
Tests	6	1	0	–	–	–	–
First-class	–	440	13	33.84	3/6	–	–

MAYNE, Lawrence Charles

WA, LHB/RFM
Born: 23 January 1942
Westonia, Western Australia

Laurie Mayne was a Western Australian fast-medium bowler who toured the West Indies in 1965 and India and South Africa in 1969–

181

70. After some steady performances for WA as Graham McKenzie's opening partner from 1961–62, Mayne's Test debut came at Sabina Park, Jamaica, in the first Test of the series. He bowled particularly well to take eight wickets, but could not repeat that form on the rest of the tour, or on his trip to India and South Africa, where a knee injury restricted him. The Springbok batsmen, Graeme Pollock and Barry Richards, were particularly severe on his bowling. Despite his lack of success at Test level, Mayne was a very useful first-class player.

BATTING	M	Inn	NO	HS	Runs	Ave	100s	50s	C/S
Tests	6	11	2	13	76	9.50	–	–	3
First-class	58	74	22	72	667	12.82	–	2	21

BOWLING	Balls	Runs	Wkts	Ave	BB	5wl	10wM
Tests	1251	628	19	33.05	4/43	–	–
First-class	–	6162	203	30.35	7/75	6	–

MECKIFF, Ian

Vic, RHB/LF
Born: 6 January 1935
Mentone, Victoria

Without doubt one of the most controversial figures in Australian cricket history, Ian Meckiff was a left-arm fast bowler with what many considered a suspect action. Meckiff made his Test debut against South Africa in 1957–58, but it was against England in 1958–59 that the controversy began. In that series he formed an effective opening partnership with another left-hander, Alan Davidson, and at Melbourne took 6/38 to dismiss England for 87. As argument raged about his action, he toured India and Pakistan in 1959–60 and played against the West Indies in 1960–61. With a remodelled action, Meckiff returned to the Australian team for the first Test of the 1963–64 series against South Africa. In his first over he was repeatedly no-balled by umpire Col Egar and never played again. Although he was under great strain throughout his career, the dignity with which Meckiff accepted the criticism of his action and his ultimate cricketing fate shows the extraordinary character of the man.

BATTING	M	Inn	NO	HS	Runs	Ave	100s	50s	C/S
Tests	18	20	7	45*	154	11.84	–	–	9
First-class	74	89	20	55	778	11.27	–	1	37

BOWLING	Balls	Runs	Wkts	Ave	BB	5wI	10wM
Tests	3734	1423	45	31.62	6/38	2	–
First-class	–	6282	269	23.35	6/29	12	1

MEULEMAN, Kenneth Douglas

Vic, WA, RHB/LBG
Born: 5 September 1923
Melbourne, Victoria

Ken Meuleman had the misfortune to have his cricket career coincide with those of Arthur Morris and Sid Barnes, two of Australia's finest opening batsmen. He made his debut for Victoria in 1945–46 and was chosen for the short tour of New Zealand, where he played his single Test. On a difficult wicket he failed to score in his only innings. In 1952–53 he moved to Western Australia, where he did much to establish that state in the Sheffield Shield. He averaged over 50 for them and his highest score of 234 not out was made against South Australia at Perth in 1956–57. Meuleman retired in 1960–61, leaving behind the record of a very fine player, a batsman unlucky not to have played far more Test cricket.

BATTING	M	Inn	NO	HS	Runs	Ave	100s	50s	C/S
Tests	1	1	0	0	0	0.00	–	–	1
First-class	117	184	19	234*	7855	47.60	22	41	35

BOWLING	Runs	Wkts	Ave	BB	5wI	10wM
First-class	956	19	50.31	3/7	–	–

MIDWINTER, William Evans

Vic, RHB/RMF(r)
Born: 19 June 1851
St Briavels, Forest of Dean, England
Died: 3 December 1890
Kew Asylum, Victoria

Billy Midwinter could claim to have had cricket's most unusual career, being the only man to have played for both England and Australia in Tests between the two countries. Born in England, Midwinter came to Australia at an early age and began his cricket here. He played in the first Test as an aggressive batsman and fast-medium round-arm bowler. Supposedly part of the 1878 team, he was abducted by WG Grace to play for Gloucestershire, for whom he had a birth qualification. Midwinter then became the first cricketer to commute between England and Australia, which he did for the next few seasons, and to the displeasure of many players and officials. He toured Australia with an English team in 1881–82, playing in four Tests, toured England with Australia in 1884 and ended his Test career for Australia in 1886–87. Midwinter died in Kew asylum, aged 39, following the deaths of his wife and children.

BATTING	M	Inn	NO	HS	Runs	Ave	100s	50s	C/S
Tests	8	14	1	37	174	13.38	–	–	5
First-class	160	264	27	137*	4497	18.97	3	12	123

BOWLING	Balls	Runs	Wkts	Ave	BB	5wI	10wM
Tests	949	333	14	23.78	5/78	1	–
First-class	–	7287	420	17.35	7/27	26	3

MILLER, Keith Ross

Vic, NSW, RHB/RF
Born: 28 November 1919
Sunshine, Victoria

Keith 'Nugget' Miller can rightly lay claim to being Australia's finest all-round cricketer. He was a magnificent batsman, always looking to get on with the game, a fast bowler of genius and a great slips fields-man. As a batsman, attack was his motto and he produced some of the biggest hits ever seen on the world's major grounds. His fast bowling could be as devastating as it was unpredictable, a blistering bouncer could be followed by a wrong 'un, and if he was a player of moods, his overall record remains one of great consistency. Given the chance, he would also have made an excellent Test captain. With his good looks, his long mane of hair and his extraordinary skills, he captivated cricket crowds for a decade.

Although he made his first-class debut for Victoria in 1937–38, it was not until after the war, in which he served as a Mosquito pilot, that he became known. Playing in the Victory Tests and then the Services side under Lindsay Hassett, it was obvious that a special talent had arrived. Miller settled in New South Wales following the 1946–47 season, after making his Test debut against New Zealand in 1945–46, with his friend and fellow fast bowler Ray Lindwall. It was against England at Brisbane in 1946–47 that he really arrived, making 79 and taking 7/60. Good performances in that series and against India next season took Miller to England in 1948 where he was a key member of Australia's best-ever team.

Initially not chosen to tour South Africa in 1949–50, he arrived as a late replacement and played an important part in the series. His Test place was never again questioned until he retired after the 1956 tour of England. Even on that final tour, when the years were starting to catch up with him, he took 5/72 and 5/80 to win the Lord's Test. Throughout his 55 Tests, Miller's record was good enough for him to gain selection as a batsman or bowler, and it is certain that he would have made many more runs if he had not been required to do so much bowling.

Miller led New South Wales with great flair and success for a number of seasons, but never captained Australia. In 1954 he was certainly favoured ahead of Ian Johnson for the job, but perhaps his personality and desire always to see cricket as a game to be enjoyed counted against him.

BATTING	M	Inn	NO	HS	Runs	Ave	100s	50s	C/S
Tests	55	87	7	147	2958	36.97	7	13	38
First-class	226	326	36	281*	14183	48.90	41	63	136

BOWLING	Balls	Runs	Wkts	Ave	BB	5wI	10wM
Tests	10461	3906	170	22.97	7/60	7	1
First-class	–	11087	497	22.30	7/12	16	1

MINNETT, Roy Baldwin

NSW, RHB
Born: 13 June 1888
St Leonards, New South Wales
Died: 21 October 1955
Manly, New South Wales

Roy Minnett was a right-handed batsman for New South Wales and Australia in the period before the First World War. He made his first-class debut in 1906–07, the youngest of three brothers to play for the state. Minnett scored 90 in his first Test innings, against England at Sydney in the first match of the 1911–12 series. He also made half centuries in the fourth and fifth Tests to gain selection for the 1912 tour of England. He played his other four Tests during that tour, but had little success. For a player of such obvious ability it is surprising that he made only two first-class centuries, the highest of which was 216 not out against Victoria at Sydney, in his best season, 1911–12.

BATTING	M	Inn	NO	HS	Runs	Ave	100s	50s	C/S
Tests	9	15	0	90	391	26.06	–	3	–
First-class	55	85	9	216*	2203	28.98	2	12	18

BOWLING	Balls	Runs	Wkts	Ave	BB	5wl	10wM
Tests	589	290	11	26.36	4/34	–	–
First-class	–	2152	86	25.02	8/50	3	1

MISSON, Francis Michael

NSW, RHB/RFM
Born: 19 November 1938
Darlinghurst, New South Wales

Frank Misson was a right-arm fast-medium bowler who made his debut for New South Wales in 1958–59. Selected to play in the second Test

186

of the 1960–61 series against the West Indies he dismissed opener Conrad Hunte with his second ball, but took only one other wicket in the game. He missed the next match, but played in the last two, recording his best figures of 4/58 in the fifth Test at Melbourne. Misson was taken to England in 1961 and played in the first two Tests. Thereafter Graham McKenzie took over, and Misson was unable to win back his place. During that tour, Misson and Victorian Bill Lawry produced a series of practical jokes that had all team members, and captain Richie Benaud (whose shoes were once nailed to the floor) wondering what was coming next. Misson continued to play for New South Wales until 1963–64.

BATTING	M	Inn	NO	HS	Runs	Ave	100s	50s	C/S
Tests	5	5	3	25*	38	19.00	–	–	6
First-class	71	77	17	51*	1052	17.53	–	2	58

BOWLING	Balls	Runs	Wkts	Ave	BB	5wl	10wM
Tests	1197	616	16	38.50	4/58	–	–
First-class	–	5511	177	31.13	6/75	1	–

MOODY, Thomas Masson

WA, RHB/RM
Born: 2 October 1965
Adelaide, South Australia

A tall Western Australian batsman and useful medium pace bowler, Tom Moody has been on the fringe of Test selection for a number of seasons without establishing himself in the side. In form he is a destroyer of bowling, using his great height and reach to drive the ball with incredible power. Moody was selected for a number of Australian tours, including the 1989 tour of England, before he made his Test debut at Perth in 1989–90 against New Zealand. He made a half century in his first game and 106 in his second, against Sri Lanka in Brisbane, but soon found himself out of the side. A question mark over his ability to deal with short–pitched fast bowling was probably the main factor. He has slaughtered English county bowlers, once making a century in 26 minutes, albeit against fairly friendly bowling. At Sydney in 1990–

91, he hit leg-spinner Adrian Tucker for 30 runs in one over, an Australian record. Moody finally won his Test place back, for the fifth Test against India at Perth in 1991–92, and scored 50 and 101. He had a poor tour of Sri Lanka, where he was used as an opening batsman, and on returning to Australia his form so deserted him that he was unable to push for a recall.

BATTING	M	Inn	NO	HS	Runs	Ave	100s	50s	C/S
Tests	8	14	0	106	456	32.57	2	3	9
First-class	146	243	19	210	10227	45.66	32	44	122

BOWLING	Balls	Runs	Wkts	Ave	BB	5wl	10wM
Tests	432	147	2	73.50	1/17	–	–
First-class	–	2716	82	33.30	7/43	1	1

MORONEY, John

NSW, RHB
Born: 24 July 1919
Randwick, New South Wales

Opening batsman 'Jack' Moroney could be considered unlucky to play in only seven Tests. He made his first-class debut for New South Wales in 1945–46, and a good season in 1948–49 gained him a trip to South Africa in 1949–50. With Sid Barnes out of the side, Moroney opened with Arthur Morris and made nearly 1500 runs on the tour, including 118 and 101 not out in the fourth Test. However, he made a pair in the first Test against England in 1950–51 and was dropped. He played only one more Test, against the West Indies in 1951–52. While he was not a spectacular strokeplayer or a great fieldsman, he could hit hard when in top form. Moroney's dogged approach to batting produced an enviable first-class record.

BATTING	M	Inn	NO	HS	Runs	Ave	100s	50s	C/S
Tests	7	12	1	118	383	34.81	2	1	–
First-class	57	93	16	217	4023	52.24	12	22	19/1

BOWLING	Runs	Wkts	Ave	BB	5wl	10wM
First-class	15	0	–	–	–	–

MORRIS, Arthur Robert

NSW, LHB/SLC
Born: 19 January 1922
Dungog, New South Wales

Left-handed Arthur Morris was one of Australia's finest opening batsmen, and he was a key member of the country's Test sides for nearly a decade after the Second World War. A player who possessed an excellent technique, enabling him to adapt to all conditions, Morris also had plenty of attacking strokes and was a ferocious player of the hook shot. He batted his side out of many a crisis, setting up numerous victories along the way.

Morris had a sensational first-class debut for New South Wales when he made 148 and 111 in season 1940–41. He made this something of a habit, later scoring centuries on his first appearances in England, South Africa and the West Indies. The war interrupted any further cricketing plans, and it was 1946–47 before he could return to first-class cricket.

After scoring well in the early part of the season, he was chosen for the first Test against England. Morris made 155 in the third Test, and a century in each innings of the fourth, forming an excellent opening partnership with Sid Barnes during the series. On the 1948 tour of England he finished on top of the averages, with 696 runs at 87 in the series, including 182 at Leeds and 196 at The Oval, and scored just under 2000 runs on the tour.

Morris toured South Africa successfully in 1949–50, and became vice-captain of Australia and captain of New South Wales. He captained Australia twice in Tests: against the West Indies at Adelaide in 1951–52 and against England at Sydney in 1954–55. Neither was a success as Australia lost both games. In his later series against England, 1950–51 and 1953, Alec Bedser devised a leg trap which reduced Morris' scoring capacity and dismissed him cheaply on a number of occasions, and like all Australian batsmen, he struggled against the extreme speed of Frank Tyson in 1954–55. Despite that, eight of his twelve centuries were made against England.

Morris' last tour was to the West Indies in 1955, where he averaged over 50, scoring his last Test century at Trinidad. He retired from cricket after that trip when his wife contracted cancer, from which she subsequently died at the age of 33. He remarried some years later, and even returned to cricket in 1963 when he played in India with a Commonwealth side. Even at 41 he was still able to exhibit considerable skill.

BATTING	M	Inn	NO	HS	Runs	Ave	100s	50s	C/S
Tests	46	79	3	206	3533	46.86	12	12	15
First-class	162	250	15	290	12614	53.67	46	46	73

BOWLING	Balls	Runs	Wkts	Ave	BB	5wI	10wM
Tests	111	50	2	25.00	1/5	–	–
First-class	–	592	12	49.33	3/36	–	–

MORRIS, Samuel

Vic, RHB/RM
Born: 22 June 1855
Hobart, Tasmania
Died: 20 September 1931
Albert Park, Victoria

Sam Morris was the first black man to represent Australia in Test cricket. He was not an aborigine, but was born in Hobart of West Indian parents who had come in search of gold. Morris moved to Victoria at a young age where he learned his cricket in the Daylesford area. He made his debut in 1881–82, a selection no doubt prompted by an innings of 280 for Richmond against St Kilda, believed to be the first double century scored by a black player. Morris' only Test was at Melbourne in 1884–85 when the selectors were forced to choose an entirely new team after a dispute over money. Morris' right-handed batting and medium pace bowling were not greatly successful, but his fielding thrilled the crowd. He was a useful player at first-class level and a very good grade cricketer. Morris became curator, first at Richmond, then at Carlton and finally at Melbourne University until he lost his eyesight. Blindness did not stop him from attending matches, and in 1930–31, shortly before his death, he had the pleasure of meeting Learie Constantine and the first West Indian team when they toured Australia.

BATTING	M	Inn	NO	HS	Runs	Ave	100s	50s	C/S
Tests	1	2	1	10*	14	14.00	–	–	–
First-class	21	39	5	64*	623	18.32	–	5	13

BOWLING	Balls	Runs	Wkts	Ave	BB	5wI	10wM
Tests	136	73	2	36.50	2/73	–	–
First-class	–	809	31	26.09	5/21	1	–

MOSES, Henry

NSW, LHB/RAB
Born: 13 February 1858
Windsor, New South Wales
Died: 7 December 1938
Strathfield, New South Wales

'Harry' Moses was a very good left-handed batsman who never produced the runs at Test level to match his first-class form. He made his first-class debut in 1881–82 and played his first Test against England at Sydney in 1886–87. By making 31 and 24 he top scored in both innings. Business prevented him touring England, but he played in every home Test until a leg injury sustained in the first match of the 1891–92 series forced him out of the side. For New South Wales he was a brilliant player, with an excellent defence and a very good technique on damaged pitches, of which there were plenty at the time. His highest score, a monumental 297 not out, was made against England for New South Wales in 1887–88, and his first-class average is an outstanding one for the period.

BATTING	M	Inn	NO	HS	Runs	Ave	100s	50s	C/S
Tests	6	10	0	33	198	19.80	–	–	1
First-class	48	89	8	297*	2898	35.77	4	15	25

BOWLING	Runs	Wkts	Ave	BB	5wl	10wM
First-class	52	1	52.00	1/19	–	–

MOSS, Jeffrey Kenneth

Vic, LHB
Born: 29 June 1947
Melbourne, Victoria

Jeff Moss was a much under–rated Victorian left-handed batsman. He favoured an aggressive approach to the game and was unlucky not to have played in more Tests. Moss made his first-class debut in 1976–77, and some good form in 1978–79, including his highest score of 220 against South Australia, saw him chosen for the second Test against Pakistan, in Perth. With scores of 22 and 38 not out in a winning side, he was well worth his place. Moss played in the 1979 World Cup, but after the settlement with World Series Cricket, he was not chosen again. He continued to make runs for Victoria, including another double century in a record partnership of 390 with Julien Wiener in 1981–82. Unbelievably, Victoria dispensed with his services a couple of games later, when he was still in form and with plenty of runs left in him.

BATTING	M	Inn	NO	HS	Runs	Ave	100s	50s	C/S
Tests	1	2	1	38*	60	60.00	–	–	–
First-class	51	86	8	220	3416	43.79	9	14	33

BOWLING	Runs	Wkts	Ave	BB	5wl	10wM
First-class	43	0	–	–	–	–

MOULE, William Henry

Vic, RHB/RM
Born: 31 January 1858
Brighton, Victoria
Died: 24 August 1939
St Kilda, Victoria

Moule was a right-handed batsman and medium paced bowler who made his first-class debut for Victoria in 1878–79. Despite demonstrating nothing in the way of good form, he was chosen to tour England in 1880. He played little cricket and his selection to play in the only Test, at the Oval, must be viewed as a fortunate one. Despite this, he did not perform too badly, taking 3/23 and scoring 34 of a last-wicket partnership of 88 with his captain Murdoch, a stand which avoided an innings defeat. He played very little cricket after the tour, as he became a prominent member of the legal profession and later a judge. He was also the last survivor of the first Australian Test team to play in England.

BATTING	M	Inn	NO	HS	Runs	Ave	100s	50s	C/S
Tests	1	2	0	34	40	20.00	–	–	1
First-class	9	15	3	34	137	11.41	–	–	7

BOWLING	Balls	Runs	Wkts	Ave	BB	5wl	10wM
Tests	51	23	3	7.66	3/23	–	–
First-class	–	106	5	21.20	3/23	–	–

MURDOCH, William Lloyd

NSW, RHB/WK
Born: 18 October 1854
Sandhurst, Victoria
Died: 18 February 1911
Melbourne, Victoria

Billy Murdoch was the first great Australian batsman, a player of immense concentration, quick footwork and attractive cuts and drives. According to reports, he also specialised in the under-the-leg stroke, a leg glance played under the batsman's raised leg. In addition to his batting, Murdoch was a respected leader, captaining Australia on four of his five tours of England, winning five and losing seven of his 16 games in charge.

Murdoch began his career as a wicketkeeper, and he must have been quite useful as Fred Spofforth refused to play in the first Test in 1877 unless he was behind the stumps. The selectors were unmoved and gave the job to the Victorian Jack Blackham. However, Spofforth played in the next Test, and Murdoch soon gave 'keeping away to concentrate on his batting. He toured England for the first time in 1878, but with little success. He made up for it on his next four tours: 1880, 1882, 1884 and 1890, when he topped the batting averages on every occasion. At The Oval in 1880 he scored 153 not out, beating WG Grace's score by a run and denying England an innings win. In 1882 he captained Australia to victory in the Ashes Test and at The Oval in 1884 he made 211, the first double century in Test cricket.

At first-class level, his innings of 321 for New South Wales against Victoria at Sydney in 1881–82 was the highest score made in Australia and remained so for some time. It was the controversial run out of the hero Murdoch which drove the Sydney crowd to riot against Lord Harris's English team at Sydney in 1878–79; the worst crowd disturbance in Australian cricket history.

Murdoch returned after a six-year absence to lead Australia to England in 1890 and was the side's best batsman, but was replaced after the tour because at 36 he was thought to be too old. He proved the experts wrong by moving to England, where he captained Sussex for a number of years, then played for London County with his old friend WG Grace. Murdoch even represented England in one Test against South Africa in 1891–92 and made his last century at the age of 49.

A popular and amusing man, Murdoch collapsed and died while watching Australia play South Africa in a Test at Melbourne.

BATTING	M	Inn	NO	HS	Runs	Ave	100s	50s	C/S
Tests	18	33	5	211	896	32.00	2	1	13/1
First-class	391	679	48	321	16953	26.86	19	85	218/25

BOWLING	Runs	Wkts	Ave	BB	5wl	10wM
First-class	430	10	43.00	2/11	–	–

MUSGROVE, Henry Alfred

Vic, RHB
Born: 27 November 1860
Surbiton, Surrey, England
Died: 2 November 1931
Darlinghurst, New South Wales

Musgrove, a right-handed batsman who made his debut in 1881–82, was another player whose only Test was the controversial second game of the 1884–85 series when the entire Australian team refused to play. The selectors chose a new team, one of whom was Musgrove. He owed his selection to a century made against the Englishmen in a game at Ballarat. His Test appearance was a failure, and apart from one innings of 62, for the Non–Smokers against the Smokers in a total of 803 in 1886–87, his first-class career is a poor one. In addition to his Test match, Musgrove played four games for Victoria and took the field twice on the 1896 tour of England, which he managed. In later life Musgrove became famous as a partner of JC Williamson, the theatrical entrepreneur.

BATTING	M	Inn	NO	HS	Runs	Ave	100s	50s	C/S
Tests	1	2	0	9	13	6.50	–	–	–
First-class	7	12	0	62	99	8.25	–	1	3

BOWLING	Runs	Wkts	Ave	BB	5wl	10wM
First-class	18	0	–	–	–	–

NAGEL, Lisle Ernest

Vic, RHB/RFM
Born: 6 March 1905
Bendigo, Victoria
Died: 23 November 1971
Mornington, Victoria

Lisle Nagel was a six foot six inch, fast-medium bowler from Victoria, who swung the ball considerably and gained disconcerting bounce from his great height. He made his first-class debut in 1927–28 and earned his Test selection with a performance of 8/32 for an Australian XI against England at Melbourne in 1932–33. In bowling the Englishmen out for 60, Nagel ensured a place for the first Test of the Bodyline series. He could not repeat the effort and was not chosen again. Nagel's one tour was to India with an Australian team in 1935–36, where he bowled well despite injury and inhospitable pitches. Nagel's twin brother Vernon also played for Victoria.

BATTING	M	Inn	NO	HS	Runs	Ave	100s	50s	C/S
Tests	1	2	1	21*	21	21.00	–	–	–
First-class	26	39	6	44	407	12.33	–	–	12

BOWLING	Balls	Runs	Wkts	Ave	BB	5wI	10wM
Tests	262	110	2	55.00	2/110	–	–
First-class	–	1900	67	28.35	8/32	3	–

NASH, Laurence John

Tas, Vic, RHB/RF
Born: 2 May 1910
Fitzroy, Victoria
Died: 24 July 1986
Heidelberg, Victoria

Laurie Nash was a talented all-rounder who could have made many more Test appearances if he had possessed a less abrasive personality. Although he was born in Melbourne, Nash grew up in Tasmania, developing into a fast bowler with an ungainly action and a batsman of great determination, if little style. He made his first-class debut in 1929–30, but it was at Hobart against South Africa in 1931–32 that he bowled himself into the Test team by taking 7/50. Playing in the fifth Test he took 4/18 and 1/4 as the Springboks were bowled out for 36 and 45. In 1932 he moved to Victoria to play Australian Rules football, a game in which he is regarded as an all–time great, and played only grade cricket. In 1936–37 he re–emerged to take 4/37 for Victoria against the English side, in his only game for the state. That performance earned him a place in the fifth Test team, and he took 4/70 as Australia retained the Ashes. With Australia searching for a fast bowler throughout the thirties, Nash could have been the answer.

BATTING	M	Inn	NO	HS	Runs	Ave	100s	50s	C/S
Tests	2	2	0	17	30	15.00	–	–	6
First-class	22	36	2	110	953	28.02	1	5	19

BOWLING	Balls	Runs	Wkts	Ave	BB	5wI	10wM
Tests	311	126	10	12.60	4/18	–	–
First-class	–	1955	69	28.33	7/50	3	–

NITSCHKE, Holmesdale Carl

SA, LHB
Born: 14 April 1905
Adelaide, South Australia
Died: 29 September 1982
Adelaide, South Australia

'Slinger' Nitschke was an aggressive South Australian opening batsman and fine fieldsman. He had the misfortune to have his career coincide with the likes of Woodfull and Ponsford, which restricted him to just two Tests, both of them as a middle-order batsman. Nitschke made his first-class debut in 1929–30. He had a good season in 1930–31, making 830 runs at 55.33, and this certainly contributed to his Test selection for the first two games of the 1931–32 series against South Africa. Forced to bat out of position he achieved little, his best effort being 47 in the second Test. Perhaps he should have been given another chance. Although that never happened, Nitschke did play some excellent cricket for South Australia, scoring nine centuries in a career that lasted until 1934–35. In later life he became a racehorse breeder; his horses winning a number of important races.

BATTING	M	Inn	NO	HS	Runs	Ave	100s	50s	C/S
Tests	2	2	0	47	53	26.50	–	–	3
First-class	45	82	3	172	3320	42.02	9	16	22

BOWLING	Runs	Wkts	Ave	BB	5wl	10wM
First-class	27	0	–	–	–	–

NOBLE, Montague Alfred

NSW, RHB/RM, OB
Born: 28 January 1873
Sydney, New South Wales
Died: 22 June 1940
Randwick, New South Wales

Monty Noble was a top flight all-rounder who bowled a mixture of off spin and medium pace, batted soundly in the middle order and was an extremely capable captain. His unusual grip enabled him to curve the ball in flight, making him a far more difficult proposition than most off spinners of the time. He made his first-class debut for New South Wales in 1893–94, but took a few seasons to establish himself in the side. Once this was done, the tall all-rounder graduated to Test cricket in 1897–98 against England, playing in four of the five Tests.

Noble toured England for the first time in 1899 and made a century in his first innings. Twice he batted in a stubborn, defensive manner in order to save two of the Tests. On his second tour, in 1902, he made his highest score, 284 against Sussex at Hove. This, plus four successive hundreds for New South Wales, showed that he had the strokes when required. Noble's only Test century, 133, was made against England at Sydney in 1903–04. His best bowling display had come in the previous Australian series, 1901–02, when he took 7/17 to dismiss England for 66. He captured a further six wickets in the second innings.

After touring England in 1905, Noble inherited the Australian captaincy when Joe Darling retired at the end of that trip. He successfully led Australia to a 4–1 victory against England in 1907–08 and again in England on the 1909 tour, when the series was won 2–1 after losing the first Test. He retired from Test cricket after that tour, but continued to play for New South Wales for a number of years, his final appearance coming in 1919–20.

He was a stickler for the conventions of the game and possessed a great knowledge of cricket. Tactically he was very sound, and when it came to analysing technique there was no-one better. In addition to his career in dentistry, he found time to write and comment on the game. His book, *The Game's the Thing*, is a classic, and in it his analysis of friend and team mate Victor Trumper is probably the finest piece ever written on that great batsman. Noble even found time to be involved in the first synthetic radio broadcasts. To have a grandstand at the SCG named after him is a fitting tribute to his contribution to cricket.

BATTING	M	Inn	NO	HS	Runs	Ave	100s	50s	C/S
Tests	42	73	7	133	1997	30.25	1	16	26
First-class	248	377	34	284	13975	40.74	37	66	191

BOWLING	Balls	Runs	Wkts	Ave	BB	5wl	10wM
Tests	7159	3025	121	25.00	7/17	9	2
First-class	–	14445	625	23.11	8/48	33	7

NOBLET, Geffery

SA, RHB/RFM
Born: 14 September 1916
Adelaide, South Australia

Noblet was a tall, South Australian fast-medium bowler who could swing the ball either way, and deliver a useful slower ball with an off-spin grip. He delivered the ball with an unusual action which caused some eyebrows to be raised, but he was never called for throwing. Some good performances at first-class level saw Noblet chosen to tour

South Africa in 1949–50, where he made his debut in the fifth Test. His only other games were the third Test against the West Indies in 1951–52 and the fifth Test against South Africa in 1952–53. He was certainly unlucky to have his career coincide with those of Lindwall, Miller and Bill Johnston, a fact which probably cost him a number of matches. After his playing days were over Noblet became a prominent administrator with the South Australian Cricket Association.

BATTING	M	Inn	NO	HS	Runs	Ave	100s	50s	C/S
Tests	3	4	1	13*	22	7.33	–	–	1
First-class	71	99	29	55*	975	13.92	–	2	44

BOWLING	Balls	Runs	Wkts	Ave	BB	5wI	10wM
Tests	774	183	7	26.14	3/21	–	–
First-class	–	5432	282	19.26	7/29	13	2

NOTHLING, Otto Ernest

NSW, Qld, RHB/RFM
Born: 1 August 1900
Teutoburg, Queensland
Died: 26 September 1965
Chelmer, Queensland

A big, hard-hitting batsman and medium-pace bowler, Otto Nothling made his first-class debut for New South Wales in 1922–23, but moved to Queensland in 1927–28, where he played an important role in that state's first seasons in the Sheffield Shield. Nothling made his only Test appearance at Sydney in the second Test of the 1928–29 series against England. Although he failed to take a wicket he did make 44 in Australia's second innings, but England won the match by eight wickets. Nothling's only century came against New South Wales at Sydney in 1929–30, and he captained his state on three occasions. After his playing days he became a prominent administrator, ending his career as president of the Queensland Cricket Association.

BATTING	M	Inn	NO	HS	Runs	Ave	100s	50s	C/S
Tests	1	2	0	44	52	26.00	–	–	–
First-class	21	38	2	121	882	24.50	1	6	15

BOWLING	Balls	Runs	Wkts	Ave	BB	5wI	10wM
Tests	276	72	0	–	–	–	–
First-class	–	1478	36	41.05	5/39	2	–

O'BRIEN, Leo Patrick Joseph

Vic, LHB/RM
Born: 2 July 1907
West Melbourne, Victoria

Leo O'Brien was a left-handed Victorian batsman who played five Tests between 1932 and 1936. He made his first-class debut in 1929–30, and played his first Test in the second game of the Bodyline series. It was thought that his technique and courage, in addition to being left-handed, might enable him to cope with the English pace attack, but he made only 10 and 11. He returned to make his highest score in the fifth Test, his only other game in that series, when he compiled a brave 61. O'Brien missed the tour to England in 1934, but did go to South Africa in 1935–36, where he made 59 and 48 in the last two Tests. A failure in the second game of the 1936–37 series against England was his last opportunity at Test level.

BATTING	M	Inn	NO	HS	Runs	Ave	100s	50s	C/S
Tests	5	8	0	61	211	26.37	–	2	3
First-class	61	97	7	173	3303	36.70	7	16	24

BOWLING	Runs	Wkts	Ave	BB	5wl	10wM
First-class	127	3	42.33	1/3	–	–

O'CONNOR, John Denis Alphonsus

NSW, SA, LHB/RM
Born: 9 September 1875
Burrowa, New South Wales
Died: 23 August 1941
Lewisham, New South Wales

O'Connor was a medium pace bowler for New South Wales and South Australia in the first decade of this century. Although he made his first-class debut in 1904–05, he won his way into the Test team after some good performances with South Australia, for whom he started playing in 1906–07. O'Connor played his first Test against England at Adelaide in 1907–08, taking eight wickets in the match, including 5/40 in the second innings. He did very little in two other games of that series, but was selected to tour England in 1909. He played only the first Test, but produced some useful bowling in the minor games. Despite his failure to establish a place in Test cricket, O'Connor proved an excellent bowler at first-class level, with a best of 7/36 against Victoria at Melbourne in 1908–09.

BATTING	M	Inn	NO	HS	Runs	Ave	100s	50s	C/S
Tests	4	8	1	20	86	12.28	–	–	3
First-class	50	77	18	54	695	11.77	–	2	32

BOWLING	Balls	Runs	Wkts	Ave	BB	5wI	10wM
Tests	692	340	13	26.15	5/40	1	–
First-class	–	5255	224	23.45	7/36	18	5

O'DONNELL, Simon Patrick

Vic, RHB/RFM
Born: 26 January 1963
Deniliquin, New South Wales

Simon O'Donnell has shown himself to be a man of great personal courage as well as a very fine all-round cricketer. A hard–hitting batsman and useful medium pace bowler, O'Donnell gained selection for the 1985 tour of England, where he made his Test debut. While he played some useful innings, his bowling was largely ineffective. In subsequent seasons he created a reputation as a valuable one-day player. After being a vital member of Australia's 1987 World Cup-winning side, O'Donnell was diagnosed as having cancer. In a remarkable fightback he beat the disease, won his way back into the Australian one-day team and was given the captaincy of Victoria. While he was unable to reclaim a Test place, O'Donnell became one of the world's best one-day players, able to turn a game with some huge hitting or tight bowling. He was a surprise winner of the International Cricketer of the Year Award in 1990–91, a season in which he also led Victoria to the Sheffield Shield. An injury early in 1991–92 cost him his place in the one-day team, and so far, he has been unable to get it back.

BATTING	M	Inn	NO	HS	Runs	Ave	100s	50s	C/S
Tests	6	10	3	48	206	29.42	–	–	4
First-class	83	133	16	130	4603	39.34	7	31	60

BOWLING	Balls	Runs	Wkts	Ave	BB	5wl	10wM
Tests	940	504	6	84.00	3/37	–	–
First-class	–	5642	151	37.36	6/54	2	–

OGILVIE, Alan David

Qld, RHB
Born: 3 June 1951
Southport, Queensland

David Ogilvie was a right-handed batsman who had one spectacular season for Queensland, which he was sadly unable to repeat. Ogilvie set Australia alight in 1977–78 when he made 1215 runs at 50.62 in first-class cricket. In the initial season of World Series Cricket it was natural that he would be given a chance. He was selected in the first three Tests against India in 1977–78 and later that season toured the West Indies, where he played a further two Tests. While he usually managed to get a start, he was out too often when it seemed he should have gone on to a big score. Apart from that one season, when he scored six of his eight centuries, Ogilvie did little. A blow on the head from a Bob Willis bouncer in 1978–79 may also have damaged his confidence against the quicker bowlers, and he soon faded from the scene.

BATTING	M	Inn	NO	HS	Runs	Ave	100s	50s	C/S
Tests	5	10	0	47	178	17.80	–	–	5
First-class	51	93	5	194	3006	34.15	8	10	44

BOWLING	Runs	Wkts	Ave	BB	5wI	10wM	
First-class	4	0	–	–	–	–	

O'KEEFFE, Kerry James

NSW, RHB/LBG
Born: 25 November 1949
Hurstville, New South Wales

Kerry O'Keeffe was a useful right-handed batsman and a talented leg-break bowler who gave Australia good service in 24 Tests without producing any spectacular performances. The tall, fair–haired O'Keeffe made his first-class debut in 1968–69 and played in two of the final three Tests of the 1970–71 series against England. Two seasons in county cricket with Somerset helped win him a place on the 1973 tour of the West Indies. Over the next few seasons he was in and out of the Australian side. His best bowling of 5/101 was taken against New Zealand in 1976–77 and his highest score of 85 was also made against the Kiwis, at Adelaide in 1973–74. O'Keeffe's last Tests were played on tour in England in 1977, where he finished second in the first-class averages. He joined World Series Cricket and retired after the 1979–80 season.

BATTING	M	Inn	NO	HS	Runs	Ave	100s	50s	C/S
Tests	24	34	9	85	644	25.76	–	1	15
First-class	169	233	73	99*	4169	26.05	–	13	113

BOWLING	Balls	Runs	Wkts	Ave	BB	5wI	10wM
Tests	5384	2018	53	38.07	5/101	1	–
First-class	–	13382	476	28.11	7/38	24	5

OLDFIELD, William Albert Stanley

NSW, RHB/WK
Born: 9 September 1894
Alexandria, New South Wales
Died: 10 August 1976
Killara, New South Wales

Bert Oldfield was Australia's wicketkeeper for the greater part of the period between the wars. He was a small man whose 'keeping was typified by its neatness and excellent footwork. Oldfield's fame rests on his work to Australian spinners such as Grimmett, O'Reilly and Mailey. Each was a unique bowler, providing special challenges for a 'keeper, yet Oldfield mastered them all, and his 52 stumpings are a record in Test cricket. He came to prominence with the AIF team in 1919, and moved to Test cricket in 1920–21, touring England in 1921. For those two seasons he shared the job with Hanson Carter, but when Carter retired after the English tour Oldfield took over. He held the position until he missed selection on the tour to England in 1938, visiting England in 1926, 1930 and 1934, and South Africa in 1935–36. It was obvious on this last tour that his work was slipping, particularly to the left-arm spin of Fleetwood–Smith, and it was perhaps surprising that he retained the position for the 1936–37 series against England. Oldfield was the unfortunate player to be hit by Harold Larwood in the third Test of the 1932–33 Bodyline series, suffering a fractured skull. Despite that, he was a capable batsman. At his peak, which lasted a considerable time, Australia can have had few better 'keepers.

BATTING	M	Inn	NO	HS	Runs	Ave	100s	50s	C/S
Tests	54	80	17	65*	1427	22.65	–	4	78/52
First-class	245	315	57	137	6135	23.77	6	21	399/262

O'NEILL, Norman Clifford

NSW, RHB/RM, LBG
Born: 19 February 1937
Carlton, New South Wales

Norm O'Neill was an aggressive right-handed batsman who possessed all the strokes, most of which he hit with crashing power. He was also a brilliant fieldsman and a useful leg-spin bowler. O'Neill had a stunning debut season in first-class cricket, scoring over 1000 runs in 1957–58 while the Test team was touring South Africa. In 1958–59 further good form ensured he would make his Test debut, which he duly did against England at Brisbane, scoring 71 not out in the second innings. He hit three Test centuries on the 1959–60 tour of India and Pakistan, and his highest first-class score came on that tour. O'Neill's best Test performance of 181 was made against the West Indies at Brisbane in the Tied Test of 1960–61. On the first of his English tours, in 1961, he was in excellent form with 1981 runs at 60.03. He was not the same force in 1964, but still managed 1369 runs at 45.63. As his career wore on he became something of a poor starter, leading to the nickname 'Nervous Norm'. But once the initial period was survived, all the strokes were still there. O'Neill's last Tests were played on tour in the West Indies in 1965. He missed selection against England in 1965–66 and to South Africa next season. His form was still good, as he topped the Sheffield Shield aggregates in the latter season and toured New Zealand with an Australian 'B' team. O'Neill's son, Mark, was a successful all-rounder for Western Australia and New South Wales for a number of seasons.

BATTING	M	Inn	NO	HS	Runs	Ave	100s	50s	C/S
Tests	42	69	8	181	2779	45.55	6	15	21
First-class	188	306	34	284	13859	50.95	45	63	104

BOWLING	Balls	Runs	Wkts	Ave	BB	5wl	10wM
Tests	1392	667	17	39.23	4/41	–	–
First-class	–	4060	99	41.01	4/40	–	–

O'Reilly, William Joseph

NSW, LHB/LBG
Born: 20 December 1905
White Cliffs, New South Wales
Died: 6 October 1992
Sutherland, New South Wales

Bill 'Tiger' O'Reilly was one of cricket's greatest bowlers. In fact, no less an authority than Sir Donald Bradman has repeatedly insisted that O'Reilly was the best bowler he ever saw. A tall, aggressive character, he charged up to the wicket and bowled his leg spinners, top spinners and wrong 'uns at a brisk medium pace. Although he did not gain great spin, he seemed always able to extract something from the wicket, and the pace and bounce of his bowling was a constant threat. If there was anything in the pitch, he could be lethal. Despite the pace at which he bowled and the effort that went into every delivery, O'Reilly could keep going for long spells without ever losing control. He was also his own man; efforts to change his bowling were quietly, but firmly, resisted. No less a person than Arthur Mailey told O'Reilly to change his grip, but the young man insisted he would do things his way.

Born in the country, O'Reilly had his first opportunity to play grade cricket when he came to Sydney to complete his education, but a series of outback teaching appointments delayed his chances in first-class cricket. He had played for New South Wales in 1927–28, but made no real impact until 1931–32, when he gained selection for the last two Tests against South Africa. O'Reilly really emerged as a force in the 1932–33 Bodyline series, taking 27 wickets at 26.81, including 10 in the Melbourne Test, Australia's only win.

He did even better on his first English tour in 1934, with 28 wickets at 24.92 in the Tests, and over 100 in the first-class games. The combination of O'Reilly and Grimmett also proved too much for South Africa in 1935–36, the two taking 71 wickets in the series. O'Reilly's share was 27 at 17.03 and he took 95 at 13.56 on the tour.

When the selectors dispensed with Grimmett for the 1936–37 series against England, O'Reilly soldiered on, with 25 wickets at 22.20 as Australia won 3–2. In 1938, on his second English tour, he helped ensure the retention of the Ashes with 10 wickets in the fourth Test, Australia's only victory, and he took 22 in the series. That performance gave him 100 wickets against England and over 20 wickets in every series he played against them, mostly on pitches loaded in favour of the batsmen. O'Reilly returned to play one Test against New Zealand in 1945–46, before retiring to write on the game. In a journalistic career lasting many years his opinions were expressed with the same forthright, whole–hearted approach he brought to his bowling. O'Reilly was strong in his championing of spin bowling, and his dislike of the one-day game. His death after a long period of illness was greeted with universal regret at the passing of a great Australian.

BATTING	M	Inn	NO	HS	Runs	Ave	100s	50s	C/S
Tests	27	39	7	56*	410	12.81	–	1	7
First-class	135	167	41	56*	1655	13.13	–	1	65

BOWLING	Balls	Runs	Wkts	Ave	BB	5wl	10wM
Tests	10024	3254	144	22.59	7/54	11	3
First-class	–	12850	774	16.60	9/38	63	17

OXENHAM, Ronald Keven

Qld, RHB/RM
Born: 28 July 1891
Nundah, Queensland
Died: 16 August 1939
Nundah, Queensland

Ron Oxenham was a very good all-rounder, arguably one of the best produced by Queensland. He bowled medium paced cutters, was an aggressive striker of the ball and a fine fieldsman close to the wicket. Although he made his first-class debut in 1911–12, Queensland's lack of competition meant that he did not make the Test team until the third Test of the 1928–29 series when he was 37 years old, and probably past his best. Although he played well in that series he was overlooked for the 1930 tour of England. Oxenham returned to play against the West Indies in 1930–31 and South Africa in 1931–32. It was against the latter that he produced his best bowling of 4/39. In that same season he made his highest first-class score, 162 not out, in Brisbane against Victoria. He played no further Test cricket, but did tour India with an Australian team in 1935–36. Oxenham was badly injured in a car accident in 1937. He never fully recovered and died in 1939, aged 48.

BATTING	M	Inn	NO	HS	Runs	Ave	100s	50s	C/S
Tests	7	10	0	48	151	15.10	–	–	4
First-class	97	166	22	162*	3693	25.64	4	19	45

BOWLING	Balls	Runs	Wkts	Ave	BB	5wI	10wM
Tests	1802	522	14	37.28	4/39	–	–
First-class	–	6891	369	18.67	9/18	22	8

P

PALMER, George, Eugene

Vic, Tas, RHB/RM
Born: 22 February 1860
Mulwala, New South Wales
Died: 22 August 1910
Baddaginnie near Benalla, Victoria

A bowler of medium-pace spinners and cutters and a useful batsman, Palmer was an important player in early Australian teams. He bowled well enough to gain a trip to England in 1880, where he made his Test debut. Over the next few seasons he rivalled Spofforth as the country's finest bowler. Against England in 1881–82 he took 20 wickets in two Tests, including 7/68 in the second game at Sydney, to give Australia the series. Palmer's best bowling, 7/65, was taken at Melbourne in the first Test of the 1882–83 series. He toured England again in 1882, 1884 and 1886. On the last visit he became the first Australian to score 1000 runs and take 100 wickets on an English tour. Palmer's first-class career ended in Tasmania, where he spent some time playing and coaching.

BATTING	M	Inn	NO	HS	Runs	Ave	100s	50s	C/S
Tests	17	25	4	48	296	14.09	–	–	13
First-class	133	200	31	113	2728	16.14	1	10	108

BOWLING	Balls	Runs	Wkts	Ave	BB	5wI	10wM
Tests	4517	1678	78	21.51	7/65	6	2
First-class	–	10500	594	17.67	8/41	54	16

PARK, Roy Lindsay

Vic, RHB
Born: 30 July 1892
Ballarat, Victoria
Died: 23 January 1947
Middle Park, Victoria

Roy Park was a very good right-handed batsman who had an unfortunate Test career. Chosen to play in the second game of the 1920–21 series against England, he was bowled first ball in his only innings. His wife is said by Arthur Mailey to have dropped her wool as he was facing his first delivery, bent down to pick it up, and missed her husband's entire Test career. Despite that, he was a talented player, captaining Victoria on his first-class debut in 1912–13. He earned a place on the 1914–15 tour of South Africa, abandoned due to the war. In 1919–20 he returned to make his highest score, 228 against South Australia, and in 1920–21 he made three centuries to earn his Test place. Park probably deserved another chance, but the competition for Test places was intense. He continued to make runs for Victoria until his retirement in 1925.

BATTING	M	Inn	NO	HS	Runs	Ave	100s	50s	C/S
Tests	1	1	0	0	0	0.00	–	–	–
First-class	36	67	3	228	2514	39.28	9	10	13

BOWLING	Balls	Runs	Wkts	Ave	BB	5wI	10wM
Tests	6	9	0	–	–	–	–
First-class	–	139	3	46.33	1/15	–	–

PASCOE, Leonard Stephen

NSW, RHB/RF
Born: 13 February 1950
Bridgetown, Western Australia

The son of Yugoslav migrants (his surname was Durtanovich), Len Pascoe was a fast bowler whose aim was to project the ball as rapidly as possible from one end of the pitch to the other. There was little science to his bowling, but he was very quick indeed. Although some of the aggression was tempered as he grew older, no-one could doubt the whole–hearted effort he displayed, and he was very popular with the crowds. Forming one of the most lethal attacks ever seen in grade cricket with his friend Jeff Thomson, Pascoe graduated to Shield cricket in 1974–75 and to Tests when he toured England in 1977. After World Series Cricket he returned to the Test team, touring England again in 1980, where he took his best figures, at Lord's in the Centenary Test. A knee operation unfortunately caused him to miss the 1981 tour. He played again the following summer, but was unable to hold his place in the side.

BATTING	M	Inn	NO	HS	Runs	Ave	100s	50s	C/S
Tests	14	19	9	30*	106	10.60	–	–	2
First-class	74	77	25	51*	472	9.07	–	1	22

BOWLING	Balls	Runs	Wkts	Ave	BB	5wl	10wM
Tests	3403	1668	64	26.06	5/59	1	–
First-class	–	7314	289	25.30	8/41	10	2

PELLEW, Clarence Everard

SA, RHB/RM
Born: 21 September 1893
Port Pirie, South Australia
Died: 9 May 1981
Adelaide, South Australia

'Nip' Pellew was a right-handed batsman, brilliant fielder and later a fine coach, one of two brothers and two cousins to play for South Australia. He made his first-class debut in 1913–14, but had to wait until after the First World War to make a significant impact on the game. Pellew played successfully for the AIF team at the end of the war, then returned to South Australia, for whom he made his highest score, 271, against Victoria at the Adelaide Oval in 1919–20. He scored at a run a minute, going through four bats in the process. Such form put him into the Australian team against England in 1920–21 and he made 116 in his second Test and another hundred in the next game.

He was a certainty for the tour of England in 1921, but did little in the series. Pellew retired in 1923, but returned for a few games in 1928–29.

BATTING	M	Inn	NO	HS	Runs	Ave	100s	50s	C/S
Tests	10	14	1	116	484	37.23	2	1	4
First-class	91	147	12	271	4536	33.60	9	21	45

BOWLING	Balls	Runs	Wkts	Ave	BB	5wI	10wM
Tests	78	34	0	–	–	–	–
First-class	–	849	12	70.75	3/119	–	–

PHILLIPS, Wayne Bentley

SA, LHB/WK
Born: 1 March 1958
Adelaide, South Australia

An aggressive left-handed batsman and wicketkeeper, South Australian Wayne Phillips had a brilliant Test debut, making 159 against Pakistan at Perth in 1983–84. Although he played some fine innings over the next few seasons, he never produced the quantity of runs his ability appeared to warrant. This could have been due to the fact that he was required to keep wicket after Rod Marsh retired. To be truthful he was not a top class 'keeper and the work appeared to limit his batting. He still produced some fine innings, none better than his 120 against the West Indies at Barbados in 1983–84 when he took on some fearsome pace bowling with a thrilling display of aggressive strokes. He toured England in 1985 and New Zealand in 1985–1986, but after the latter trip poor form saw him dropped. Some harsh words about the selectors may also have counted against a recall. In 1990–91 he fought his way back into Shield cricket after being dropped, but was unable to recapture his best form and the comeback was short–lived.

BATTING	M	Inn	NO	HS	Runs	Ave	100s	50s	C/S
Tests	27	48	2	159	1485	32.28	2	7	52/-
First-class	114	199	16	260	6907	37.74	13	33	154/7

BOWLING	Runs	Wkts	Ave	BB	5wI	10wM
First-class	13	0	–	–	–	–

PHILLIPS, Wayne Norman

Vic, RHB/OB
Born: 7 November 1962
Geelong, Victoria

The diminutive Victorian opener was a surprise choice to replace the out–of–form Geoff Marsh for the final Test of the 1991–92 series against India. Although not a dashing player, Phillips had performed steadily for his State since scoring a century on debut against the West Indies in 1988–89, and developed a reputation as a hard man to dismiss. Initially chosen in the middle order, he moved to the role of opener where he provided a sound base for stroke players like Dean Jones, Darren Lehmann and Simon O'Donnell to build on. He was a leading force in Victoria's 1990–91 Sheffield Shield triumph, scoring 91 not out and hitting the winning run. With innings of eight and 14, his Test debut was not a success. Phillips began the next season with a double century, but the emergence of young players like Matthew Hayden, Michael Slater and Justin Langer have probably put paid to his chances.

BATTING	M	Inn	NO	HS	Runs	Ave	100s	50s	C/S
Tests	1	2	0	14	22	11.00	–	–	–
First-class	50	88	7	205	3185	39.32	7	16	21

BOWLING	Runs	Wkts	Ave	BB	5wI	10wM		
First-class	124	1	124.00	1/59	–	–		

PHILPOTT, Peter Ian

NSW, RHB/LBG
Born: 21 November 1934
Manly, New South Wales

Peter Philpott was a leg-spinning all-rounder who played eight Tests for Australia in the mid-sixties. Although he made his debut for New

South Wales in 1954–55, Philpott had to wait until 1964–65 to be selected for Australia. The presence of Richie Benaud no doubt limited his Test opportunities, and it was not until Benaud retired that Philpott made his debut, against the West Indies at Kingston, Jamaica. After taking 49 wickets on tour, including 18 in the five Tests, he had three Tests against England in 1965–66, taking 5/90 at Brisbane, before losing his place in the side. At first-class level he was a more than useful batsman, scoring four centuries. His game must also have been affected by a weak heart, which required open heart surgery in 1980. After playing cricket all over the world, Philpott has become an excellent coach and was in charge of the South Australian Shield team for some time.

BATTING	M	Inn	NO	HS	Runs	Ave	100s	50s	C/S
Tests	8	10	1	22	93	10.33	–	–	5
First-class	76	109	17	156	2886	31.36	4	15	55

BOWLING	Balls	Runs	Wkts	Ave	BB	5wl	10wM
Tests	2262	1000	26	38.46	5/90	1	–
First-class	–	7427	245	30.31	7/53	12	2

PONSFORD, William Harold

Vic, RHB
Born: 19 October 1900
North Fitzroy, Victoria
Died: 13 April 1991
Kyneton, Victoria

Victorian opening batsman Bill Ponsford may have lacked the charisma that brought thousands through the gate, but if the business of batting is to score runs then he must be ranked among the finest of all time. He shunned publicity, but accumulated runs with a certainty that was awesome, creating many records along the way. The prospect of bowling to him and to Don Bradman, whose feats have tended to overshadow Ponsford's, must have given bowlers many sleepless nights.

After breaking into the Victorian team in 1920, he established himself in 1922–23 with a world-record innings of 429 against Tasmania.

Five years later he made 437 against Queensland, the only player to make over 400 twice. This latter score was achieved during a run of form that saw him make 11 hundreds in 18 innings. In fact during December 1927 he scored 133, 47, 437, 202, 38 and 336 to reach 1000 Shield runs in a month. Scoring of such proportions had never been seen before, nor would it be again.

Ponsford made his Test debut against England at Sydney in 1924–25, scoring 110. He made another century in the second Test. At first-class level he formed an opening partnership with Bill Woodfull that realised 22 century partnerships before it ended with their retirements after the 1934 tour of England.

Ponsford toured England in 1926, 1930 and 1934, averaging over 55 in all. If there was any weakness in his batting it was against the best fast bowling, but he did make a century against Larwood at The Oval in 1930, and in the most vicious of the Bodyline Tests, at Adelaide in 1932–33, he batted with great courage to score 85. The extreme pace of Larwood found him a little slow on his feet, and he was struck on a number of occasions. In fact he did have a flat spot in the early thirties. After some excellent play against the West Indies in 1930–31, he struggled against South Africa in 1931–32—and then came Bodyline.

However, the Victorian fought back to end his career with one last glorious tour of England. In his last two Tests he made 181 and 266, setting record partnerships of 451 and 388 for the fourth and second wickets with Bradman. He averaged 94.83 in his last Test series, a fitting end to a wonderful career. Ponsford is the only player to make centuries in each of his first and last two Tests.

For Victoria he was outstanding, averaging 86 and creating the then Australian record partnership of 456 with Edgar Mayne. Scoring runs was Ponsford's game and he did it as well as anyone ever has.

BATTING	M	Inn	NO	HS	Runs	Ave	100s	50s	C/S
Tests	29	48	4	266	2122	48.22	7	6	21
First-class	162	235	23	437	13819	65.18	47	43	71

BOWLING	Runs	Wkts	Ave	BB	5wI	10wM
First-class	41	0	–	–	–	–

POPE, Roland James

NSW, RHB
Born: 18 February 1864
Sydney, New South Wales
Died: 27 July 1952
Manly, New South Wales

Dr 'Rowley' Pope was a useful right-handed batsman who played one Test against England at Melbourne in 1884–85, the game in which the original team refused to play. Batting in the middle order, he failed in both innings. But playing cricket was only part of Pope's life. At his own expense, he accompanied many Australian touring teams as a kind of unofficial camp follower. While he was never a member of an Australian team to England, Pope did play several games when required. After the war, he journeyed to England again in 1921 and 1926. He became famous for the amount of luggage he carried. On a trip to America in 1932 Arthur Mailey restricted Pope to just 36 bags. In that luggage he carried every conceivable object. A player wanting a button–hook was sent to Pope, who promptly produced one. Author Jack Pollard reports the only time Pope was defeated was when Edgar Mayne wanted a bicycle pump on the boat home from England in 1921. Needless to say, he always packed one from then on. Although he may not have been a great player, Pope lived an enviable life in cricket, and no doubt enjoyed every minute of it.

BATTING	M	Inn	NO	HS	Runs	Ave	100s	50s	C/S
Tests	1	2	0	3	3	1.50	–	–	–
First-class	20	33	7	47	318	12.23	–	–	13

BOWLING	Runs	Wkts	Ave	BB	5wl	10wM
First-class	19	0	–	–	–	–

R

RACKEMANN, Carl Gray

Qld, RHB/RF
Born: 3 June 1960
Wondai, Queensland

A big, blond fast bowler, Carl Rackemann never established a permanent place in the Australian side despite his considerable ability. Early in his career he was injury prone, and it was almost an achievement for him to play two Tests in succession. Injury cost him an early Test debut in 1981, when he was unable to join the side as a reinforcement in England, and he finally made his debut in the second Test against England in 1982–83. He had much better luck against Pakistan in 1983–84 when he took 16 wickets in the first two Tests, but missed the rest of the series. In the West Indies in 1983–84 he took five wickets in his only match. Joining the rebel tour to South Africa disqualified him from the Test team for some time, but he gained selection to tour England in 1989. Injury again prevented him playing any serious part. Rackemann had an extended Test run in 1989–90; he bowled well, but took few wickets. After one game against England in 1990–91 he lost his place in the side. Rackemann became Queensland captain for a season in 1991–92. Illness caused him to miss a number of games at the beginning of the next season, but he came back with some displays that showed he was still a force to be reckoned with.

BATTING	M	Inn	NO	HS	Runs	Ave	100s	50s	C/S
Tests	12	14	4	15*	53	5.30	–	–	2
First-class	127	137	47	31*	569	6.32	–	–	32

BOWLING	Balls	Runs	Wkts	Ave	BB	5wI	10wM
Tests	2719	1137	39	29.15	6/86	3	1
First-class	–	12331	466	26.46	8/84	18	3

RANSFORD, Vernon Seymour

Vic, LHB/SLA
Born: 20 March 1885
South Yarra, Victoria
Died: 19 March 1958
Brighton, Victoria

Vernon Ransford was a very good left-handed batsman and brilliant outfielder who represented Australia in 20 Tests before the First World War and played for Victoria between 1903 and 1927. After a promising debut, Ransford forced his way into the Test side for the 1907–08 series against England, then batted well in the next season to ensure a trip to England in 1909. He came second to Bardsley with 1783 runs on the tour, including his only Test century, 143 not out at Lord's. Ransford played against South Africa in 1910–11 and England in 1911–12, before his Test career ended when he was one of six players who refused to tour England in 1912. He continued to play for Victoria, for whom his record is excellent, for many seasons.

BATTING	M	Inn	NO	HS	Runs	Ave	100s	50s	C/S
Tests	20	38	6	143*	1211	37.84	1	7	10
First-class	142	219	24	190	8268	42.40	25	32	74

BOWLING	Balls	Runs	Wkts	Ave	BB	5wI	10wM
Tests	43	28	1	28.00	1/9	–	–
First-class	–	888	29	30.62	6/38	1	–

REDPATH, Ian Ritchie

Vic, RHB/RM
Born: 11 May 1941
Geelong, Victoria

Ian Redpath was a gritty right-handed batsman with an excellent technique against fast bowling, and was always at his best in a crisis. He made his Test debut against South Africa in 1963–64, scoring 97, and although he toured England in 1964, he did not establish a place until the tour of South Africa in 1966–67. He toured England again in 1968, and finally made his first Test century against the West Indies in 1968–69. His highest score of 171 was made at Perth against England in 1970–71. He missed another tour of England in 1972, but did well in the West Indies as Keith Stackpole's opening partner. At Auckland in 1973–74, Redpath carried his bat through the innings, making 159 not out. His last two series were his best, 472 runs at 42.90 against England in 1974–75 and 575 runs at 52.27 against the West Indies in 1975–76. He came out of retirement to join World Series Cricket, but injury restricted his appearances, and he returned to his antique business.

BATTING	M	Inn	NO	HS	Runs	Ave	100s	50s	C/S
Tests	66	120	11	171	4737	43.45	8	31	83
First-class	226	391	24	261	14993	41.99	32	84	211

BOWLING	Balls	Runs	Wkts	Ave	BB	5wl	10wM
Tests	64	41	0	–	–	–	–
First-class	–	466	13	35.84	3/24	–	–

REEDMAN, John Cole

SA, RHB/RM
Born: 9 October 1865
Gilberton, South Australia
Died: 23 March 1924
Gilberton, South Australia

'Dinny' Reedman was a right-handed South Australian batsman and a usefully accurate medium pacer. He made his debut in 1887–88 and played his only Test against England at Sydney in 1894–95. In a sensational game, Australia lost after making 586 and forcing England to follow on. Reedman contributed little and returned to South Australia. He continued to play at first-class level until 1908–09. While his two centuries were made in the 1890s, his best bowling of 7/54 and 6/95 was taken against Victoria in 1904–05. Reedman may have lacked technical graces, but was a solid, stubborn player and a tough opponent, who gave South Australia great value.

BATTING	M	Inn	NO	HS	Runs	Ave	100s	50s	C/S
Tests	1	2	0	17	21	10.50	–	–	1
First-class	81	151	8	113	3338	23.34	2	15	68

BOWLING	Balls	Runs	Wkts	Ave	BB	5wI	10wM
Tests	57	24	1	24.00	1/12	–	–
First-class	–	3787	118	32.09	7/54	6	1

REID, Bruce Anthony

WA, LHB/LF
Born: 14 March 1963
Osborne Park, Western Australia

A very tall, gangling left-arm fast bowler, Bruce Reid made an amazing comeback when it seemed his Test career was over. His height, which providing awkward bounce, and an ability to move the ball both ways, along with the left-hander's angle of delivery made him a difficult proposition for the best of batsmen. After making his Test debut in 1985–86, he had useful series against England in 1986–87 and New Zealand in 1987–88, consistently taking wickets without producing large hauls. He seemed on the road to stardom with some devastating bowling on the dead tracks of Pakistan, when his back gave out. After a couple of aborted comebacks, Reid re–emerged in 1990–91 with a steel rod inserted in his spine and a remodelled action. He bowled beautifully to destroy the England batting, topping the bowling averages with 27 wickets at 16 and producing his best figures, 6/97 and 7/51, in the second Test at Melbourne. Reid had a disappointing tour of the West Indies where he could not recapture his form. Back in Australia he took 12 wickets (6/66 and 6/60) against India in the second Test of the 1991–92 series, before falling prey to injury yet again.

Reid's only game against the West Indies in 1992–93 provided seven wickets, before he succumbed to a shoulder injury. If he could remain fit, he could be the world's best bowler.

BATTING	M	Inn	NO	HS	Runs	Ave	100s	50s	C/S
Tests	27	34	14	13	93	4.65	–	–	5
First-class	80	90	34	30	477	8.52	–	–	16

BOWLING	Balls	Runs	Wkts	Ave	BB	5wI	10wM
Tests	6244	2784	113	24.64	7/51	5	2
First-class	–	8014	296	27.07	7/51	10	3

REIFFEL, Paul Ronald

Vic, RHB/RFM
Born: 19 April 1966
Box Hill, Victoria

A strong, fast-medium bowler and useful batsman, Paul Reiffel made his first-class debut in 1987–88, but really came to prominence in 1990–91 when he was Victoria's leading wicket–taker in their Sheffield Shield winning season. He took 49 wickets at 23.75, including his career best of 6/57 against Tasmania, and also made 86 to show promise as an all-rounder. Reiffel spent most of 1991–92 as Australia's twelfth man, before making his debut at Perth in the fifth Test against India. Steady bowling returned figures of 0/46 and 2/34. He showed enough promise to be persisted with, and in 1992–93 became an important part of the Australian one-day side. His accurate bowling under pressure was rewarded with some good returns and a place in the side to tour New Zealand, where he played in all three Tests. While he produced nothing in the way of spectacular returns, he did enough to gain selection in the 1993 Ashes team. On the early part of that tour he struggled for form, but gradually came to terms with English conditions. Selected for the fourth Test he bowled superbly to take 5/65 and 3/87. In the following game, at Edgbaston, he captured 6/71 in the first innings. Reiffel's form helped compensate for the loss of McDermott and gave the impression that he could have a long term future in the Australian team.

BATTING	M	Inn	NO	HS	Runs	Ave	100s	50s	C/S
Tests	7	8	0	42	106	13.25	–	–	3
First-class	61	67	20	86	1029	21.89	–	3	26

BOWLING	Balls	Runs	Wkts	Ave	BB	5wl	10wM
Tests	1630	726	26	27.92	6/71	2	–
First-class	–	6074	202	30.07	6/57	7	2

RENNEBERG, David Alexander

NSW, RHB/RF
Born: 23 September 1942
Balmain, New South Wales

Dave Renneberg was a big, strong fast bowler who gave great service to New South Wales and played in eight Tests between 1966 and 1968. After making his first-class debut in 1964–65, he graduated to Test cricket on the 1966–67 tour of South Africa. He played in all five Tests but took only 11 wickets, although he did manage 5/97 at Johannesburg. He was more successful in three Tests against India in 1967–68, where he took his best figures of 5/39. This earned him a trip to England in 1968, but the presence of McKenzie, Connolly, Hawke and Freeman kept him out of the Test side. He never had another chance, retiring from first-class cricket in 1970–71.

BATTING	M	Inn	NO	HS	Runs	Ave	100s	50s	C/S
Tests	8	13	7	9	22	3.66	–	–	2
First-class	90	109	43	26	466	7.06	–	–	35

BOWLING	Balls	Runs	Wkts	Ave	BB	5wl	10wM
Tests	1598	830	23	36.08	5/39	2	–
First-class	–	8527	291	29.30	8/72	13	1

RICHARDSON, Arthur John

SA, WA, RHB/OB
Born: 24 July 1888
Sevenhill near Clare, South Australia
Died: 23 December 1973
Adelaide, South Australia

Arthur Richardson was a very capable South Australian all-rounder in the period following the First World War. He was a hard-hitting batsman and off-break bowler, who made his first-class debut in 1918–19, although he had played against Fiji in 1907–08 at the age of 19 in a non-first-class fixture. Selected in the first Test of the 1924–25 series against England, he made 98 on debut. Although he did little else in that series, his first-class form remained good enough to ensure a trip to England in 1926. At Leeds he scored his only Test century, aged nearly 38. For South Australia he was a valuable player, scoring two double centuries against MCC sides, including his highest score of 280 in 1922–23. Richardson became an outstanding coach, an occupation which took him all over the cricketing world, even to the West Indies, where he umpired two Tests in 1934–35.

BATTING	M	Inn	NO	HS	Runs	Ave	100s	50s	C/S
Tests	9	13	0	100	403	31.00	1	2	1
First-class	86	139	13	280	5238	41.57	13	16	34

BOWLING	Balls	Runs	Wkts	Ave	BB	5wI	10wM
Tests	1812	521	12	43.41	2/20	–	–
First-class	–	6555	209	31.36	6/28	7	1

RICHARDSON, Victor York

SA, RHB/RM
Born: 7 September 1894
Parkside, South Australia
Died: 30 October 1969
Fullarton, South Australia

Vic Richardson was a fine all-round sportsman, capable of excelling at any game he attempted. Although he was a very good Australian Rules footballer, baseballer, gymnast, hockey player and athlete, cricket was probably his best game. He made his first-class debut in 1918–19 and was South Australia's captain from 1921 until 1935. An absolutely fearless cricketer, whether batting aggressively or fielding close to the wicket, he made his Test debut against England in 1924–25, scoring 138 in his second game. Richardson toured England in 1930 as Woodfull's vice-captain. In 1932–33 he stood up bravely to Bodyline, making 83 in the fourth Test. His final Tests were played in 1935–36 when he led the Australian team to South Africa. While his batting was past its best, he set a world record for the most catches in his final Test. The players on this tour all agree that it was the most enjoyable experience of their cricketing careers. Following his retirement from active participation Richardson became a much respected radio commentator. The family involvement in cricket was further maintained by his grandsons, the Chappell brothers, and Richardson's memory is honoured by the gates at the Adelaide Oval which bear his name.

BATTING	M	Inn	NO	HS	Runs	Ave	100s	50s	C/S
Tests	19	30	0	138	706	23.53	1	1	24
First-class	184	297	12	231	10727	37.63	27	47	213/4

BOWLING	Runs	Wkts	Ave	BB	5wI	10wM
First-class	545	8	68.12	3/22	–	–

RIGG, Keith Edward

Vic, RHB
Born: 21 May 1906
Malvern, Victoria

Keith Rigg was unlucky to represent Australia in only eight Tests. He was a very good right-handed batsman, but had the misfortune to play in an era when Australia possessed a large number of talented cricketers. He made his debut for Victoria in 1926–27, scoring 62 in a total of 1107. After being twelfth man for four Tests against the West Indies in 1930–31 he made his debut in the fifth. He had more luck against South Africa in 1931–32 making 127 in the second Test. Following that, his only other Tests were the last three in the 1936–37 series against England. It was unfortunate that he could not establish a place in the Test team, or even gain a place in a touring side, as he was a consistently high run-scorer for Victoria with his attractive batting, being involved in a number of large partnerships. Rigg was also a Victorian captain and selector.

BATTING	M	Inn	NO	HS	Runs	Ave	100s	50s	C/S
Tests	8	12	0	127	401	33.41	1	1	5
First-class	87	143	11	167*	5544	42.00	14	30	58

BOWLING	Runs	Wkts	Ave	BB	5wl	10wM
First-class	30	0	–	–	–	–

RING, Douglas Thomas

Vic, RHB/LBG
Born: 14 October 1918
Hobart, Tasmania

Doug Ring is primarily remembered as a leg-spin bowler, but he was also a useful batsman who played a number of valuable innings in his 13 Tests for Australia. He made his first-class debut in 1938–39 for Victoria, but had to wait until 1947–48 to make his Test debut, against India. In the face of strong opposition he won a place in the 1948 side to England, playing in only the fifth Test. He was more successful against the West Indies in 1951–52, taking 6/80 and making some good contributions with the bat. Ring's best bowling of 6/72 came next season against South Africa at Brisbane. He also made two fifties in the series and toured England again in 1953. Unfortunately, he played only one Test on the tour, his last. Against strong competition, Ring achieved much, and for Victoria he was a consistently successful performer.

BATTING	M	Inn	NO	HS	Runs	Ave	100s	50s	C/S
Tests	13	21	2	67	426	22.42	–	4	5
First-class	129	169	22	145	3418	23.25	1	20	93

BOWLING	Balls	Runs	Wkts	Ave	BB	5wl	10wM
Tests	3024	1305	35	37.28	6/72	2	–
First-class	–	12847	451	28.48	7/88	21	2

RITCHIE, Gregory Michael

Qld, RHB/RM
Born: 23 January 1960
Stanthorpe, Queensland

A solidly built right-handed batsman, Greg Ritchie was an extremely talented player who, although he played some fine innings at Test level, probably never realised his full potential. Ritchie made his debut in Pakistan on the 1982 tour and scored 106 not out in his second Test, at Faisalabad. Despite his good form he did not reappear for Australia until the 1983–84 tour of the West Indies. He seemed to have established a Test place, particularly after the 1985 tour of England when he made 94 at Lord's and 146 at Trent Bridge. He made his third Test century against India in 1985–86, but from there his form fell away until he lost his place in the side. A tendency to put on weight and the detrimental effect this must have had on his cricket may have been a contributing factor. Ritchie captained Queensland in 1989–90, but then retired at the end of that season. He reappeared for one season in 1991–92, and showed that he was still capable player at first-class level.

BATTING	M	Inn	NO	HS	Runs	Ave	100s	50s	C/S
Tests	30	53	5	146	1690	35.20	3	7	14
First-class	159	254	24	213*	10170	44.22	24	54	115

BOWLING	Balls	Runs	Wkts	Ave	BB	5wl	10wM
Tests	6	10	0	–	–	–	–
First-class	–	247	5	49.40	1/2	–	–

RIXON, Stephen John

NSW, RHB/WK
Born: 25 February 1954
Albury, New South Wales

An extremely talented wicketkeeper and a useful right-handed batsman, Steve Rixon made his debut for New South Wales in 1974–75. He had his chance at Test level in 1977–78 when he became Australia's 'keeper in the first season of World Series Cricket. Rixon played in the five Tests against India, then toured the West Indies. Although he kept well and batted competently in some tight situations, he lost the job to John Maclean in 1978–79. With the return of Rod Marsh, Rixon had to settle for the deputy's position, which he filled in England on the 1981 tour. After Marsh's retirement Wayne Phillips took over as 'keeper, but when he was injured, Rixon returned to play in the last three Tests against the West Indies in 1984–85. He chose to tour South Africa with the rebel Australians in 1985. After those tours he returned to set a record number of appearances for New South Wales before retiring. Rixon has retained a major involvement with cricket through his appointment as coach of the New South Wales Shield team.

BATTING	M	Inn	NO	HS	Runs	Ave	100s	50s	C/S
Tests	13	24	3	54	394	18.76	–	2	42/5
First-class	151	221	35	128	4303	23.13	6	14	394/66

BOWLING	Runs	Wkts	Ave	BB	5wI	10wM
First-class	20	0	–	–	–	–

ROBERTSON, William Roderick

Vic, RHB/LB
Born: 6 October 1861
Deniliquin, New South Wales
Died: 24 June 1938
Brighton, Victoria

William Robertson was a leg-break bowler and right-handed batsman whose only Test was in the controversial second game of the 1884–85 series when the selectors were forced to chose an entirely new team following a dispute over payments. He achieved little and was not chosen again. Robertson made his first-class debut earlier in the 1884–85 season, and the highlight of his short career came for Victoria against Alfred Shaw's English team when he took his best figures of 5/46 in a game which ended in a tie. At grade level Robertson was a member of the strong East Melbourne Club.

BATTING	M	Inn	NO	HS	Runs	Ave	100s	50s	C/S
Tests	1	2	0	2	2	1.00	–	–	–
First-class	7	13	5	33	109	13.62	–	–	3

BOWLING	Balls	Runs	Wkts	Ave	BB	5wI	10wM
Tests	44	24	0	–	–	–	–
First-class	–	466	15	31.06	5/46	1	–

ROBINSON, Richard Daryl

Vic, RHB/WK
Born: 8 June 1946
East Melbourne, Victoria

Extremely tall for a wicketkeeper, Richie Robinson was particularly agile behind the stumps and he was a quite brilliant batsman, always prepared to attack the bowling. He made his first-class debut for Victoria in 1971–72 and on the strength of his batting toured England in 1975 as Rod Marsh's deputy. A good season in 1976–77, including his highest score of 185 against South Australia, saw him chosen as the second 'keeper on the 1977 English tour. Problems with the batting led to him playing his three Tests, all as a batsman, while Marsh kept wicket. The experiment was not a success, as Robinson was unable to maintain his first-class form at Test level. He joined World Series Cricket, but returned to play for Victoria until his retirement in 1981–82. Robinson was also a very competent leader, captaining his State for a number of seasons. Recently he has established a reputation as a coach, a position he held with the Queensland team.

BATTING	M	Inn	NO	HS	Runs	Ave	100s	50s	C/S
Tests	3	6	0	34	100	16.66	–	–	4/-
First-class	97	153	33	185	4776	39.80	7	22	289/40

ROBINSON, Rayford Harold

NSW, SA, RHB/LBG
Born: 26 March 1914
Stockton, New South Wales
Died: 10 August 1965
Stockton, New South Wales

Ray Robinson's career is very much a case of what might have been. He had exceptional talent as a right-handed batsman, but faults in his character prevented him from making the most of his extraordinary ability. Following his debut for New South Wales in 1934–35, he quickly established his place with an outstanding season in 1935–36. Good form at the beginning of the 1936–37 earned him selection in the first Test at Brisbane against England. He failed in both innings as Australia was caught on a wet wicket. The further chances that his ability obviously warranted never materialised. In 1937–38 Robinson moved to South Australia, but with little success. He returned to New South Wales and represented them until the war. After he was discharged he drifted into and out of various occupations. Unable to claim a spot in the New South Wales side, he moved to New Zealand in 1946–47 where he represented Otago for three seasons.

BATTING	M	Inn	NO	HS	Runs	Ave	100s	50s	C/S
Tests	1	2	0	3	5	2.50	–	–	1
First-class	46	81	4	163	2441	31.70	4	13	24

BOWLING	Runs	Wkts	Ave	BB	5wl	10wM	
First-class	1654	44	37.59	4/45	–	–	

RORKE, Gordon Frederick

NSW, LHB/RF
Born: 27 June 1938
Mosman, New South Wales

A tall and very fast bowler, Gordon Rorke's action attracted much criticism because of the length of his drag, which saw him deliver the ball from well in front of the popping crease. There were also some who believed he threw, although he was never called. He made his first-class debut in 1957–58 and played his first Test next season in the 1958–59 series against England. He did well, but his Test career was short–lived when he caught hepatitis on the 1959–60 tour of India and Pakistan. Following the illness he was never able to recapature the rhythm and speed which had taken him to the top. Rorke struggled on in first-class cricket until he lost his place in 1964. In addition to the illness, he was forced to adjust to rule changes specifically designed to curb his unique drag.

BATTING	M	Inn	NO	HS	Runs	Ave	100s	50s	C/S
Tests	4	4	2	7	9	4.50	–	–	1
First-class	36	35	12	35	248	10.78	–	–	10

BOWLING	Balls	Runs	Wkts	Ave	BB	5wI	10wM
Tests	703	203	10	20.30	3/23	–	–
First-class	–	2165	88	24.60	6/52	3	–

RUTHERFORD, John Walter

WA, RHB/LB
Born: 25 September 1929
Bungulluping, Western Australia

The first player chosen from Western Australia to play Test cricket, John Rutherford was a sound right-handed opening batsman. He made his first-class debut in 1952–53 and steady play over the next few seasons earned him a place on the 1956 team to tour England, India and Pakistan. Despite some poor Australian batting he was not chosen for any of the English Tests, his one game was against India at Bombay where he made 30 in his only innings. The presence of Jim Burke and Colin McDonald no doubt restricted Rutherford's chances, but he proved a good player for his State, making five centuries, including a top score of 167 against South Australia in 1955–56. His other century was made in a Test Trial which helped secure his trip to England.

BATTING	M	Inn	NO	HS	Runs	Ave	100s	50s	C/S
Tests	1	1	0	30	30	30.00	–	–	–
First-class	67	115	9	167	3367	31.76	6	15	53

BOWLING	Balls	Runs	Wkts	Ave	BB	5wI	10wM
Tests _____	36	15	1	15.00	1/11	–	–
First-class _____	–	1313	29	45.27	3/12	–	–

RYDER, John

Vic, RHB/RFM
Born: 8 August 1889
Collingwood, Victoria
Died: 3 April 1977
Fitzroy, Victoria

A tall, aggressive right-handed batsman and useful medium-fast bowler, Jack Ryder was an important figure in Australian cricket during the twenties. He made his first-class debut in 1912 and had early success as a bowler. His batting came to the fore after the war and he made his Test debut in 1920–21 against England. He toured England in 1921, but did not play in a Test until the side stopped in South Africa on the way home. Ryder gave his best display in the third Test of the 1924–25 series, hitting the English bowlers for 201 not out and 88. He toured England again in 1926 and inherited the Australian captaincy at the end of that trip. In 1928–29 he had the almost impossible task of leading a young Australian side against a powerful English team. Although he scored 492 runs at 54.66 he lost the captaincy to Bill Woodfull for the 1930 tour of England. After retirement Ryder served as a Test selector for many years.

BATTING	M	Inn	NO	HS	Runs	Ave	100s	50s	C/S
Tests _____	20	32	5	201*	1394	51.62	3	9	17
First-class _____	177	274	37	295	10499	44.29	24	55	132

BOWLING	Balls	Runs	Wkts	Ave	BB	5wI	10wM
Tests _____	1897	743	17	43.70	2/20	–	–
First-class _____	–	7064	237	29.80	7/53	9	1

S

SAGGERS, Ronald Arthur

NSW, RHB/WK
Born: 15 May 1917
Sydenham, New South Wales
Died: 13 March 1987
Harbord, New South Wales

Ron Saggers was unlucky to have his career coincide with that of Don Tallon, otherwise this very capable wicketkeeper would certainly have played more than six Tests. Although he made his first-class debut in 1939–40, Saggers had to wait until after the Second World War to push his claim for Test selection. This came when he was chosen as Tallon's deputy for the 1948 tour of England. Both 'keepers claimed 43 victims on the trip, but Saggers had to be content with one Test, the fourth at Leeds, when Tallon was injured. Saggers became Australia's 'keeper on the 1949–50 tour of South Africa when Tallon was unavailable. His 'keeping to the spinners was impressive, particularly his speed in stumping, a feature of his entire career. Saggers retired from first-class cricket following that tour.

BATTING	M	Inn	NO	HS	Runs	Ave	100s	50s	C/S
Tests	6	5	2	14	30	10.00	–	–	16/8
First-class	77	93	14	104*	1888	23.89	1	8	147/74

231

SAUNDERS, John Victor

Vic, LHB/LM, SLA
Born: 3 February 1876
Melbourne, Victoria
Died: 21 December 1927
Toorak, Victoria

A tall, left-arm bowler who varied his pace according to the conditions, John Saunders was a valuable member of the Australian attack in the first years of this century. He made his first-class debut in 1899–1900 and played his maiden Test in the fourth game of the 1901–02 series. He took 4/119 and 5/43, but missed the next Test, when he fractured his right collarbone attempting to take a catch in Victoria's game against the Englishmen. However, he recovered to be chosen for the 1902 tour of England where he took 127 wickets, including 18 in the Tests. On the way home he took his best figures of 7/34 against South Africa at Johannesburg. He did not tour England in 1905, but ended his Test career against England in 1907–08 when he took 31 wickets in the series. At first-class level he was a matchwinner for Victoria, and if there was any help in the pitch he was positively lethal. After touring New Zealand, he settled there in 1910 and played for Wellington until 1914. It is thought that while there he was a major influence on Clarrie Grimmett, whom he persuaded to come to Australia to further his career.

BATTING	M	Inn	NO	HS	Runs	Ave	100s	50s	C/S
Tests	14	23	6	11*	39	2.29	–	–	5
First-class	107	170	47	29*	586	4.76	–	–	72

BOWLING	Balls	Runs	Wkts	Ave	BB	5wI	10wM
Tests	3565	1796	79	22.73	7/34	6	–
First-class	–	12065	553	21.81	8/106	48	9

SCOTT, Henry James Herbert

Vic, RHB/RM
Born: 26 December 1858
Toorak, Victoria
Died: 23 September 1910
Scone, New South Wales

'Tup' Scott was a right-handed batsman with a defensive outlook and the first Victorian to captain Australia, something he did with little success. He made his first-class debut in 1877–78 and some good form in 1883–84 saw him chosen to tour England in 1884, where he scored just under 1000 runs. In the second Test at Lord's he made 75, caught by his captain Murdoch, fielding substitute for England, and 31 not out, and in the third game at The Oval he made 102. He returned to England as captain in 1886, but it was a disastrous tour as injuries and arguments destroyed his team. Although he batted well, it was not enough to lift his side. After the season ended, Scott stayed in England to complete a medical degree, a decision which ended his career. He returned to Australia after completing his degree, and died of typhoid fever at the age of 51 in Scone, where he had his practice.

BATTING	M	Inn	NO	HS	Runs	Ave	100s	50s	C/S
Tests	8	14	1	102	359	27.61	1	1	8
First-class	85	141	15	123	2863	22.72	4	14	57

BOWLING	Balls	Runs	Wkts	Ave	BB	5wI	10wM
Tests	28	26	0	–	–	–	–
First-class	–	494	18	27.44	6/33	1	–

SELLERS, Reginald Hugh Durning

SA, RHB/LBG
Born: 20 August 1940
Bulsar, India.

Rex Sellers was a leg-spin bowler, born in India, who migrated to Australia as a teenager. He made his first-class debut for South

233

Australia in 1959–60, but it was not until a good season in 1963–64 that he forced himself into Test calculations. His performances that summer earned him a trip to England in 1964. He did not bowl well in English conditions and was forced to battle a hand injury sustained on the voyage to England, but did manage to play his only Test, against India at Calcutta, on the way home. It was not a successful outing as he made nought and bowled only a few overs. Still bothered by the hand injury, Sellers announced his retirement on his return to Australia.

BATTING	M	Inn	NO	HS	Runs	Ave	100s	50s	C/S
Tests	1	1	0	0	0	0.00	–	–	1
First-class	53	80	20	87	1089	18.15	–	2	41

BOWLING	Balls	Runs	Wkts	Ave	BB	5wI	10wM
Tests	30	17	0	–	–	–	–
First-class	–	4653	121	38.45	5/36	4	1

SERJEANT, Craig Stanton

WA, RHB
Born: 1 November 1951
Nedlands, Western Australia

Craig Serjeant looked to be a very good right-handed batsman, but one who never managed to make the quantities of runs that would have been in keeping with his ability. He made his first-class debut in 1976–77 and did so well in his maiden season that he was chosen to tour England in 1977. After making 81 on debut at Lord's he seemed to have the world at his feet, but was left out of the side before the end of the series. One of the few in that team who did not join World Series Cricket, Serjeant played against India in 1977–78 and toured the West Indies later that season. In the third Test at Georgetown, Guyana, he made 124 to ensure an Australian victory. After that series he lost form and played no further Test cricket. He did, however, continue to play for Western Australia until he retired in 1983, captaining the side on a few occasions.

BATTING	M	Inn	NO	HS	Runs	Ave	100s	50s	C/S
Tests	12	23	1	124	522	23.72	1	2	13
First-class	80	134	19	159	4030	35.04	9	20	90

BOWLING	Runs	Wkts	Ave	BB	5wI	10wM
First-class	4	0	–	–	–	–

SHEAHAN, Andrew Paul

Vic, RHB
Born: 30 September 1948
Werribee, Victoria

An elegant right-handed batsman and an absolutely brilliant cover fieldsman, Paul Sheahan's Test record does not reflect the ability he seemed to possess. He made his first-class debut in 1965–66 and moved into Test cricket against India in 1967–68, scoring 81 and 35 in his first Test. This ensured him a place in the 1968 team to tour England. Despite being a regular choice for the next few seasons, he did not produce consistently heavy scoring, although he did play the occasional excellent innings, including his two centuries: 114 against India in 1969–70 and 127 against Pakistan in 1972–73. He toured England again in 1972, and had the pleasure of being at the crease when Australia won the fifth Test at The Oval to square the series. Sheahan retired from cricket in 1973–74 to concentrate on his teaching career, a move which has proved successful. The unfortunate aspect for Australian cricket was that, at 26 years of age, he may have been on the verge of realising his potential.

BATTING	M	Inn	NO	HS	Runs	Ave	100s	50s	C/S
Tests	31	53	6	127	1594	33.91	2	7	17
First-class	133	206	33	202	7987	46.16	19	38	34

BOWLING	Runs	Wkts	Ave	BB	5wl	10wM
First-class	66	1	66.00	1/19	–	–

SHEPHERD, Barry Kenneth

WA, LHB/OB
Born: 23 April 1937
Donnybrook, Western Australia

A solidly built left-handed batsman, Barry Shepherd's record indicates that he was a little unlucky to play for Australia on only nine occasions.

235

He always approached his batting in an aggressive frame of mind. After making his debut seven years earlier, he managed to force his way into the Australian team for the third Test of the 1962–63 series against England, making 71 not out. In spite of this he could never be sure of a game, but when chosen he usually did well. He had innings of 96, 70 and 78 against South Africa in 1963–64, but missed the 1964 tour of England. He did manage to tour the West Indies in 1964–65, where he played the last of his Tests. At first-class level he was a very dependable batsman for Western Australia, for whom he scored 12 centuries, three of them over 200. As a captain he was a shrewd tactician who made the best of limited resources during his 39 games in charge.

BATTING	M	Inn	NO	HS	Runs	Ave	100s	50s	C/S
Tests	9	14	2	96	502	41.83	–	5	2
First-class	110	186	14	219	6834	41.16	13	36	72

BOWLING	Balls	Runs	Wkts	Ave	BB		5wI	10wM
Tests	26	9	0	–	–		–	–
First-class	–	343	4	85.75	1/1		–	–

SIEVERS, Morris William

Vic, RHB/RFM
Born: 13 April 1912
Wonthaggi, Victoria
Died: 10 May 1968
Brunswick, Victoria

Morrie Sievers was a tall, Victorian fast-medium bowler and a capable batsman. He made his debut in 1933–34 and was chosen to tour South Africa in 1935–36. The selection would seem to have been a lucky one; the first-choice player, left-arm bowler and fellow Victorian Hans Ebeling, was unavailable. Although he produced some good performances in the first-class games, he was unable to force his way into the Test side. His three Tests came in the 1936–37 series against England. In the third game at Melbourne he produced his best bowling of 5/21 as England crumbled on a sticky wicket. Rather surprisingly Sievers was dropped for the next Test and was not chosen again, although he continued to represent Victoria for a number of seasons, for whom he was a more than useful performer.

BATTING	M	Inn	NO	HS	Runs	Ave	100s	50s	C/S
Tests	3	6	1	25*	67	13.40	–	–	4
First-class	58	87	17	76	2075	29.64	–	14	56

BOWLING	Balls	Runs	Wkts	Ave	BB	5wI	10wM
Tests	602	161	9	17.88	5/21	1	–
First-class	–	3870	116	33.36	6/43	4	–

SIMPSON, Robert Baddeley

NSW, WA, RHB/LBG
Born: 3 February 1936
Marrickville, New South Wales

Bob Simpson was a top class opening batsman, a useful leg spinner and one of the finest slips fieldsmen of all time. In addition, he captained Australia successfully, produced an amazing comeback, and in recent times has been the guiding force behind the Test side's remarkable improvement. He made his first-class debut in 1952–53 for New South Wales, but moved to Western Australia in 1956–57 for five years to further his Test chances. The move was a success, gaining him a place on the 1957–58 trip to South Africa where he made his Test debut.

It was not until the 1960–61 series against the West Indies that he established a place in the side. He toured England in 1961 where he began his opening partnership with Bill Lawry. Simpson became captain of Australia in 1963–64 and finally, in his thirtieth Test, at Old Trafford in 1964, he made his first Test century, a monumental 311, adding 201 with Lawry and winning the series. Against Pakistan on the way home he hit a century in each innings at Karachi. There were further big stands with Lawry: 382 against the West Indies at Barbados in 1965 and 244 against England at Adelaide in 1965–66, Simpson ending up with 201 and 225 respectively.

After 52 Tests, he announced his retirement in 1967–68, but continued to play grade cricket, and in 1977–78, at the age of 41, made a remarkable comeback. With the 'official' Test side struggling as a result of World Series Cricket, he returned to defeat India 3–2. Batting in the middle order, he had innings of 89, 176, 100 and 51 to show he was still a force to be reckoned with. Leading the side in the West Indies he was less successful against a strong pace attack, losing the series 3–1 to powerful opposition. A dispute with the Australian Cricket Board saw him retire in 1978–79, when his leadership would certainly have given Mike Brearley some food for thought.

With Australia struggling in the mid–eighties, Simpson again returned, this time as coach, and has succeeded in once more placing the Test team near the top of the international tree. His influence on players like Border, Jones, Boon and many others has been enormous. For over 30 years Bob Simpson has made an immense contribution to Australian cricket, and his influence looks like being felt for some time to come.

BATTING	M	Inn	NO	HS	Runs	Ave	100s	50s	C/S
Tests	62	111	7	311	4869	46.81	10	27	110
First-class	257	436	62	359	21029	56.22	60	100	383

BOWLING	Balls	Runs	Wkts	Ave	BB	5wl	10wM
Tests	6681	3001	71	42.26	5/57	2	–
First-class	–	13287	349	38.07	5/33	6	–

SINCOCK, David John

SA, RHB/SLC
Born: 1 February 1942
North Adelaide, South Australia

David Sincock was a left-arm wrist-spin bowler, who could not always summon the accuracy needed to secure a place in the Test team. Although he may have bowled some poor deliveries, there was always the possibility that he could produce a ball which would remove the opposition's best player. He made his first-class debut in 1960–61, taking 6/52 in his first game. His elevation to Test level seemed certain, and arrived in 1964–65 against Pakistan. He played one Test against the West Indies in 1965 and another against England in 1965–66, but he paid too dearly for his wickets and could not pose the same threat to Test batsmen as he did in the first-class arena.

BATTING	M	Inn	NO	HS	Runs	Ave	100s	50s	C/S
Tests	3	4	1	29	80	26.66	–	–	2
First-class	46	65	17	61*	838	17.45	–	4	27

BOWLING	Balls	Runs	Wkts	Ave	BB	5wI	10wM
Tests	724	410	8	51.25	3/67	–	–
First-class	–	5863	159	36.87	7/48	10	1

SLATER, Keith Nichol

WA, RHB/RFM, OB
Born: 12 March 1936
Midland, Western Australia

Keith Slater began as a fast-medium bowler, but changed to off spin in mid-career. He delivered the ball with a strange jerk in his action which led to suspicions of throwing. Slater was picked for the third Test of the 1958–59 series against England, a series in which the actions of Ian Meckiff and others had aroused criticism. He took only two wickets, and was not chosen again. As a batsman he was a useful performer, his only century being made against Queensland in 1963–64. Although he never produced outstanding performances, he was capable of securing a vital wicket or making a few runs when they were most needed. As such he was an extremely valuable player to his side. These days he can be heard commentating on the game as part of the ABC's team.

BATTING	M	Inn	NO	HS	Runs	Ave	100s	50s	C/S
Tests	1	1	1	1*	1	–	–	–	–
First-class	74	117	13	154	2198	21.13	1	13	50

BOWLING	Balls	Runs	Wkts	Ave	BB	5wI	10wM
Tests	256	101	2	50.50	2/40	–	–
First-class	–	5922	140	42.30	4/33	–	–

SLATER, Michael Jonathon

NSW, RHB
Born: 21 February, 1970
Wagga Wagga, New South Wales

A small, nimble-footed opening batsman, Michael Slater made his first-class debut in 1991–92. He played only two games at the end of the season, but showed enough promise to be given the opportunity of a full season in 1992–93. He amply repaid the selectors' faith by scoring 1019 runs at 59.94—winning a trip to England in the process. Slater lost out to Matthew Hayden for the one-day games, but won selection to partner Mark Taylor in the first Test at Old Trafford. With scores of 58 and 27 he ensured a place in the second Test team at Lord's. There, he struck the first ball to the mid wicket boundary, reached a century in just over three hours, and finished with 152 in an opening partnership of 260 with Taylor. Slater possesses all the shots, and his aggressive approach ensures that bowlers will struggle to tie him down. If he can continue the way he has started, the youngster could have an impressive Test career ahead of him.

BATTING	M	Inn	NO	HS	Runs	Ave	100s	50s	C/S
Tests	6	10	0	152	416	41.60	1	2	2
First-class	29	50	6	152	2392	54.36	7	15	17

SLEEP, Peter Raymond

SA, RHB/LBG
Born: 4 May 1957
Penola, South Australia

A talented batsman and a useful leg-spin bowler, Peter Sleep was given a number of chances to establish a place in the Test side. He made his first-class debut in 1976–77 and played his first Test against Pakistan in 1978–79. Sleep toured India in 1979–80, with some success, and

Pakistan in 1982, before dropping out of contention. Continued good form for South Australia won him a recall against England in 1986–87. At Sydney in the second innings of the fifth Test he took 5/72 to bowl Australia to victory. Next season against New Zealand he scored 211 runs at 52.75 in the three Tests, including his best score of 90, at Melbourne. His bowling, however, proved less effective and he lost his leg-spinning place to Trevor Hohns. He played once against Sri Lanka at Hobart in 1989–90, scoring 47 not out and taking 3/26 and 2/75, and once against Pakistan. In 1990–91 a run of poor form saw Sleep dropped from the South Australian team. He returned once more in 1991–92. In his final seasons he moved further down the batting order and concentrated more on his bowling. In his last game before retiring to England he took seven Western Australian wickets in a fitting end to his career.

BATTING	M	Inn	NO	HS	Runs	Ave	100s	50s	C/S
Tests	14	21	1	90	483	24.15	–	3	5
First-class	173	283	49	182	7971	34.06	14	39	103/1

BOWLING	Balls	Runs	Wkts	Ave	BB	5wI	10wM
Tests	2982	1397	31	45.06	5/72	1	–
First-class	–	14273	363	39.32	8/133	9	–

SLIGHT, James

Vic, RHB
Born: 20 October 1855
Geelong, Victoria
Died: 9 December 1930
Elsternwick, Victoria

James Slight was a right-handeded batsman who made his first-class debut for Victoria in 1874–75, a season in which he and BB Cooper produced the first double century opening partnership, 218, for South Melbourne against East Melbourne. He was very successful at grade level, but was unable to translate that form onto the first-class arena. Chosen for the 1880 tour, he suffered from illness and made only 41 runs in the six innings he played. He did, however, manage to be selected in the only Test match of the tour, at The Oval, where he made 11 and nought. Slight continued to represent Victoria until 1887–88 with generally little success, although 'Johnny' Moyes did describe him as 'one of the stars of the day'. Two of Slight's brothers also played first-class cricket.

BATTING	M	Inn	NO	HS	Runs	Ave	100s	50s	C/S
Tests	1	2	0	11	11	5.50	–	–	–
First-class	19	34	1	53	415	12.57	–	1	4

BOWLING	Runs	Wkts	Ave	BB	5wl	10wM
First-class	37	3	12.33	2/4	–	–

SMITH, David Bertram Miller

Vic, RHB
Born: 14 September 1884
Richmond, Victoria
Died: 29 July 1963
Hawthorn, Victoria

David Smith was a right-handed batsman of aggressive intent, who made his first-class debut for Victoria in 1908–09. His promise earned him a place in the Australian side which toured New Zealand under Warwick Armstrong in 1909–10, the year in which he made his highest score, 146, against South Australia. Smith was chosen as a replacement in the 1912 team to tour England when six of the top players withdrew. He played in two Tests on that tour, but achieved little of note. In fact his entire tour was rather disappointing as he made only 316 runs at 13.73. He did, however, have the satisfaction of making 100 against Surrey at The Oval. Injury forced his retirement from the game following that tour. Smith was also a champion Australian Rules player.

BATTING	M	Inn	NO	HS	Runs	Ave	100s	50s	C/S
Tests	2	3	1	24*	30	15.00	–	–	–
First-class	46	77	3	146	1764	23.83	3	6	16

BOWLING	Runs	Wkts	Ave	BB	5wl	10wM
First-class	22	1	22.00	1/22	–	–

SMITH, Stephen Barry

NSW, RHB
Born: 18 October 1961
Sydney, New South Wales

An aggressive right-handed batsman, Steve Smith did not do justice to his considerable ability in his three Test matches. His attacking approach made him an ideal one-day player and he produced some excellent innings in the World Series Cup. On his day he was capable of destroying any attack in the world and much was hoped for when he was chosen to tour the West Indies in 1983–84, but he failed in his three Tests. During the last of these he had a finger fractured by a delivery from Joel Garner. It was still thought that he had plenty of time to erase that poor start, but Smith disqualified himself from the Australian team by accepting an invitation to tour South Africa. After the two rebel tours he returned to New South Wales, but following a further season of Shield cricket he decided to continue his first-class career in South Africa. His is very much a case of what might have been.

BATTING	M	Inn	NO	HS	Runs	Ave	100s	50s	C/S
Tests	3	5	0	12	41	8.20	–	–	1
First-class	90	155	9	263	5248	35.94	12	26	66

BOWLING	Runs	Wkts	Ave	BB	5wI	10wM
First-class	77	1	77.00	1/35	–	–

SPOFFORTH, Frederick Robert

NSW, Vic, RHB/RFM
Born: 9 September 1853
Balmain, New South Wales
Died: 4 June 1926
Ditton Hill, Surbiton, England

Fred 'the Demon' Spofforth was the first great Australian bowler and one of the finest in the history of the game. His fast-medium bowling was delivered with a high action and cunningly disguised variations of pace. In addition, he was capable of cutting the ball both ways, and throughout his career he possessed an armoury more than capable of dismissing the best of batsmen. Behind a somewhat satanic countenance lurked a finely tuned tactical mind, which delighted in setting traps for unwary batsmen.

Spofforth came into top-class cricket in 1874, but missed the first Test in 1876–77 when he refused to play because Jack Blackham and not Murdoch had been chosen to keep wicket. The dispute was soon settled and Spofforth played in the second Test of that season. He toured England in 1878 and was a sensation, taking an amazing 764 wickets at 6.04 in all matches. The highlight of the tour came when he and Harry Boyle dismissed a strong MCC side for 33 and 19. Against Lord Harris's team in 1878–79 he took 6/48 and 7/62 and Test cricket's first hat-trick. Touring England again in 1880 he was just as devastating, with 763 wickets at 5.49, but injury prevented him from playing in the only Test.

It was the 1882 tour which brought Spofforth his greatest moment. In the only Test, at The Oval, he took 7/46 and 7/44, with Australia winning the game by seven runs to create the legend of the Ashes. In their second innings England needed only 84 to win, but 'the Demon' proved irresistible. While it is argued that he was not as good a bowler in Australia, he still produced some fine performances. In 1882–83 he took 18 wickets at 22.66 in the series, and in 1884–85 he took 4/54 and 6/90 in the third Test and 5/30 in the fourth. He toured England again in 1884 and 1886, and if he wasn't as devastating as on earlier visits he was still a force to be reckoned with.

In 1887 he moved to England where he became a successful businessman. He found time to play for Derbyshire and was still able to produce some dazzling displays. In 1896, playing for Wembley Park, he took 11 wickets against the touring Australians. Perhaps the last word on this legendary player should come from a country match in 1881–82, when he supposedly bowled all ten batsmen in each innings. The scorecard of this game is yet to come to light, but if the story is true it is a display unlikely to have ever been equalled.

BATTING	M	Inn	NO	HS	Runs	Ave	100s	50s	C/S
Tests	18	29	6	50	217	9.43	–	1	11
First-class	155	236	41	56	1928	9.88	–	3	83

BOWLING	Balls	Runs	Wkts	Ave	BB	5wl	10wM
Tests	4185	1731	94	18.41	7/44	7	4
First-class	–	12759	853	14.95	9/18	84	32

STACKPOLE, Keith Raymond

Vic, RHB/LB
Born: 10 July 1940
Collingwood, Victoria

A solidly built opening batsman with an attacking frame of mind, Keith Stackpole gloried in the hooking and cutting of fast bowling. The son of a state cricketer, Stackpole made his first-class debut in 1959–60, and his ability to bowl leg spin aided his Test selection against England in 1965–66. He was then chosen to tour South Africa in 1966–67, where he made 134 in the second Test. He dropped out of the side for a time, but re–established himself against the West Indies in 1968–69 when Bill Lawry had the inspired idea of sending him in first. Taking on the fast bowlers was perfectly suited to his aggressive approach, and he maintained his place until he retired in 1973–74. Although no bowler was safe against him, perhaps his most spectacular battles were against England and John Snow. In 1970–71 he scored 627 runs at 52.25, including 207 at Brisbane. The battle was continued in England in 1972 when he made 485 runs at 55.88. In the West Indies in 1973 much was expected of local fast bowler Uton Dowe. Stackpole carved him up to such an extent that the captain Rohan Kanhai was given the eleventh commandmant by the crowd, 'Dowe shall not bowl'. Although he retired before Australia reached a dominant position in world cricket during the seventies, he had laid much of the groundwork for that success.

BATTING	M	Inn	NO	HS	Runs	Ave	100s	50s	C/S
Tests	43	80	5	207	2807	37.42	7	14	47
First-class	167	279	22	207	10100	39.29	22	50	166

BOWLING	Balls	Runs	Wkts	Ave	BB	5wI	10wM
Tests	2321	1001	15	66.73	2/33	–	–
First-class	–	5814	148	39.28	5/38	2	–

STEVENS, Gavin Byron

SA, RHB
Born: 29 February 1932
Adelaide, South Australia

Gavin Stevens was a talented opening batsman who may have played in many more Tests had he not contracted hepatitis on his only tour, to India and Pakistan in 1959–60. He made his first-class debut in 1952–53, taking some time to establish himself as a Test prospect, something he achieved in 1957–58 when he made a century in each innings against New South Wales. With Jim Burke retiring at the end of the 1958–59 series, Australia was looking for an opening batsman, and Stevens seemed to fit the bill, particularly after he took 259 off the New South Wales bowlers during that season. Stevens played his only four Tests on that 1959–60 tour, his failures almost certainly accounted for by his illness.

BATTING	M	Inn	NO	HS	Runs	Ave	100s	50s	C/S
Tests	4	7	0	28	112	16.00	–	–	2
First-class	47	86	6	259*	3061	38.26	7	11	34

BOWLING	Runs	Wkts	Ave	BB	5wl	10wM		
First-class	123	3	41.00	2/16	–	–		

TABER, Hedley Brian

NSW, RHB/WK
Born: 29 April 1940
Wagga Wagga, New South Wales

Brian Taber was a top-class wicketkeeper, whose neat work behind the stumps was of great benefit in 16 Tests. He made his first-class debut in 1964–65, securing over 30 dismissals in each of his first two seasons. When Barry Jarman was unavailable to tour South Africa in 1966–67, Taber was given the job and captured eight victims in his first Test. He toured England as Jarman's deputy in 1968 and replaced him as Australia's 'keeper for the fifth Test against the West Indies in 1968–69, a season in which he equalled the world record of 12 dismissals in a match, and for the tour of India and South Africa in 1969–70. Although a useful batsman, his lack of runs at Test level may have been a cause for his replacement by Rod Marsh in 1970–71. Taber toured England as Marsh's deputy in 1972, before retiring in 1973–74. Since then he has established a reputation as an excellent coach.

BATTING	M	Inn	NO	HS	Runs	Ave	100s	50s	C/S
Tests	16	27	5	48	353	16.04	–	–	56/4
First-class	129	182	35	109	2648	18.01	1	8	345/50

BOWLING	Runs	Wkts	Ave	BB	5wI	10wM
First-class	6	0	–	–	–	–

TALLON, Donald

Qld, RHB/WK
Born: 17 February 1916
Bundaberg, Queensland
Died: 7 September 1984
Bundaberg, Queensland

Don Tallon could lay claim to being the country's finest wicketkeeper. He was a brilliant stumper and a safe catch, able to make the difficult appear simple. As a batsman he was more than capable, and the tragedy is that he lost many of his best years to the Second World War. He made his first-class debut in 1933–34 and established such a reputation that he was considered unlucky not to tour England in 1938. In 1938–39 he set a world record of 12 dismissals in a match. The long–awaited Test debut finally came in New Zealand in 1945–46. Against England in 1946–47 he removed 20 batsmen, and following a fine series against India, he was a vital member of the 1948 side which demolished England. Unavailable for the 1949–50 tour of South Africa, he returned to play against England in 1950–51, but lost his place to Gil Langley next season. Tallon's last Test came on the 1953 tour of England.

BATTING	M	Inn	NO	HS	Runs	Ave	100s	50s	C/S
Tests	21	26	3	92	394	17.13	–	2	50/8
First-class	150	228	21	193	6034	29.14	9	27	303/129

BOWLING	Runs	Wkts	Ave	BB	5wl	10wM
First-class	202	0	–	–	–	–

TAYLOR, John Morris

NSW, RHB
Born: 10 October 1895
Stanmore, New South Wales
Died: 12 May 1971
Turramurra, New South Wales

A stylish, attacking right-handed batsman, and the idol of the young Don Bradman, Johnny Taylor played 20 Tests in the period following the First World War. He made his first-class debut in 1913–14, but really came to notice with the first AIF team in England in 1919. This led to his Test selection against England in 1920–21. He was chosen to tour England in 1921, playing in all five Tests, and he also played against South Africa on the way home. Against England at Sydney in 1924–25 he made his only Test century, adding 127 with Arthur Mailey for the last wicket, still an Australian Test record. He toured England again in 1926 before retiring from first-class cricket in 1926–27. Perhaps he may have been a little too aggressive to make the number of runs his ability seemed to warrant, but he was well worth watching.

BATTING	M	Inn	NO	HS	Runs	Ave	100s	50s	C/S
Tests	20	28	0	108	997	35.60	1	8	11
First-class	135	195	7	180	6274	33.37	11	38	68

BOWLING	Balls	Runs	Wkts	Ave	BB	5wl	10wM
Tests	114	45	1	45.00	1/25	–	–
First-class	–	53	1	53.00	1/25	–	–

TAYLOR, Mark Anthony

NSW, LHB
Born: 27 October 1964
Leeton, New South Wales

A solidly built left-handed opening batsman of endless concentration and plenty of strokes, Mark Taylor served a long apprenticeship in the New South Wales side before making his debut in the fourth Test against the West Indies at Adelaide in 1988–89. This involved splitting up the successful partnership of David Boon and Geoff Marsh. Taylor did little in the fourth and fifth Tests, but was selected to tour England in 1989. He was nothing short of sensational, scoring 839 runs at 83.90, including 219 at Trent Bridge and 136 at Headingley. Back in Australia in 1989–90 he continued his good form, scoring four more Test centuries against Sri Lanka and Pakistan. Much was expected of him against England in 1990–91, but the tactic of bowling around the wicket restricted him. Taylor fought back well in the West Indies to end the series with a fighting century in an Australian victory. In recent series at home and on tour in Sri Lanka he struggled and was dropped for the fifth Test of the 1992–93 series against the West Indies. Taylor fought back with some improved performances in New Zealand, then renewed his liking for English conditions with another successful tour in 1993. As captain of New South Wales and vice-captain of Australia, Taylor has shown enough leadership potential to be rated as a future Test captain, possibly the successor to Allan Border.

BATTING	M	Inn	NO	HS	Runs	Ave	100s	50s	C/S
Tests	46	84	5	219	3588	45.42	10	20	62
First-class	146	252	11	219	10739	44.56	28	55	203

BOWLING	Balls	Runs	Wkts	Ave	BB	5wl	10wM
Tests	24	15	0	–	–	–	–
First-class	–	57	1	57.00	1/4	–	–

TAYLOR, Peter Laurence

NSW, Qld, LHB/OB
Born: 22 August 1956
North Sydney, New South Wales

New South Wales off-spinner Peter Taylor had one of cricket's more sensational Test debuts. Chosen for the fifth Test of the 1986–87 series against England after six first-class games, the man dubbed 'Peter Who?' by the press took 6/78 and 2/76, made some useful runs, particularly a second innings 42, and won the Man of the Match Award in an Australian victory. While he was an integral member of Australia's one-day team, he did not establish himself in the Test side. With the bat he was a stubborn lower order player, who always sold his wicket dearly. His highest score of 87 was made against New Zealand at Wellington in 1989–90. Dropped from the New South Wales team on his return, Taylor moved to Queensland in 1990–91. He earned a trip to the West Indies (one Test) and played two Tests at home against India in 1991–92. He enjoyed little success in those matches and retired at the end of the season. Taylor's coolness under pressure made him an extremely valuable one-day player, and it was in this area that he produced his best cricket.

BATTING	M	Inn	NO	HS	Runs	Ave	100s	50s	C/S
Tests	13	19	3	87	425	26.56	–	2	10
First-class	63	81	19	105*	1919	30.95	1	10	45

BOWLING	Balls	Runs	Wkts	Ave	BB	5wI	10wM
Tests	2101	989	25	39.56	6/78	1	–
First-class	–	4820	129	37.36	6/78	3	–

THOMAS, Grahame

NSW, RHB
Born: 21 March 1938
Croydon Park, New South Wales

Despite some excellent displays at first-class level, New South Wales right-hander Grahame Thomas was unable to secure a regular Test place. He made his debut in 1957–58, steadily developing a reputation with some brilliant displays, and could have been considered unlucky not to tour England in 1961 and 1964. His chance finally came when he was chosen to tour the West Indies in 1964–65, making his debut in the first Test. He played in all five Tests, making his highest score of 61 in the second game, in Trinidad. Despite making 229 early in 1965–66 he had to wait until the third Test of the series against England. Two half-centuries in those games helped him gain selection to South Africa in 1966–67. He did not play in any of the Tests on tour and retired on his return to Australia. For such an attractive and aggressive player, the scorer of 17 first-class centuries, the lack of success at Test level was a disappointment.

BATTING	M	Inn	NO	HS	Runs	Ave	100s	50s	C/S
Tests	8	12	1	61	325	29.54	–	3	3
First-class	100	154	12	229	5726	40.32	17	23	92/2

BOWLING	Runs	Wkts	Ave	BB	5wI	10wM
First-class	30	0	–	–	–	–

THOMS, George Ronald

VIC, RHB
Born: 22 March 1927
Footscray, Victoria

George Thoms was a right-handed batsman who opened for Victoria in 19 games between 1946 and 1953. For most of that time he was paired with Colin McDonald, and the two developed an excellent understanding. Two centuries in 1951–52, including his highest score of 150 against Western Australia, earned Thoms a place in the fifth Test team to play the West Indies at Sydney. He made 16 and 28, but was not chosen again. At the time Australia possessed a number of fine opening batsmen, and it was players like Arthur Morris, Jim Burke and McDonald himself who prevented Thoms from receiving another chance. After one more season in first-class cricket he retired to his medical practice.

BATTING	M	Inn	NO	HS	Runs	Ave	100s	50s	C/S
Tests	1	2	0	28	44	22.00	–	–	–
First-class	19	32	0	150	1137	35.53	3	5	10

BOWLING	Runs	Wkts	Ave	BB	5wI	10wM
First-class	14	1	14.00	1/8	–	–

THOMSON, Alan Lloyd

VIC, RHB/RFM
Born: 2 December 1945
Reservoir, Victoria

Alan 'Froggy' Thomson was an unusual fast-medium bowler, who delivered the ball off the wrong foot. He made his first-class debut in 1968–69, and bowled so well during the next two seasons that he became a Test possible for the 1970–71 series against England. He confirmed his place by taking 6/80 and 3/101 against them for Victoria, and duly made his debut in the first Test at Brisbane. In four Tests he lacked the pace to trouble the English batsmen, who made him pay dearly for his wickets. Despite a successful career for Victoria until 1974 the selectors were not prepared to risk him again.

BATTING	M	Inn	NO	HS	Runs	Ave	100s	50s	C/S
Tests	4	5	4	12*	22	22.00	–	–	–
First-class	44	55	23	34*	260	8.12	–	–	12

BOWLING	Balls	Runs	Wkts	Ave	BB	5wl	10wM
Tests	1519	654	12	54.50	3/79	–	–
First-class	–	4917	184	26.72	8/87	12	3

THOMSON, Jeffrey Robert

NSW, Qld, RHB/RF
Born: 16 August 1950
Greenacre, New South Wales

In all cricket history there may have been a few bowlers capable of delivering a cricket ball at a similar speed to Jeff Thomson, but it is hard to imagine anyone bowling faster. With his unusual slinging action Thomson was capable of awesome speed, and if there was any uneven bounce in the pitch he could be positively lethal. Against such pace there is no time to alter a stroke, and a fraction of a second spent hesitating could end an innings. In addition, he could make the ball lift alarmingly from just short of a length. With Dennis Lillee at the other end, the threat was simply doubled.

The Bankstown boy made his first-class debut in 1972–73 and was chosen for the second Test against Pakistan later that season. He played with a broken bone in his foot and did little to impress. A move to Queensland saw his career take off, and he was chosen for the first Test of the 1974–75 series against England. On a pitch of doubtful quality he was frighteningly fast in taking 3/59 and 6/46. He took 33 wickets at 17.93 and left a number of batsmen nursing bruises and broken bones. Injury prevented him playing in the final Test, but he was back to torment England in 1975 taking 16 wickets at 28.56, despite the lack of pace in the pitches. He was also at his lethal best

when capturing 29 wickets against the West Indies in 1975–76, and
was a major factor in Australia's 5–1 victory.

Playing against Pakistan in the first Test of the next season he col-
lided with Alan Turner and dislocated his collarbone. He returned a
few months later to tour England in 1977 and take 23 wickets. Declining to join World Series Cricket, he was Australia's leading bowler in
the 1977–78 series against India and the West Indies. He did join World
Series in its second season and after that appeared to lose form for a
time. Certainly, after the shoulder injury he was not as consistently fast.

True to character, 'Thommo' came back. He bowled well in 1981–82
and the next season, in the absence of an injured Lillee, he led the
attack against England taking 22 wickets in four Tests. The rebel tour
of South Africa meant that a number of players were unavailable for
selection for the 1985 tour of England, a fact that undoubtedly contributed to Thomson's selection for the tour. Although no longer the
threat of old, he did manage to secure his 200th Test wicket. Unable
to win the Sheffield Shield for Queensland as a player, he became state
coach in 1990–91 in the hope of capturing what seems to have become
an impossible dream.

BATTING	M	Inn	NO	HS	Runs	Ave	100s	50s	C/S
Tests	51	73	20	49	679	12.81	–	–	20
First-class	187	216	64	61	2065	13.58	–	2	63

BOWLING	Balls	Runs	Wkts	Ave	BB	5wI	10wM
Tests	10535	5601	200	28.00	6/46	8	–
First-class	–	17864	675	26.46	7/27	28	3

THOMSON, Nathaniel Frampton Davis

NSW, RHB/RM(r)/WK
Born: 29 May 1839
Surry Hills, New South Wales
Died: 2 September 1896
Burwood, New South Wales

Nat Thomson has the distinction of being the first player dismissed in
a Test match. He opened the batting with Charles Bannerman in the

254

first game at Melbourne in 1876–77 and was bowled for one. Thomson had begun his first-class career back in 1857–58, and was well into the veteran stage by the time Test cricket began. Although he did not succeed in the first Test, he had a little more luck in the return match, making 41 in the second innings. He continued to play first-class cricket until 1879–80, taking part in the famous New South Wales versus England match in 1878–79 which saw a riot occur when local hero Murdoch was dismissed, but he was not considered again for Test selection. Undoubtedly Thomson was a better than average player, but the international game had come a little too late for him to take advantage of it.

BATTING	M	Inn	NO	HS	Runs	Ave	100s	50s	C/S
Tests	2	4	0	41	67	16.75	–	–	3
First-class	27	51	1	73	705	14.10	–	3	23/7

BOWLING	Balls	Runs	Wkts	Ave	BB	5wl	10wM
Tests	112	31	1	31.00	1/14	–	–
First-class	–	512	23	22.26	3/13	–	–

THURLOW, Hugh Motley

Qld, RHB/RF
Born: 10 January 1903
Townsville, Queensland
Died: 3 December 1975
Rosalie, Queensland

Hugh 'Pud' Thurlow was a right-arm fast bowler who led the Queensland attack between 1928–29 and 1934–35. His only Test came against South Africa at Adelaide in 1931–32. It was an unsuccessful selection as he failed to take a wicket and was run out for nought in his only innings, leaving his partner, Don Bradman, on 299 not out. Despite his lack of success at Test level, he was a good first-class bowler, quite capable of upsetting the best of batsmen. In fact it was Thurlow who struck Alan Kippax with a bouncer, an injury which certainly affected that great batsman's play for the remainder of his career.

BATTING	M	Inn	NO	HS	Runs	Ave	100s	50s	C/S
Tests	1	1	0	0	0	0.00	–	–	–
First-class	31	58	20	23	202	5.31	–	–	10

BOWLING	Balls	Runs	Wkts	Ave	BB	5wl	10wM
Tests	234	86	0	–	–	–	–
First-class	–	3431	80	42.88	6/59	5	–

TOOHEY, Peter Michael

NSW, RHB
Born: 20 April 1954
Blayney, New South Wales

Peter Toohey was a small, aggressive right-handed batsman, who bore some similarities to Doug Walters. In fact it looked for a short time as if he would go some way towards emulating that player's feats. He made his first-class debut in 1974–75 and was brought into the Test side for the first game of the 1977–78 series against India. With innings of 82 and 57, he won the Man of the Match Award and had much to do with Australia's success during the first season of World Series Cricket. He played well in the rest of that series, passing 50 on three more occasions. A broken thumb kept him out of two Tests against the West Indies in 1977–78, but he returned to make 122 and 97 in the last two games. Apart from an innings of 81 not out at Perth in 1978–79, he performed poorly against the English bowlers and lost his Test place. Although he continued to play for New South Wales for a number of seasons, Toohey was unable to recapture the form which had made him one of the world's most promising players.

BATTING	M	Inn	NO	HS	Runs	Ave	100s	50s	C/S
Tests	15	29	1	122	893	31.89	1	7	9
First-class	74	163	12	158	5735	37.98	12	31	67

BOWLING	Balls	Runs	Wkts	Ave	BB	5wl	10wM
Tests	2	4	0	–	–	–	–
First-class	–	9	0	–	–	–	–

TOSHACK, Ernest Raymond Herbert

NSW, RHB/LM
Born: 15 December 1914
Cobar, New South Wales

A miserly left-arm medium pace bowler, Ernie Toshack was an important member of the Australian attack in the period after the Second World War. Although his principal task was to tie up an end for the likes of Miller and Lindwall operating at the other end, he did much more than that, as his impressive Test record will confirm. If there was anything in the pitch, he could be unplayable. Toshack built up a reputation in country cricket before moving to Sydney with Keith Miller after the War. He took little time to reach the top, making his Test debut in New Zealand in 1945–46, taking six wickets in the match. Toshack took 17 English wickets in 1946–47, while against India at Brisbane in 1947–48 he returned the amazing figures of 5/2 and 6/29. To tour England in 1948 he had to pass a medical examination of a troublesome knee injury. Although the knee did eventually let him down, he took 50 wickets on tour, including 11 in the Tests. An operation enabled him to continue for another two seasons, but he did not play Test cricket again, although he was put on standby for the 1949–50 South African tour when Bill Johnston was injured.

BATTING	M	Inn	NO	HS	Runs	Ave	100s	50s	C/S
Tests	12	11	6	20*	73	14.60	–	–	4
First-class	48	45	13	20*	185	5.78	–	–	10

BOWLING	Balls	Runs	Wkts	Ave	BB	5wl	10wM
Tests	3140	989	47	21.04	6/29	4	1
First-class	–	3973	195	20.37	7/81	12	1

TRAVERS, Joseph Patrick Francis

SA, LHB/SLA
Born: 10 January 1871
Adelaide, South Australia
Died: 15 September 1942
Adelaide, South Australia

Travers was a left-arm slow bowler who represented South Australia between 1895–96 and 1906–07. His only Test was the fifth against England at Melbourne in 1901–02 as replacement for the injured Saunders. Although Australia won the game by 32 runs, Travers was given very little to do. He missed selection for the 1902 tour of England and could certainly have been given another chance, especially considering his first-class form. His best figures of 9/30 were taken against Victoria in 1900–01, and he held his own in a state attack that contained great bowlers like George Giffin and Ernie Jones. With hindsight, perhaps Travers deserved a little better.

BATTING	M	Inn	NO	HS	Runs	Ave	100s	50s	C/S
Tests	1	2	0	9	10	5.00	–	–	1
First-class	37	69	23	77	760	16.52	–	2	25

BOWLING	Balls	Runs	Wkts	Ave	BB	5wI	10wM
Tests	48	14	1	14.00	1/14	–	–
First-class	–	3673	117	31.39	9/30	6	1

TRIBE, George Edward

Vic, LHB/SLC
Born: 4 October 1920
Yarraville, Victoria

A left-arm wrist-spin bowler, George Tribe was a master purveyor of cricket's most difficult deliveries, and he was also a more than useful batsman. He made his debut in 1945–46, taking 33 wickets in his first season. Tribe's three Tests were played against England in 1946–47, and produced just two wickets, a poor return for such a gifted player. As he was unable to force his way into a strong Australian side, Tribe took his talents to English league cricket. He toured India successfully on two occasions with Commonwealth teams, and in 1952 he began a county career with Northamptonshire. Beginning with 40 wickets in his first four games, Tribe completed the thousand run-hundred wicket double in his first years. In fact he achieved the double in seven of his eight seasons, and during the fifties he was undoubtedly the best left-arm spinner in the world; sadly Australia saw too little of him.

BATTING	M	Inn	NO	HS	Runs	Ave	100s	50s	C/S
Tests	3	3	1	25*	35	17.50	–	–	–
First-class	308	454	82	136*	10177	27.34	7	48	243

BOWLING	Balls	Runs	Wkts	Ave	BB	5wI	10wM
Tests	760	330	2	165.00	2/48	–	–
First-class	–	28321	1378	20.55	9/43	93	23

TROTT, Albert Edwin

Vic, RHB/RFM
Born: 6 February 1873
Abbotsford, Victoria
Died: 30 July 1914
Willesden Green, London, England

An immensely talented all-rounder, Albert Trott had a sensational Test debut against England in 1894–95, when, in three Tests, he had innings of 38 not out, 72 not out and 85 not out, and at Adelaide took 8/43. When he missed the 1896 touring team, captained by his brother, Harry, he took his skills to England, qualifying for Middlesex in 1898. He produced some spectacular cricket, particularly in his first few years, scoring 1000 runs and taking over 200 wickets in each of the 1899 and 1900 seasons. Against the Australians in 1899 he struck MA Noble over the pavilion at Lord's, and against Somerset in 1900 he took all 10 wickets. He played 2 Tests for England against South Africa in 1898–99 in which he took 17 wickets at 11.64, but his powers declined with age. In desperate poverty, Trott shot himself at the age of 41.

BATTING	M	Inn	NO	HS	Runs	Ave	100s	50s	C/S
Tests	3	5	3	85*	205	102.50	–	2	4
First-class	375	602	53	164	10696	19.48	8	44	449

BOWLING	Balls	Runs	Wkts	Ave	BB		5wI	10wM
Tests	474	192	9	21.33	8/43		1	–
First-class	–	35316	1674	21.09	10/42		132	41

TROTT, George Henry Stevens

Vic, RHB/LB
Born: 5 August 1866
Collingwood, Victoria
Died: 10 November 1917
Albert Park, Victoria

Harry Trott's performances were not as spectacular as those of his younger brother Albert, but he was a very capable all-rounder with his right-handed batting and leg-spin bowling. He made his first-class debut in 1885–86 and played his maiden Test on tour in England in 1888. He toured again in 1890, 1893 and 1896, captaining the side on the final visit. It was at Lord's on this tour that he made his only Test century. Trott won five and lost three Tests as leader, and many contemporaries were high in their praise of his tactical skills. He was also immensely popular, and had much to do with the early careers of players like Hugh Trumble, Joe Darling and Clem Hill. Sadly his health broke down in 1898 and he was confined to a mental institution. Incredibly, he emerged to play for Victoria again from 1903–04 to 1907–08. Like his brother, Harry Trott did not live to a ripe old age, the years of health problems eventually taking their toll.

BATTING	M	Inn	NO	HS	Runs	Ave	100s	50s	C/S
Tests	24	42	0	143	921	21.92	1	4	21
First-class	222	393	19	186	8797	23.52	9	40	183

BOWLING	Balls	Runs	Wkts	Ave	BB		5wI	10wM
Tests	1890	1019	29	35.13	4/71		–	–
First-class	–	9700	386	25.12	8/36		17	2

TRUMBLE, Hugh

Vic, RHB/OB
Born: 12 May 1867
Abbotsford, Victoria
Died: 14 August 1938
Hawthorn, Victoria

A magnificent off-spin bowler and useful batsman, Hugh Trumble was a key figure in Australian teams at the turn of the century. He was also an excellent judge of batsmen and a master at spotting weaknesses. With his long fingers he could get plenty of spin and he had the height to gain bounce from the wicket. Added to this was the ability to vary his pace without any noticable change in his action. At his peak he was arguably the best bowler in the world.

Trumble made his first-class debut in 1887–88, but did not play Test cricket until 1890 on his first tour of England. He toured England again in 1893, 1896, 1899 and 1902, being the side's key bowler on each of the last three occasions. During those trips there were some fine performances: at The Oval in 1896 he took 6/59 and 6/30, at Old Trafford in 1902 he picked up 10 wickets in a classic game which Australia won by three runs, while in the next match at The Oval he took 8/65 and 4/108 as England won by a single wicket.

Although he did have great success in England, he was no less a matchwinner in Australia. In 1897–98 he took 19 wickets as Australia won the series. He captained Australia to victory in each of the last two Tests of the 1901–02 series, and also performed the hat-trick in the last game at Melbourne. Persuaded to play in the second Test against England in 1903–04, he took 4/107 and 5/34. He continued for the remainder of the series, and in his last game at Melbourne, Trumble ended his Test career with 7/28, bowling his side to victory and taking his second hat-trick in Test cricket. It was a fitting end to a wonderful career.

Although his bowling was his main weapon, he was quite a capable batsman, usually scoring his runs when they were most needed. He scored four fifties in Tests and ended up with a creditable average for a lower order batsman. Trumble also gave great service to Victoria, his best effort being 7/89 and 8/113 against South Australia in 1889–90.

In retirement, he became an astute writer on the game and was the secretary of the Melbourne Cricket Club for many years, but it is as Australia's finest off-spin bowler that he is best remembered.

BATTING	M	Inn	NO	HS	Runs	Ave	100s	50s	C/S
Tests	32	57	14	70	851	19.79	–	4	45
First-class	213	344	67	107	5395	19.47	3	20	329

BOWLING	Balls	Runs	Wkts	Ave	BB	5wI	10wM
Tests	8099	3072	141	21.78	8/65	9	3
First-class	–	17153	929	18.46	9/39	69	25

TRUMBLE, John William

Vic, RHB/OB
Born: 16 September 1863
Kew, Victoria
Died: 17 August 1944
Brighton, Victoria

John Trumble was a useful all-rounder, if not in the class of his younger brother Hugh. After making his first-class debut in 1883–84, he was one of the replacement team chosen for the second Test of the 1884–85 series against England. Scoring 59, he held his place for the next Test, something most of his team mates failed to do. He performed well enough to gain a place on the 1886 tour of England. Unfortunately he achieved little, on what was a disappointing trip. His play for Victoria was never spectacular, but he could make valuable runs or take useful wickets, and he was also a good fieldsman. A career in the legal profession restricted his cricket after the 1886 tour, but he continued to play first-class cricket until 1889–90.

BATTING	M	Inn	NO	HS	Runs	Ave	100s	50s	C/S
Tests	7	13	1	59	243	20.25	–	1	3
First-class	63	104	11	87	1761	18.93	–	7	33

BOWLING	Balls	Runs	Wkts	Ave	BB	5wI	10wM
Tests	600	222	10	22.20	3/29	–	–
First-class	–	2627	109	24.10	6/33	5	1

TRUMPER, Victor Thomas

NSW, RHB/RM
Born: 2 November 1877
Darlinghurst, New South Wales
Died: 28 June 1915
Darlinghurst, New South Wales

Victor Trumper was a true genius of Australian cricket. A right-handed batsman capable of destroying any attack under any conditions, he had every stroke in the book and a few others of his own invention. He possessed a special magic which remained in the memory, and it was the manner of their making rather than the number of runs he scored that stamped him as something special. Such was his appeal that thousands would attend a grade game just to see him. Because he was capable of winning any match, his was the wicket most wanted by the opposition. He was also a useful bowler and an athletic fieldsman.

Trumper made his first-class debut in 1894–95, but created no real impression until 1898–99 when he scored two double centuries. Under pressure from MA Noble, Trumper was a late inclusion on the 1899 tour of England. He failed in his first Test, but scored 135 not out in the second at Lord's. That, plus 300 not out against Sussex, saw him given the same payments as the rest of the team. He was not so successful against England at home in 1901–02, but on his second English tour he was a sensation. In a wet summer he scored 2570 runs with 11 centuries. At Old Trafford in the fourth Test he became the first player to make a century before lunch. It was the pinnacle of his career—his other tours to England in 1905 and 1909 were not as successful. Through this period he formed a fine opening partnership with Reg Duff, the two sharing many impressive and fast-scoring stands. As Duff's career declined, Trumper continued on. Against England in 1903–04 he made 185 not out in the first Test, 74 out of a team total of 122 on a difficult pitch in the second, 113 and 59 in the third, and 88 in the fifth. At Sydney in 1907–08 he made 166 against England. He was in good form against South Africa in 1910–11, and also in his last series, against England in 1911–12, when he scored his final Test century in the first Test and made 50 in his last Test innings. He should have had one more series in 1912, but was one of six who refused to tour England over a managerial dispute.

Trumper's death, from Bright's Disease in 1915 at the age of 37, was universally mourned and forced even the War news off the front pages. No cricketer has been more greatly admired.

BATTING	M	Inn	NO	HS	Runs	Ave	100s	50s	C/S
Tests	48	89	8	214*	3163	39.04	8	13	31
First-class	255	401	21	300*	16939	44.57	42	87	171

BOWLING	Balls	Runs	Wkts	Ave	BB	5wI	10wM
Tests	546	317	8	39.62	3/60	–	–
First-class	–	2031	64	31.73	5/19	2	–

TURNER, Alan

NSW, LHB
Born: 23 July 1950
Camperdown, New South Wales

Alan Turner was a left-handed opening batsman whose solid performances for New South Wales in the seventies enabled him to force his way into the Test side. Turner made his first-class debut in 1968–69, and toured New Zealand with a 'B' team in 1969–70. A good season in 1974–75 saw him chosen to tour England in 1975. He played in the World Cup games, scoring a century against Sri Lanka, then made his Test debut at Edgbaston. Turner scored his only Test century, against the West Indies at Adelaide in 1975–76. In 1976–77 he had the misfortune to collide with Jeff Thomson when going for a catch, an incident which badly injured the fast bowler's shoulder. He toured New Zealand in 1976–77, but missed selection in the Centenary Test and the 1977 tour of England, and retired in 1978 after just one more season.

BATTING	M	Inn	NO	HS	Runs	Ave	100s	50s	C/S
Tests	14	27	1	136	768	29.53	1	3	15
First-class	105	196	10	156	5744	30.88	7	31	80

BOWLING	Runs	Wkts	Ave	BB	5wI	10wM
First-class	10	1	10.00	1/6	–	–

TURNER, Charles Thomas Biass

NSW, RHB/RM
Born: 16 November 1862
Bathurst, New South Wales
Died: 1 January 1944
Manly, New South Wales

Known as 'the Terror', Charlie Turner succeeded Fred Spofforth as Australia's premier bowler. A right-arm medium pacer with strong fingers and plenty of variations, Turner could devastate the best of batting, but he had the misfortune to play in a period when Australia's own batting was so poor that it was usually unable to capitalise on his masterly bowling. He was also a useful batsman, scoring two first-class centuries, and he may have made many more runs had he not been required to do so much bowling.

Turner made his debut for New South Wales in 1882–83, although he had already built a strong reputation in country cricket. He made his Test debut in 1886–87, taking 6/15 to bowl England out for 45, and went on to take 29 wickets in his first four games, all of which were lost. In consecutive innings those returns were 6/15, 2/53, 5/41, 4/69, 5/44 and 7/43. In 1887–88 he became the first, and so far only, bowler to take a hundred wickets in an Australian season, when he removed 106 batsmen at an average of 13.59.

He was an obvious choice to tour England in 1888 and here his partnership with left-armer JJ Ferris really blossomed. The pair were sensational, taking 534 wickets on tour, Turner's share being 314 at 11.12, including 21 in the three Tests. He took five or more wickets in every Test innings in which he bowled: 5/27 and 5/36 at Lord's, 6/112 at The Oval and 5/86 at Old Trafford. In a multitude of dazzling displays, he took 8/13 and 9/37 against an England XI at Hastings and 9/17 against another England XI at Stoke. At the end of the tour he had taken 494 first-class wickets at 11.12 in just under two years.

On his other trips to England he was not quite so successful. In 1890 he took 215 wickets at 12.67 and in 1893 it was 149 at 14.25. On those tours he no longer had the services of Ferris, who had moved to England, but he was still capable of winning a game with a devastating burst.

Turner retired in 1894–95 with 101 Test wickets at 16.53, and while others have taken more wickets, no-one has paid as little for them. It is an average which is unchallenged, and is just one of many astounding achievements by a bowler who must rank as one of the finest of all time.

BATTING	M	Inn	NO	HS	Runs	Ave	100s	50s	C/S
Tests	17	32	4	29	323	11.53	–	–	8
First-class	155	261	13	103	3856	15.54	2	11	85

BOWLING	Balls	Runs	Wkts	Ave	BB	5wl	10wM
Tests	5179	1670	101	16.53	7/43	11	2
First-class	–	14147	993	14.24	9/15	102	35

V

VEIVERS, Thomas Robert

Qld, LHB/OB
Born: 6 April 1937
Beenleigh, Queensland

An economical, rather than devastating, off-spin bowler and useful batsman, the solidly built Tom Veivers was an important member of the Australian teams of the sixties. He made his first-class debut in 1958–59 and played his maiden Test, against South Africa, in 1963–64. Although he achieved little, he went to England in 1964 where he was a vital player. At Old Trafford, in a total of 611, he bowled 95 overs to take 3/155, the most overs delivered by an Australian in a Test ininngs. In addition to his bowling, he made some important contributions with the bat. He was unable to tour the West Indies in 1965, but returned to play against England in 1965–66 and tour South Africa in 1966–67. Unfortunately Veivers retired from first-class cricket in 1967–68, at the age of 30, when most believed his best was yet to come.

BATTING	M	Inn	NO	HS	Runs	Ave	100s	50s	C/S
Tests	21	30	4	88	813	31.26	–	7	7
First-class	106	162	24	137	5100	36.95	4	37	52

BOWLING	Balls	Runs	Wkts	Ave	BB	5wI	10wM
Tests	4191	1375	33	41.66	4/68	–	–
First-class	–	7393	191	38.70	5/63	3	–

VELETTA, Michael Robert John

WA, RHB/WK
Born: 30 October 1963
Subiaco, Western Australia

Mike Veletta is a dogged right-handed opening batsman, a brilliant fieldsman in any position and a useful wicketkeeper. He has been given a number of opportunities at Test level without being able to reproduce any of the form shown for Western Australia. There he has formed a successful opening partnership with Geoff Marsh which has produced a number of large stands. Veletta first came to international prominence with some good innings in the 1987 World Cup. He made his Test debut against New Zealand in 1987–88, and despite playing all five Tests that summer, he achieved little. After two Tests against the West Indies in 1988–89 he lost his place, although he did tour England in 1989, play one game against Pakistan in 1989–90 and visit the West Indies in 1990–91. Perhaps the last selection owed more to his ability to act as a reserve 'keeper, than to his batting form. He is an enthusiastic and dedicated player, but his chances at the highest level must be running out.

BATTING	M	Inn	NO	HS	Runs	Ave	100s	50s	C/S
Tests	8	11	0	39	207	18.81	–	–	12
First-class	130	214	23	262	7823	40.96	20	39	161/2

BOWLING	Runs	Wkts	Ave	BB	5wl	10wM
First-class	12	0	–	–	–	–

WAITE, Mervyn George

SA, RHB/RM, OB
Born: 7 January 1911
Kent Town, South Australia
Died: 16 December 1985
Georgetown, South Australia

Merv Waite was a useful all-rounder for South Australia from his debut in 1930–31. He was an aggressive lower order batsman and a bowler who could send down either medium pace or off spin depending on the conditions. Chosen to tour England in 1938 he played in the last two Tests, but made little impact. After playing a minor role in the fourth Test victory, he opened the bowling at The Oval, sending down 72 overs for 150 runs and the wicket of Denis Compton, whom he bowled for one, in a total of 7/903. He performed reasonably well in other tour games, making 760 runs at 25.33 and taking 57 wickets at 26.03. Waite's sole hundred came against Queensland in 1939–40, but the War removed any chance of improving his Test figures.

BATTING	M	Inn	NO	HS	Runs	Ave	100s	50s	C/S
Tests	2	3	0	8	11	3.66	–	–	1
First-class	103	155	15	137	3888	27.77	1	23	66

BOWLING	Balls	Runs	Wkts	Ave	BB	5wI	10wM
Tests	552	190	1	190.00	1/150	–	–
First-class	–	6071	192	31.61	7/101	5	–

WALKER, Maxwell Henry Norman

Vic, RHB/RFM
Born: 12 September 1948
West Hobart, Tasmania

Max Walker bowled his fast-medium deliveries with an unusual action, earning himself the name 'Tangles'. Despite this, he was able to move the ball sharply into the batsman and also deliver a useful leg cutter. Coming to Melbourne to play football, he triumphed as a cricketer, making his Test debut against Pakistan in 1972–73 and taking 6/15 in only his second game. His best series was on tour in the West Indies in 1973, when, in the absence of Lillee and Massie, he took 26 wickets at 20.73, leading Australia to a 2–0 victory. For the rest of his career he served as a support for Lillee, Thomson and company, a task which he did with great success. Against England at Melbourne in 1974–75, with both fast bowlers injured, Walker took 8/143. He toured England in 1977, then joined World Series Cricket. Walker was a very popular player, adored by fans, and is now a successful sports commentator.

BATTING	M	Inn	NO	HS	Runs	Ave	100s	50s	C/S
Tests	34	43	13	78*	586	19.53	–	1	12
First-class	135	170	40	78*	2014	15.49	–	3	49

BOWLING	Balls	Runs	Wkts	Ave	BB	5wl	10wM
Tests	10094	3792	138	27.47	8/143	6	–
First-class	–	13209	499	26.47	8/143	21	–

WALL, Thomas Welbourn

SA, RHB/RF
Born: 13 May 1904
Semaphore, South Australia
Died: 26 March 1981
Adelaide, South Australia

'Tim' Wall was Australia's most successful fast bowler of the thirties. He made up in accuracy what he might have lacked in speed, and performed valuable service for Australia from his Test debut against England in 1928–29, when he took 3/123 and 5/66, until he retired after touring England in 1934. He had previously toured there in 1930. Against South Africa in 1931–32 he produced his best figures of 5/14 in the first Test. Wall's best season was 1932–33 when he took 16 wickets at 25.56 in the Bodyline series, including 5/72 at Adelaide. During the same season he became the first bowler to take 10 wickets in a Shield innings when he took 10/36 to dismiss a strong New South Wales side, with six Test players, including Bradman, for 113. Only Peter Allan (Qld) and Ian Brayshaw (WA), have since equalled Wall's feat.

BATTING	M	Inn	NO	HS	Runs	Ave	100s	50s	C/S
Tests	18	24	5	20	121	6.36	–	–	11
First-class	108	135	33	53*	1071	10.50	–	1	54

BOWLING	Balls	Runs		Wkts	Ave	BB		5wI	10wM
Tests	4812	2010		56	35.89	5/14		3	–
First-class	–	9877		330	29.93	10/36		10	2

WALTERS, Francis Henry

NSW, Vic, RHB/RM
Born: 9 February 1860
East Melbourne, Victoria
Died: 1 June 1922
at sea near Bombay, India

Walters was an aggressive batsman and a medium pace bowler who made his first-class debut for Victoria in 1880–81. His only Test came against England at Melbourne in the fifth game of the 1884–85 series. He was a failure there, but was given a chance to redeem himself when chosen for the 1890 English tour. He did not grasp the opportunity, making only 402 runs at 10.05. Walters continued to play well for Victoria until he moved to New South Wales, for whom he played in 1895–96 and made his highest score of 150 against Queensland. He had previously made two centuries for Victoria in the early nineties and 122 for Combined Australia against the 1888 Australian team at Sydney in 1888–89. All four of his centuries were made on the Sydney Cricket Ground.

BATTING	M	Inn	NO	HS	Runs	Ave	100s	50s	C/S
Tests	1	2	0	7	12	6.00	–	–	2
First-class	56	96	9	150	1755	20.17	4	5	31

BOWLING	Runs	Wkts	Ave	BB	5wI	10wM
First-class	81	1	81.00	1/17	–	–

WALTERS, Kevin Douglas

NSW, RHB/RM
Born: 21 December 1945
Dungog, New South Wales

Doug Walters was a dashing right-handed batsman, capable of turning a match with a brilliant innings, taking a vital wicket with his seemingly innocuous medium pace, or a dazzling catch. The one blot on his career was his failure to come to terms with English conditions, despite touring there in 1968, 1972, 1975 and 1977.

Walters had a stunning debut against England in 1965–66, making 155 and 115 in his first two Tests. National Service interrupted his career, but he returned to bat well against India in 1967–68. Next year he tore the West Indies to pieces making 76, 118, 110, 50, 242 and 103. The last two innings were the first time anyone had made a double century and a century in the one Test.

Ian Chappell greatly valued Walters' ability to win Test matches, something he proved repeatedly over the years. At Jamiaca on the 1973 West Indies tour he scored 100 in a session on the first day and Australia won by 44 runs. In the next match at Georgetown he took 5/66 in a 10-wicket win. Sent in on a green pitch at Auckland in 1973–74, and with Australia one down in the series, he struck a dazzling 104 not out to set up a victory.

Perhaps Walters' greatest feat came at Perth against England in 1974–75. Three not out at tea on the first day, he slaughtered the bowling to score 100 in the final session. That figure and his own century were brought up when he hit Bob Willis over square leg for six off the last ball of the day. Australia went on to win by nine wickets. Also in that series, at Adelaide, he scored an important 55 against Derek Underwood on a wet wicket to take Australia from 5/84 to an eventual 163-run victory. In 1976–77 he made his highest score, 250, against New Zealand at Christchurch.

Walters joined World Series Cricket, and when it seemed his Test days were over he returned to the Australian side in 1980–81, batting superbly against a New Zealand attack led by Richard Hadlee. On a not very good Melbourne wicket he made 107, and later that summer scored 78 and 18 not out as Australia lost to India. It was to be his final Test as he missed selection on the 1981 tour of England.

Although he never courted publicity, Walters was incredibly popular, and he gave much to the game with his dry humour and his amazing batting displays.

BATTING	M	Inn	NO	HS	Runs	Ave	100s	50s	C/S
Tests	74	125	14	250	5357	48.26	15	33	43
First-class	258	426	57	253	16180	43.84	45	81	149

BOWLING	Balls	Runs	Wkts	Ave	BB	5wl	10wM
Tests	3295	1425	49	29.08	5/66	1	–
First-class	–	6782	190	35.69	7/63	6	–

WARD, Francis Anthony

SA, RHB/LBG
Born: 23 February 1909
Sydney, New South Wales
Died: 25 May 1974
Sydney, New South Wales

A leg-break and googly bowler, Frank Ward came into the Australian side at the expense of Clarrie Grimmett, a decision many thought one of the worst in the game's history. Although he was no Grimmett, Ward was a more than useful bowler. When chosen for the first Test of the 1936–37 series against England he responded by taking 6/102 in the second innings. Despite not holding his place for the remainder of the series, Ward was selected to tour England in 1938, again ahead of Grimmett. He took 96 wickets at 18.98, but played in only the fifth Test, taking 0/142 as England scored 7/903. Ward was a better bowler than most critics were prepared to give him credit for. If his Test figures were uninspiring, his record for South Australia was impressive, and his bowling partnership with Grimmett at Shield level gave South Australia a matchwinning attack.

BATTING	M	Inn	NO	HS	Runs	Ave	100s	50s	C/S
Tests	4	8	2	18	36	6.00	–	–	1
First-class	66	80	17	62	871	13.82	–	1	42

BOWLING	Balls	Runs	Wkts	Ave	BB	5wI	10wM
Tests	1268	574	11	52.18	6/102	1	–
First-class	–	7900	320	24.68	7/51	24	5

WARNE, Shane Keith

Vic, RHB/LBG
Born: 13 September 1969
Ferntree Gully, Victoria

Australia's search for a Test slow bowler undoubtedly contributed to Shane Warne being chosen for the third Test against India, at Sydney, after only a handful of matches. The leg spinner, a product of the Cricket Academy, made his first-class debut in 1990–91 and some solid performances with a young Australian team in Zimbabwe and for Victoria led to his Test debut. After one game he was chosen for the Young Australians tour to Zimbabwe where he bowled impressively. Further solid performances for Victoria led to his Test debut. He struggled to take wickets in his two Tests, but was chosen to tour Sri Lanka in 1992–93 where his 3/11 helped produce an unlikely victory in the first Test. He worked hard on his fitness, shedding a number of kilos, and in 1992–93 his bowling had more variety, including a very dangerous 'flipper' which skidded onto the batsmen. At Melbourne Warne had his moment of triumph, taking 7/52 as Australia won by 139 runs. Touring New Zealand at the end of the season he used the 'flipper' to good effect to take seven wickets in the first Test, winning the Man of the Match award in the process, and going on to take 17 wickets in the series. Warne's 1993 Ashes tour began in sensational fashion when he bowled Mike Gatting with his first delivery of the series; a leg break which spun from outside leg stump to hit off. His control and the amount of spin he gained, meant that no batsman played him with any certainty, and he went on to produce the best bowling seen by an Australian leg spinner since the days of Clarrie Grimmett, whose record number of wickets he exceeded in the final Test. Warne has made a remarkable improvement in a short space of time and could be a key member of the Australian attack for the next decade.

BATTING	M	Inn	NO	HS	Runs	Ave	100s	50s	C/S
Tests	17	23	5	37	298	16.56	–	–	10
First-class	44	52	13	69	729	18.69	–	2	18

BOWLING	Balls	Runs	Wkts	Ave	BB	5wI	10wM
Tests	4880	1832	65	28.18	7/52	2	–
First-class	–	4338	156	27.81	7/41	5	–

WATKINS, John Russell

NSW, RHB/LBG
Born: 16 April 1943
Newcastle, New South Wales

Leg-spinner John Watkins can claim to have had one of cricket's more unusual careers. He had taken only 10 wickets in five first-class games when he was chosen to play in the third Test against Pakistan at Sydney in 1972–73. A performance of 6/38 for Northern New South Wales in a non-first-class game against the tourists probably helped his selection. He could not find a length in his six overs and appeared out of his depth, but he did have the pleasure of making 36 in a ninth wicket stand of 83 with Bob Massie. This gave Australia enough runs to win and Watkins had the honour of taking the final catch. Despite his rather ordinary bowling he was taken to the West Indies in 1973, but played in only four matches in which he collected 10 wickets. They were his final first-class games.

BATTING	M	Inn	NO	HS	Runs	Ave	100s	50s	C/S
Tests	1	2	1	36	39	39.00	–	–	1
First-class	10	15	8	36	70	10.00	–	–	10

BOWLING	Balls	Runs	Wkts	Ave	BB	5wI	10wM
Tests	48	21	0	–	–	–	–
First-class	–	726	20	36.30	4/72	–	–

WATSON, Graeme Donald

Vic, WA, NSW RHB/RM
Born: 8 March 1945
Kew, Victoria

Graeme Watson was a useful all-rounder who played for three states and World Series Cricket in a long career. He made his debut for Victoria in 1964–65 and toured South Africa in 1966–67 where he played in three Tests, making 50 at Cape Town in his first game. A move to Western Australia saw him return to the national team against the World XI in 1971–72. In that series he was struck a fearful blow in the face by a delivery from Tony Greig. Following transfusions of some 40 pints of blood, he courageously fought back to win a place on the 1972 tour of England. He played unsuccessfully in the first and last Tests, but he did make his highest score of 176 against Hampshire. In 1976–77 he played for New South Wales and then signed for World Series Cricket where he ended his career.

BATTING	M	Inn	NO	HS	Runs	Ave	100s	50s	C/S
Tests	5	9	0	50	97	10.77	–	1	1
First-class	107	162	19	176	4674	32.68	7	25	73

BOWLING	Balls	Runs	Wkts	Ave	BB	5wI	10wM
Tests	552	254	6	42.33	2/67	–	–
First-class	–	4709	186	25.31	6/61	8	–

WATSON, William James

NSW, RHB
Born: 31 January 1931
Randwick, New South Wales

A solid opening batsman, Bill Watson was a sound performer at first-class level, but failed to make much of an impression in his four Tests.

He made his first-class debut in 1953–54, and next season scored 155 against the touring English team. This no doubt helped him win a place in the fifth Test team. Although he made only 18 and three he was selected to tour the West Indies where he played his other three Tests. In a high scoring series Watson's best effort was 30 in the fourth Test at Bridgetown, Barbados. Despite his failure at Test level he did play some useful innings in the other matches. In the first-class game he was more successful, the highest of his six centuries being 206 against Western Australia at Perth.

BATTING	M	Inn	NO	HS	Runs	Ave	100s	50s	C/S
Tests	4	7	1	30	106	17.66	–	–	2
First-class	41	66	5	206	1958	32.09	6	5	26

BOWLING	Balls	Runs	Wkts	Ave	BB	5wl	10wM
Tests	6	5	0	–	–	–	–
First-class	–	40	0	–	–	–	–

WAUGH, Mark Edward

NSW, RHB/RM
Born: 2 June 1965
Canterbury, New South Wales

Mark Waugh was kept waiting 100 first-class games before making his Test debut, against England at Adelaide in 1990–91. He showed the selection was long overdue by making a magnificent 138, after having replaced his brother in the team. Before making his stunning entry into the Test arena Waugh had enjoyed a successful first-class career, which began in 1985–86. He had scored heavily for New South Wales and for Essex in the English County Championship. While not as good a bowler as Steve, he has performed well for Australia in one-day internationals and is a brilliant fieldsman. Further solid performances followed in the West Indies, but a loss of form cost him his place against India in 1991–92. Waugh endured a horror tour of Sri Lanka, but returned to some better form against the West Indies, particularly in the second Test at Melbourne where he made 112. He could not maintain his form on tour in New Zealand, and lost his place for the third Test. He returned to prominence with some excellent aggressive innings during the 1993 Ashes tour, none better than 137 and 62 not out in the fifth Test at Edgbaston, which won him the Man of the Match award and led Australia to another victory. He has such ability that he can make batting look the easiest thing in the world, and it is hard to imagine that he will not be a major force in Test cricket during the next decade.

BATTING	M	Inn	NO	HS	Runs	Ave	100s	50s	C/S
Tests	27	44	3	139*	1613	39.34	4	10	39
First-class	172	270	41	229*	13008	56.86	43	59	208

BOWLING	Balls	Runs	Wkts	Ave	BB	5wl	10wM
Tests	1344	664	17	39.06	4/80	–	–
First-class	–	4590	118	38.90	5/37	1	–

WAUGH, Stephen Rodger

NSW, RHB/RM
Born: 2 June 1965
Canterbury, New South Wales

Unlike his twin brother, Steve Waugh did not have to wait long to play his first Test. Just one season after his debut in 1984–85, he was playing Test cricket against India. Although he was an excellent one-day player with his aggressive batting and medium-pace bowling, his Test returns were very ordinary, considering his obvious ability. Gradually, he came to grips with Test cricket. Innings of 71, 79 not out and 73 against England in 1986–87 and a couple of excellent nineties against the West Indies in 1988–89 saw him starting to justify the high hopes held for him. On the 1989 English tour he really blossomed with 177 not out, 152 not out and 92. Experience in English county cricket no doubt helped. After one further hundred against Sri Lanka, he lost form and his place in the Test side. He fought back with some excellent innings for New South Wales to regain his place for the 1992–93 series against the West Indies. Although forced to bat at number three, for which many would insist he is not technically equipped, he had the satisfaction of making a century in the third Test at Sydney. Steve Waugh's future lies lower in the batting order, at five or six, where his technique has the best chance to succeed. He proved this with some useful performances on tour in New Zealand, and then returned to some of his best form during the 1993 Ashes series, where his stubborn defiance

278

helped save the third Test and his dashing 157 not out helped win the fourth.

BATTING	M	Inn	NO	HS	Runs	Ave	100s	50s	C/S
Tests	58	89	15	177*	2919	39.45	5	17	43
First-class	168	253	42	216*	9626	45.62	27	42	143

BOWLING	Balls	Runs	Wkts	Ave	BB	5wI	10wM
Tests	4862	2295	51	45.00	5/69	2	–
First-class	–	6336	192	33.00	6/51	4	–

WELLHAM, Dirk MacDonald

NSW, Tas, Qld, RHB
Born: 13 March 1959
Summer Hill, New South Wales

Dirk Wellham's Test career never fulfilled the promise he showed by making 103 on debut against England at The Oval in 1981. He earned that tour with a good season for New South Wales (for whom he also made a century on debut) but on his return he was unable to establish a Test place, although he did tour England again in 1985. He continued to play well at first-class level and became a successful captain. Wellham was tried again in Test cricket, against England in 1986–87, also without success. Had he made runs he may have become Australia's captain. When it appeared his first-class career was over he reappeared as captain and coach of Tasmania for three seasons. Although he made no centuries for them he batted well, particularly in 1990–91, his last season. In 1991–92 he moved to Queensland and enjoyed some of the best form of his long career. Wellham announced his retirement at the end of the season, but he re–emerged next season to captain Queensland in the absence of Ian Healy, becoming the only person to lead three states in the Sheffield Shield.

BATTING	M	Inn	NO	HS	Runs	Ave	100s	50s	C/S
Tests	6	11	0	103	257	23.36	1	–	5
First-class	145	233	33	167	8566	42.83	16	53	66

BOWLING	Runs	Wkts	Ave	BB	5wI	10wM	
First-class	25	1	25.00	1/11	–	–	

WESSELS, Kepler Christoffel

Qld
Born: 14 September 1957
Bloemfontein, South Africa.

Kepler Wessels came to Australia via South Africa, Sussex in English county cricket, and World Series Cricket. He became eligible for the Test team in 1982–83 and made 162 on debut against England at Brisbane. He was a Test regular until he declared himself unavailable after the first Test of the 1985–86 season. Wessels' best series was against the West Indies in 1984–85 when he overcame technical problems and some ferocious fast bowling to score 505 runs at 56.11, including his highest score of 179 at Sydney. In 1986–87 he joined the rebel Australians in South Africa and after that he decided to continue his cricket there. Although he was a controversial and not always popular player, he did give Australia excellent service. Wessels career did not end with his return to Port Elizabeth. He returned to prominence as South Africa's captain for the 1992 World Cup and for its return to Test cricket. His Australian experience has undoubtedly been of great benefit to his team, and he has shown himself to be a player still capable of scoring runs at the highest level.

BATTING	M	Inn	NO	HS	Runs	Ave	100s	50s	C/S
Tests	24	42	1	179	1761	42.95	4	9	18
First-class	246	426	37	254	19795	50.88	54	101	197

BOWLING	Balls	Runs	Wkts	Ave	BB	5wl	10wM
Tests	90	42	0	–	–	–	–
First-class	–	549	12	45.42	2/25	–	–

WHATMORE, Davenell Frederick

Vic, RHB
Born: 16 March 1954
Colombo, Ceylon (Sri Lanka)

Sri Lankan born Dav Whatmore made his first-class debut for Victoria in 1975–76. His aggressive batting and excellent slips fielding attracted the selectors' attention in 1978–79 when the Test team needed batsmen to replace those lost to World Series Cricket. Whatmore made his Test debut against Pakistan. He did enough to earn a trip to England for the 1979 World Cup and then a tour of India in 1979–80 where he played in five Tests, making 77 and 54 at Delhi. After that he was dropped from the Victorian side for a number of years, but came back in 1986–87 as an opening batsman. His aggressive approach paid off, as he scored nearly 700 runs. Next season he did even better, making over 900 runs at an average of over 50. Sadly, the Victorian selectors dispensed with his services when he still had plenty to offer.

BATTING	M	Inn	NO	HS	Runs	Ave	100s	50s	C/S
Tests	7	13	0	77	293	22.53	–	2	13
First-class	108	189	9	6116	170	33.97	10	35	147

BOWLING	Balls	Runs	Wkts	Ave	BB	5wi	10wM
Tests	30	11	0	–	–	–	–
First-class	–	109	4	27.25	1/0	–	–

WHITNEY, Michael Roy

NSW, RHB/LFM
Born: 24 February 1959
Surry Hills, New South Wales

When the 1981 team in England was hit by injury, left-arm pace bowler Mike Whitney was brought from league cricket to play in two Tests. After that he was largely forgotten, and forced to battle a knee injury, until 1987–88 when he played in the third Test against New Zealand. He saved the game with his batting by holding out for the last few overs against Richard Hadlee. His next match was the fifth Test against the West Indies at Adelaide in 1988–89. It was a triumph, as he took 7/89 and two more in the second innings. Despite that, and 50 first-class wickets in the season, he missed the 1989 tour to England. He fought back to tour the West Indies in 1991, where he bowled well in the first-class games, but did little in the Tests. The popular Whitney had more luck against India in 1991–92, taking 4/68 and 7/27, his best-ever figures, in the Perth Test and bowling well in the one-day games. The 1992–93 tour of Sri Lanka produced little, but with Bruce Reid's injury problems an opportunity opened for Whitney against the West

Indies. Unfortunately, a blow on the foot removed him from the action for the majority of the season. But Whitney is nothing if not a fighter, and it would be no surprise to see him return to the Test team once more.

BATTING	M	Inn	NO	HS	Runs	Ave	100s	50s	C/S
Tests	12	19	8	13	68	6.18	–	–	2
First-class	117	118	44	28*	415	5.61	–	–	50

BOWLING	Balls	Runs	Wkts	Ave	BB	5wI	10wM
Tests	2672	1325	39	33.97	7/27	2	1
First-class	–	11019	411	26.81	7/27	19	1

WHITTY, William James

NSW, SA, RHB/LFM
Born: 15 August 1886
Sydney, New South Wales
Died: 30 January 1974
Tantanoola, South Australia

Bill Whitty was a left-handed bowler who played one match for New South Wales in 1907–08 and then moved to South Australia where he spent the remainder of his career. He toured England in 1909, playing in one Test. The trip worked wonders on him, as he took 37 wickets against South Africa in 1910–11, including his best of 6/17 in the second Test. He toured England again in 1912 and was the leading bowler with 109 wickets, including 25 in the Tests. Sadly, the War ruined what could have been a great career. Whitty was chosen to tour South Africa in 1914–15, a trip which was cancelled. After the War he continued to bowl well in first-class cricket and was still a force when he retired in 1925–26. Had those seasons not been lost, an impressive career may have become a great one.

BATTING	M	Inn	NO	HS	Runs	Ave	100s	50s	C/S
Tests	14	19	7	39*	161	13.41	–	–	4
First-class	119	171	44	81	1464	11.52	–	1	35

BOWLING	Balls	Runs	Wkts	Ave	BB	5wI	10wM
Tests	3357	1373	65	21.12	6/17	3	–
First-class	–	11488	491	23.39	8/27	26	4

WIENER, Julien Mark

Vic, RHB/OB
Born: 1 May 1955
Melbourne, Victoria

A blond haired opening batsman, Julien Wiener made his first-class debut in 1977–78, scoring 106 against Queensland. He did so well in his first few seasons that he was chosen to play against England at Perth in 1979–80. He made 58 in the second innings, played quite well against the West Indies, and earned a tour of Pakistan in 1980. At Lahore in the third Test he made 93, his highest Test score. Strangely, Wiener did not play Test cricket again, despite some heavy scoring for Victoria, particularly in 1981–82 when he had his best season, making over 800 runs. As Australia struggled to find opening batsmen in the eighties it seems strange that he was not given another chance. At one time he looked like developing into a promising off spinner, but this declined as his batting progressed.

BATTING	M	Inn	NO	HS	Runs	Ave	100s	50s	C/S
Tests	6	11	0	93	281	25.54	–	2	4
First-class	66	123	4	221*	3609	30.32	7	13	49

BOWLING	Balls	Runs	Wkts	Ave	BB	5wI	10wM
Tests	78	41	0	–	–	–	–
First-class	–	1164	17	68.47	2/19	–	–

WILSON, John William

Vic, SA, RHB/SLA
Born: 20 August 1922
Albert Park, Victoria
Died: 13 October 1985
Melbourne, Victoria

A left-arm slow bowler, Wilson made his debut for Victoria in 1949–50, but moved to South Australia in 1950–51. He bowled well for a number of seasons before earning a place in the 1956 team to tour England. Despite a 12-wicket haul against Gloucestershire, he took only 43 wickets in all, and did not play in the Test series. The English conditions simply did not suit his style of bowling. Wilson played his single Test on the way home, against India at Bombay. It was not particularly successful as he did not bat and took only one wicket. He played one more season for South Australia before retiring.

BATTING	M	Inn	NO	HS	Runs	Ave	100s	50s	C/S
Tests	1	–	–	–	–	–	–	–	–
First-class	78	97	47	19*	287	5.74	–	–	17

BOWLING	Balls	Runs	Wkts	Ave	BB	5wI	10wM
Tests	216	64	1	64.00	1/25	–	–
First-class	–	7019	230	30.51	7/11	9	1

WOOD, Graeme Malcolm

WA, LHB/RM
Born: 6 November 1956
East Fremantle, Western Australia

Graeme Wood was a talented left-handed batsman who made nine Test centuries. He lacked consistency, however, and in his early days ended too many innings with frenetic running between the wickets. Wood made his Test debut in 1977–78 against India. Later that season he scored his first century, against the West Indies at Georgetown, an innings which led to a three-wicket win. A loss of form cost him his place in the side, but he fought back to make a century in the Centenary Test at Lord's in 1980. He was a regular player for Australia through the first half of the eighties, making many tours, including visiting England again in 1981 and 1985. On the second tour he played his highest innings, 172 at Trent Bridge. He dropped out of Test cricket after that tour, but returned to the Australian team as a middle-order batsman in 1988–89 and scored a century against the West Indies in Perth. It was to be a short–lived recovery, as he lost his place before the end of the series. Wood was a successful captain of Western Australia, but in 1989–90 he lost the leadership and was then removed from the side, on the express wishes of the players. The dispute was resolved and Wood returned to first-class cricket in 1990–91, but retired after being dropped during the next season.

BATTING	M	Inn	NO	HS	Runs	Ave	100s	50s	C/S
Tests	59	112	6	172	3374	31.83	9	13	41
First-class	227	375	41	186*	13353	39.98	35	61	155

BOWLING	Runs	Wkts	Ave	BB	5wI	10wM			
First-class	156	6	26.00	3/18	–	–			

WOODCOCK, Ashley James

SA, RHB
Born: 27 February 1947
Adelaide, South Australia

Ashley Woodcock was a very good right-handed opening batsman who made his first-class debut in 1967–68. He performed steadily at the top of the order, particularly in 1970–71 when he had South African Barry Richards as his partner. Some good form in 1973–74 earned him a place in the third Test against New Zealand at Adelaide where he made 27 in his only innings. Woodcock toured New Zealand later that season, but did not play in any of the Tests. With Australia struggling to find a suitable partner for Ian Redpath in the next two seasons, it is surprising that he was not given another chance. Despite that, he continued to make runs for South Australia until he retired in 1978–79, and it may be argued that Australia did not make the best use of his talents.

BATTING	M	Inn	NO	HS	Runs	Ave	100s	50s	C/S
Tests	1	1	0	27	27	27.00	–	–	1
First-class	85	151	4	141	4550	30.95	5	31	72

WOODFULL, William Maldon

Vic, RHB
Born: 22 August 1897
Maldon, Victoria
Died: 11 August 1965
Tweed Heads, New South Wales

Bill Woodfull is an important figure in Australian cricket history. Not only was he an excellent opening batsman with a defence so solid he was called 'the unbowlable', but he was also a superb captain who led Australia with great dignity and sportsmanship through its most difficult period. While his technique, with its minimal backlift and lack of attacking strokes, may not have excited crowds, Woodfull added an air of solidity to his side's batting. His record speaks for the success of his approach.

Woodfull made his first-class debut for Victoria in 1921–22, forming an opening partnership with Bill Ponsford which became one of Australia's finest, their efforts producing over 20 century partnerships, including 18 for the first wicket. For over a decade they gave their teams a sound start which the remaining batsmen could capitalise on. Woodfull was considered lucky to make the 1926 team to England, at the expense of Alan Kippax, who had a brilliant year, but he justified the selectors' faith by being the leading run scorer, with 1809 at 53.35, including two Test centuries.

In 1930 Woodfull was again a surprise choice, this time as captain to replace Jack Ryder, and had the pleasure of leading the side which regained the Ashes. Although the efforts of Bradman and Grimmett were the prime factors, Woodfull's innings of 155, 50, 54 and 54 certainly played a part. He led Australia successfully at home against the West Indies and South Africa, before confronting Douglas Jardine's English team in the 1932–33 Bodyline series.

Woodfull's calm dignity and the loyalty with which his players followed him meant that Australia did not retaliate, although he made his feelings about the English tactics plain. When Pelham Warner, the MCC manager came to express sympathy after Woodfull had been struck over the heart, he was told, 'There are two teams out there, but only one of them is playing cricket.' In the face of some vicious bowling he set an example by staying at the crease longer than anyone else. His best effort was to carry his bat through Australia's second innings at Adelaide for 73 not out in the toughest game of the series. In 1934 he again led the Australian team to England. His tact and diplomacy ensured the smooth running of the first post–Bodyline series, and he had the distinction of once again winning back the Ashes. It was a fitting end to a fine career.

BATTING	M	Inn	NO	HS	Runs	Ave	100s	50s	C/S
Tests	35	54	4	161	2300	46.00	7	13	7
First-class	173	245	39	284	13392	65.00	49	58	77

BOWLING	Runs	Wkts	Ave	BB	5wI	10wM	
First-class	24	1	24.00	1/12	–	–	

WOODS, Samuel Moses James

RHB/RF
Born: 13 April 1867
Ashfield, New South Wales
Died: 30 April 1931
Taunton, Somerset, England

All-rounder Sammy Woods has the unique distinction of representing Australia in Tests without ever having played first-class cricket in this country. Woods was born in Australia but educated in England at Cambridge University, which he captained at cricket and represented at rugby. He was an aggressive striker of the ball and a fine fast bowler. Most of his cricket was played for Somerset, with whom he was associated for over a quarter of a century. Woods played in the three Tests of the 1888 series when the Australian tourists were struggling for players, but he achieved little of note. He also played three times for England against South Africa and represented them at rugby. It was at Somerset, however, where he spent his life and played his best cricket. As the years slowed his bowling, he became a better batsman and displayed flair in leading a side with limited resources. Woods died a much loved figure in the county.

BATTING	M	Inn	NO	HS	Runs	Ave	100s	50s	C/S
Tests	3	6	0	18	32	5.33	–	–	1
First-class	401	690	35	215	15345	23.42	19	62	279

BOWLING	Balls	Runs	Wkts	Ave	BB	5wI	10wM
Tests	217	121	5	24.20	2/35	–	–
First-class	–	21653	1040	20.82	10/69	77	21

WOOLLEY, Roger Douglas

Tas, RHB/WK
Born: 16 September 1954
Hobart, Tasmania

Wicketkeeper-batsman Roger Woolley has the distinction of being the first Tasmanian selected from its Sheffield Shield team to play Test cricket. While his 'keeping form could fluctuate, he was a particularly exciting batsman with a wide range of strokes and an aggressive attitude. Towards the end of his career he gave up 'keeping and played strictly as a batsman. In 1977–78 he became the first Tasmanian to score a century for the Shield team. When Rod Marsh was unavailable to tour Sri Lanka in 1983 Woolley was chosen and 'kept well in the only Test at Colombo. After Marsh's retirement, Woolley was the number one 'keeper for the 1983–84 West Indies tour. However, a broken finger and the selectors' use of Wayne Phillips restricted him to just one Test in which he failed to do himself justice. Woolley captained Tasmania for a number of seasons, leading the state to its best Shield result, in 1983–84.

BATTING	M	Inn	NO	HS	Runs	Ave	100s	50s	C/S
Tests	2	2	0	13	21	10.50	–	–	7/-
First-class	85	139	20	144	4781	40.17	7	30	144/16

BOWLING	Runs	Wkts	Ave	BB	5wI	10wM	
First-class	33	0	–	–	–	–	

WORRALL, John

Vic, RHB/OB(r)
Born: 12 May 1861
Maryborough, Victoria
Died: 17 November 1937
Fairfield Park, Victoria

Worrall was an aggressive batsman, and a useful off-spin bowler who played for Victoria from 1883–84 to 1901–02, and who once made 417 not out for Carlton in a grade game. Short, thickset and tough, he made his Test debut against England in 1884–85 and toured England in 1888. His first tour was not a success as his batting was inclined to be a little reckless, perhaps a reason why he played only 11 Tests spread over 14 years. Certainly he could never command a regular place in the side. He toured England again in 1899, when he was far more successful.

In addition to some good first-class innings, Worrall made his highest Test score, 76 at Headingley out of 95, struck at a run a minute. Worrall's career ended when he made some ill-conceived remarks about his team mates and was suspended by the VCA. It was a sad conclusion to a fine career. In later life he became a respected sports journalist and is credited by many with inventing the term 'Bodyline'.

BATTING	M	Inn	NO	HS	Runs	Ave	100s	50s	C/S
Tests	11	22	3	76	478	25.25	–	5	13
First-class	142	245	23	128	4660	20.99	7	16	101

BOWLING	Balls	Runs	Wkts	Ave	BB	5wI	10wM
Tests	255	127	1	127.00	1/97	–	–
First-class	–	2426	105	23.10	5/20	4	–

WRIGHT, Kevin John

WA, SA, RHB/WK
Born: 27 December 1953
North Fremantle, Western Australia

Kevin Wright was a capable wicketkeeper and useful batsman who represented Australia during the second season of World Series Cricket. Although he made his debut for Western Australia in 1974–75, he did not gain a regular place until Rod Marsh joined World Series Cricket. He played in the last two Tests of the 1978–79 series, when the selectors decided John Maclean was not the answer behind the stumps. The red–haired Wright held his place for the two Tests against Pakistan, the 1979 World Cup and the six-Test tour of India in 1979–80. When World Series Cricket ended, Marsh returned and Wright moved to South Australia, where he played successfully for a number of seasons. His career ended when the state selectors decided that Wayne Phillips, a good bat, but not in Wright's class as a 'keeper, should take over behind the stumps. Wright retired in disgust, leaving the impression that, with a little luck, his career could have been far more substantial.

BATTING	M	Inn	NO	HS	Runs	Ave	100s	50s	C/S
Tests	10	18	5	55*	219	16.84	–	1	31/4
First-class	85	128	33	105	2551	26.85	2	10	267/26

YALLOP, Graham Neil

Vic, LHB/LM
Born: 7 October 1952
Balwyn, Victoria

Graham Yallop made his Test debut against the West Indies in 1975–76, but it was not until he toured the Caribbean in 1977–78 that he established a place in the side. In 1978–79 he had the unenviable task of captaining Australia against Mike Brearley's English team. While he was not a great leader, Yallop certainly proved himself as a batsman, scoring hundreds in the first and sixth Tests. The second of these was a spectacular innings of 121 out of a team total of 198. Injury cost him the captaincy for the second Test against Pakistan in 1978–79 and he never regained it. He was able, however, to win his Test place back after the World Series settlement. He toured England in 1981, scoring a brilliant 114 at Old Trafford. His best series was against Pakistan in 1983–84 when he made 141, 33, 68, 14, 268 and 30 in the Tests. While he destroyed leg spinner Abdul Qadir in that series, he was not so happy against pace. Bob Willis and the West Indians always troubled him. Yallop's Test career ended when he joined the rebel tour of South Africa in 1985.

BATTING	M	Inn	NO	HS	Runs	Ave	100s	50s	C/S
Tests	39	70	3	268	2756	41.13	8	9	23
First-class	164	283	30	268	11615	45.90	30	56	120/1

BOWLING	Balls	Runs	Wkts	Ave	BB	5wI	10wM
Tests	192	116	1	116.00	1/21	–	–
First-class	–	876	14	62.57	4/63	–	–

YARDLEY, Bruce

WA, RHB/RM, OB
Born: 5 September 1947
Midland, Western Australia

Bruce Yardley made his first-class debut in 1966–67, but it took a change from medium pace to off spin before he made it into Test cricket in 1977–78. In addition to his bowling he was an aggressive lower order batsman and a superb gully fieldsman. He took 15 wickets in the West Indies in 1977–78 and played some useful innings, including his highest Test score of 74 at Barbados. In and out of the Test side over the next few seasons, he returned to a permanent place with some good bowling against Pakistan and the West Indies in 1981–82. Next season against England he took 22 wickets in the series, including 5/107 and 3/101 in the first Test at Brisbane. His efforts earned him the International Cricketer of the Year Award. He followed this with 5/88 and 2/78 in the only Test in Sri Lanka at the end of the season. His bowling seemed to improve in every game, but unfortunately, this was his last Test. When he missed selection for the 1983 World Cup he retired, leaving the selectors to spend years trying to find an adequate replacement. Yardley briefly, and unsuccessfully, attempted a comeback in 1989–90.

BATTING	M	Inn	NO	HS	Runs	Ave	100s	50s	C/S
Tests	33	54	4	74	978	19.56	–	4	31
First-class	104	154	21	97*	2737	20.57	–	8	63

BOWLING	Balls	Runs	Wkts	Ave	BB	5wI	10wM
Tests	8909	3986	126	31.63	7/98	6	1
First-class	–	9625	342	28.14	7/44	20	3

Z

ZOEHRER, Timothy Joseph

WA, RHB/WK/LBG
Born: 25 September 1961
Armadale, Western Australia

When Tim Zoehrer became Australia's wicketkeeper in 1985–86 it seemed that the position was his for a long time, but his tenure lasted only 10 Tests. Although he made his first-class debut in 1980–81, it was not until Rod Marsh retired that Zoehrer could claim a regular place in the Western Australian team. After making his Test debut in New Zealand, he toured India, then played at home against England in 1986–87. He did not keep well, particularly in the fifth Test at Sydney, and some overly-aggressive behaviour did not endear him to the general public or the players. This combination of factors saw him replaced by Greg Dyer for the 1987 World Cup. In 1989 an improved Zoehrer, both behind the stumps and with the bat, toured England as Ian Healy's deputy. In 1991–92 Zoehrer emerged from wicketkeeping to display talent as a leg-spin bowler. However in 1992–93 the bowling did not progress as well as was hoped, and he gave it up to return to full time 'keeping, a move which saw him secure the reserve 'keeper's role for the 1993 tour of England.

BATTING	M	Inn	NO	HS	Runs	Ave	100s	50s	C/S
Tests	10	14	2	52*	246	20.50	–	1	18/1
First-class	135	190	22	168	4926	29.32	7	24	386/37

BOWLING	Runs	Wkts	Ave	BB	5wI	10wM
First-class	1493	35	42.66	5/58	1	–